THE CRUCIFIXION OF JESUS

Faithful History or Historical Faith?

Louay Fatoohi

SAFIS
PUBLISHING

Birmingham – UK

Published in the United Kingdom by
Safis Publishing Limited, Birmingham, UK.
www.safispub.com

ISBN   978-1-906342-27-2 (paperback)
        978-1-906342-28-9 (ebook)

First Edition

Version Identifier: 21092202

Cover image: the Greek word "ἄγνωστος" (ágnostos) means "stranger" or "unknown". It captures the conclusion of this book, which is that someone other than Jesus was crucified.

The Author

Louay Fatoohi was born in Baghdad, Iraq, in 1961. He and his wife migrated to the UK in 1992. He lives in Birmingham, England. He obtained a BSc in physics from Baghdad University, Iraq, in 1984 and a PhD in astronomy from Durham University, UK, in 1998.

Originally from a Christian family, Louay reverted to Islam in his early twenties. In addition to being his faith of choice and way of life, Islam is for him a subject of deep intellectual interest. He is interested in Qur'anic and Islamic studies in general, but his main areas of research are as follows:

- The comparative study of history in the Qur'an, Jewish and Christian scriptures, and independent historical sources
- Sufism
- The history of the Qur'anic text and revelation
- Qur'anic exegesis

Louay is a prolific author who has published over twenty-five books in English and Arabic in Islamic studies. He has also published over twenty research papers in cosmology, applied historical astronomy, and the Islamic calendar.

Contents

Introduction

In 2007, I published my comprehensive book on Jesus, *The Mystery of The Historical Jesus*. This was the first detailed study of the historical Jesus to seriously consider the Qur'anic narrative of Jesus as a credible historical account against the background of early Christian and other sources. I say "seriously" because, in non-Muslim scholarship, history in the Qur'an is typically quoted only to be dismissed. It is approached with the preconception that it is theologically and polemically driven, not to mention the all-too-common accusation that it misappropriates Jewish and Christian traditions.

That book became the main source material for three focused books, each of which zoomed in on certain aspects of Jesus' life. One of these books was *The Mystery of the Crucifixion*, which came out late in 2008. In it, I expanded only in a small way on the core material from the source book, as my limited objective was to publish a book that focused on the crucifixion and present my conclusions in a little more detail. The crucifixion is such an important event that it warranted a separate study.

Recently, I decided to update the book on the crucifixion to expand it to discuss topics that the first edition did not deal with. More specifically, I wanted to cover in more breadth and depth the Qur'anic perspective on the crucifixion and its diverse interpretations by Muslim and non-Muslim scholars. I also aimed to critique in more detail the consensus among non-Muslim scholars on the historicity of the crucifixion of Jesus. Furthermore, the new work would reflect developments in my thinking on various aspects of the crucifixion, as well as some relevant aspects of Jesus' life, since I wrote my first book on the historical Jesus almost a decade and a half ago.

As I started updating the book and expanding its scope, I was forced to revise its plan several times. It gradually became clear that to cover everything that such a detailed study needed to cover, the plan for a second edition of the earlier book had to be replaced with writing a new book. As well as adding a substantial amount of new material, I have expanded, revised, and restructured the smaller content I reused from the earlier book.

But what is the point of yet another book on the crucifixion when there are already countless books, new and old, small and large, academic and general? As I have already pointed out, the overwhelming majority of English publications share wilful neglect and/or vilification of history in the Qur'an. Jesus' history is no exception. If the Qur'an's narrative is at all cited, it is only to trivialise it and reiterate the centuries-old claim about its unreliability relative to the Gospels, which are the primary sources of the crucifixion narrative, and to just about any other secondary early source on Jesus. To be sure, the Qur'an's denial of the crucifixion of Jesus is probably the most discredited of its historical accounts. Exposing the unjustified dismissal of the Qur'an's word on the crucifixion, therefore, has broader implications for how the history it reports, in general, is viewed.

Some modern Western scholars have looked more favourably at what the Qur'an had to say about the crucifixion by interpreting it in a way that aligns it with the Gospels' narrative. Rather than denying the historicity of Jesus' execution, the Qur'an, they claim, confirms it. Some have taken the less radical view that the Qur'an does not confirm or deny the crucifixion. To justify these readings, scholars have had to make the astonishing claim that Muslims over fourteen centuries have fundamentally misunderstood the Qur'an's statement on the crucifixion. A tiny number of Muslim scholars have also adopted the view that the Muslims' rejection of the historicity of the crucifixion is a misconstrual of the Qur'an.

This book addresses various forms of such claims, some of which are theologically driven, by analysing the Qur'anic text in detail. But the book is far more than a justification of the virtual consensus of Muslim scholars that the Qur'an denies that Jesus was crucified. With this denial being the main target of the attack on the reliability of history in the Qur'an, this book shows that the acceptance of the historicity of the crucifixion has its roots more in faith than in history. Even when this acceptance is not the result of Christian faith, it is still traceable to the sources of that faith: the Gospels. None of the few early non-Christian sources that mention this event is independent of the Christian tradition. While the Qur'an is treated by non-Muslim scholars as a book of faith that has little to no reliable history, the Gospels' many well-known historical fallacies and internal contradictions and inconsistences are conveniently cast aside so that history can continue to be confidently sourced from these books.

This book also offers new insights into and observations on all relevant aspects of the Qur'anic story of Jesus to enrich our understanding of what the Qur'an really says. I have endeavoured to present all major alternatives to my preferred interpretations and address them in sufficient detail.

In summary, this book shows that, far from being a confirmed historical fact, the crucifixion of Jesus is more of a product of faith. It also explains the Qur'an's alternative history of what happened. Its combination of these two goals makes this detailed treatment of the subject from a Muslim perspective a genuinely new contribution to the literature. Muslim writings show little engagement with historical and non-Muslim scriptural and religious sources. This is often due to a lack of interest in and familiarity with the literature. While I am not as familiar with the Arabic publications on the subject, I feel confident enough to conclude that a translation of this book would also enrich the literature in the Arabic language.

I would like now to briefly review the content of the book and its roadmap. It is divided into four parts, three of which deal with the crucifixion of Jesus in three different sources: the New Testament, early non-Christian sources, and the Qur'an. Sandwiched between these is a part that dissects the belief in the historicity of the crucifixion.

Part I starts with **Chapter 1**, which highlights significant inconsistencies in the crucifixion narrative in the Gospels, although references are also made to Paul's epistles and Acts. **Chapter 2** discusses the Gospels' claim that the Old Testament has seven prophecies of the crucifixion of the Messiah. All these claims are shown to be false. The Gospel accounts of the trial of Jesus are dominated by details that are contradictory to Jewish law; these details are the subject of **Chapter 3**.

Chapter 4 focuses on the suffering Messiah, which is the central theme in the New Testament and the cornerstone of Christian theology. The chapter shows that this concept was a Christian invention that contradicted the image of the Messiah in Judaism.

Chapter 5 turns to the question of who the Gospels blame for the crucifixion of Jesus—the Jewish religious leaders or the Roman authorities—and why. It concludes that it was the Jewish leaders who indicted Jesus but only the Romans had the power to carry out capital punishment. Jesus engaged in no political activity, so the Roman governor executed him only because of the Jewish leaders. The chapter discusses the causes of the latter's escalating hostility towards Jesus. Dating the crucifixion is dealt with in **Chapter 6**.

The first six chapters can only lead to the conclusion, summarised in **Chapter 7**, that the Gospels and Paul's writings are unreliable sources on the history of Jesus, including the prominently featured crucifixion. Scholars have introduced some criteria to help in identifying reliable historical information in the New Testament. **Chapter 8** examines these criteria of authenticity and shows that the scale of the problems in the sources makes any such criteria not fit for purpose. They often end up confirming biases.

Part II deals with the references to the crucifixion of Jesus in early non-Christian sources. They are quickly introduced in **Chapter 9** before they are individually discussed in detail in the following chapters. These very brief mentions in non-Christian sources are used to claim support for the historicity of the crucifixion of Jesus in independent sources. **Chapter 10** deals with the most debated and controversial of these sources, which is a paragraph in a book by the Jewish-Roman historian Flavius Josephus. The only three classical sources from the first two centuries are then examined in **Chapter 11**, along with another three that are of some interest. **Chapter 12** deals with Jewish rabbinic writings. None of these sources is found to be free from Christian influence. They also suffer from other reliability issues. The conclusions from part II are summarised in **Chapter 13**: the crucifixion is not attested independently in early sources.

The focus of **Part III** is the *belief* in the historicity of the crucifixion. The unreliability of the Gospels and the supernaturality of the resurrection have prompted some scholars to present alternative scenarios to the crucifixion, the empty tomb claim, and Jesus' reported post-crucifixion appearances. These are discussed in **Chapter 14**. Yet, **Chapter 15** explains, the crucifixion continues to be treated by the overwhelming majority of non-Muslim scholars as an event that is as historically certain as an ancient event can be. **Chapter 16** shows that this certainty about the crucifixion is the combined result of treating theology as history and applying unjustified selectivity to sources. Dismissing the

Qur'an's alternative scenario that Jesus was not crucified is unwarranted.

We then come to **Part IV**, which focuses on the Qur'an's account of the crucifixion and related events. **Chapter 17** explains the well-known hermeneutical principle that the Qur'an interprets itself, which is used in this book to analyse the Qur'anic text. We studied in chapter 5 the possible reasons why the Jews wanted to kill Jesus as read from the Gospels against a background of historical facts. In **Chapter 18**, we look at what the Qur'an tells us about the causes of the persecution.

Chapter 19 quotes and interprets the main verse in the Qur'an on the crucifixion and its surrounding verses. It also shows that Muslim scholars have always read the Qur'an to mean that it denies that Jesus was crucified. Yet this has not stopped some Western scholars from trying to claim that the Qur'an confirms the crucifixion or is at least noncommittal. This misguided view, along with its underlying drivers, is the subject of **Chapter 20**.

Chapter 21 quotes two other verses in the Qur'an that confirm that Jesus escaped crucifixion. Various scenarios of how this could have happened are discussed in **Chapter 22**. **Chapter 23** shows that, according to the Qur'an, Jesus is no longer alive. He died after a life of normal, not supernatural, length. God's intervention to "take" Jesus is then discussed in **Chapter 24**. This intervention means that God raised Jesus to heaven, as explained in **Chapter 25**. Two Qur'anic references to the last period of Jesus on the earth and his life in heaven are discussed in **Chapter 26**. **Chapter 27** concludes this part and the whole book with a summary of its findings.

The following note is in order. I am not so naïve as to think that any study of the crucifixion, or indeed any aspect of Jesus' life, can be convincing to most people, let alone all. This was never the objective of this book nor, incidentally, any of my other works. I aimed to present an in-depth study that shows that the Qur'an offers a coherent and credible story of Jesus, undoubtedly denies that Jesus was crucified, and has no less of a claim to historicity than the New Testament, whose claims it counters. I show, as many before have done, that the inconsistency of the Gospels, individually and altogether, and their many inaccurate and wrong historical claims demand that they are not accredited with undue reliability. It is mainly this unjustified elevated status of the Gospels that has stopped scholars from seriously considering the alternative account of the crucifixion in the Qur'an.

Finally, I would like to acknowledge the help and support of my beloved wife, Shetha Al-Dargazelli, who carefully reviewed this book. Shetha's insightful comments helped me improve the book.

I would also like to thank my friend Ahmed El-Wakil for his feedback on an early incomplete draft of this book.

I

The Crucifixion in the New Testament

1

Discrepancies in the Gospel Accounts

Jesus' crucifixion is recounted in detail in the four Gospels. Jesus, who had earlier predicted his own arrest and death, was betrayed by one of his disciples, Judas Iscariot, who handed his master over to the chief Jewish priests. After being arrested and interrogated by the Jewish authorities, Jesus was found guilty of at least blasphemy and was sentenced to death. They took him to the Roman governor, Pontius Pilate, to carry out the sentence.

Pilate was particularly interested in questioning Jesus about the politically sensitive charge of claiming to be the king of the Jews. The Roman governor was not convinced that Jesus was guilty of anything and wanted to release him. The Jews, both leaders and laypeople, insisted that Pilate should crucify Jesus, and Pilate at the end bowed to their pressure and ordered the execution of the innocent man. Jesus was crucified on a Friday, but he was raised two days later. After his resurrection on Sunday, he appeared several times to his followers. This narrative is, more or less, shared by the four Gospels.

There are considerable similarities between the accounts of the four Gospels of the arrest, conviction, crucifixion, and resurrection of Jesus. Some details, though, are found in one Gospel but not another. It is difficult to understand why one Evangelist would ignore events reported by another unless he was either unaware of them or did not accept them as authentic. It may still be argued that these extra details do not constitute a problem as long as they remain compatible with the other parts of the story.

But there are also serious differences between the four narratives. Some differences may be possible to reconcile, even if the attempt may be unconvincing. Other discrepancies cannot be all integrated into one super account.

It has been known for a long time that the Gospels give highly confused and contradictory accounts of these events. For instance, the third-century Neoplatonist Greek philosopher Porphyry noted that:

> The Evangelists were inventors and not historians of the events concerning Jesus. For each of them wrote an account of the Passion which was not harmonious but as contradictory as could be.[1]

Because of the similarities they have, Mark, Matthew, and Luke are known as the "Synoptic" Gospels. This term is derived from the Greek for "view together", as they could be studied in parallel columns. But even these three contradict each other, although Matthew and Mark have fewer discrepancies between them than they have with Luke. The Synoptists have even more contradictions with John:

> The common use of the singular term "Gospel" to refer to the four Gospels in the sense of implying that they tell a coherent story is completely misleading. There are different Jesuses in the different Gospels, and there is even more than one Jesus in any one Gospel.[2]

The Book of Acts also has differences with the four Gospels.

In this chapter, we will see that comparing what the Gospels say about any episode of the story of the crucifixion reveals clear differences, including contradictions. We will not concern ourselves with listing all differences, but we will focus on particularly significant inconsistencies, mentioning them in their chronological order in the story. We will always start by citing the account in Mark and end with John, being the earliest and latest of the Gospels, respectively. The Book of Acts reports some details of the story of Jesus' passion, so these will also be cited where relevant. Paul's letters are even earlier than the Gospels, but they contain little history. There will be references to them where applicable.

1.1 Was Jesus' Arrest and Crucifixion on or before the Passover?

The contradictions between the Gospels on the story of the crucifixion start as early as their specification of the date on which Jesus was arrested and later crucified. More specifically, while all Evangelists agree that Jesus was crucified on a Friday, the Synoptists make this Friday the first day of the Passover, whereas in John it was the day of preparation for the

---

[1] Macarius, *Apocriticus*, 38.
[2] Fatoohi, *The Mystery of the Historical Jesus*, 22.

Passover, that is, one day earlier. We first need some background information on the Passover to understand all the relevant details of this contradiction.

The Passover is a major religious occasion in which the Jewish people celebrate their liberation from slavery in Egypt. It starts from 15 Nisan, which is the first month of the Jewish calendar, and lasts for seven or eight days. As the Jewish day is reckoned from sunset to sunset, so night precedes day, the Passover starts at the sunset of 15 Nisan. One essential element of this festival is offering a sacrifice, a lamb or a goat. This sacrifice must be slaughtered and prepared in the afternoon of 14 before the Passover evening starts. So, 14 is the *day of preparation for the Passover*. The Passover meal is then eaten in the evening of the first day of the Passover (Exod. 12:1-8).

According to the Synoptic Gospels, on the day before the Passover, Jesus sent his disciples to a certain man to tell him to prepare for him to have the Passover meal in his house. In the evening of the Passover, Jesus had the Passover meal with the disciples. Jesus was arrested later that night (Mark 14:12-46; Matt. 26:19-50; Luke 22:7-54) and was crucified in the morning, that is, on the morning of 15 Nisan, the first day of the Passover.

The Fourth Gospel states that after being arrested and questioned by the high priest, Jesus was taken to Pilate very early in the morning, so the arrest must have taken place at night. John then contradicts the Synoptists as he goes on to say the following about the Jewish leaders:

> They themselves did not enter the headquarters, so as to avoid ritual defilement and to be able to eat the Passover. So Pilate went out to them and said, "What accusation do you bring against this man?" (John 18:28-29)

John later confirms again that all those events took place before the Passover when he says that Pilate handed Jesus over to the Jews to crucify him on "the day of Preparation for the Passover; and it was about noon" (John 19:14). Because the Jews could not enter Pilate's residence, John claims that the governor had to come out every time he needed to speak to them, while interrogating Jesus inside. In the Synoptic Gospels, however, the dialogue between Pilate and the Jewish leaders takes place in his residence because they had already had the Passover meal. So, according to John, the crucifixion Friday was the preparation day, 14 Nisan, but for the Synoptists, it was the first day of the Passover, 15.

John's timeline of the crucifixion has Jesus die at the same time as the slaughter of the Passover sacrifices. This works very well for his description of Jesus as "the Lamb of God" in the opening chapter of his Gospel (John 1:29, 36). He also applies to Jesus' crucifixion, in the form of a prophecy, a description that the Old Testament uses for the Passover lamb (John 19:36), suggesting that in his crucifixion, Jesus played the role of the true Passover lamb (§2.6). The fact that John's dating of the crucifixion is in such agreement with his theology has made some scholars reject the historicity of his dating as deliberately manipulated and favour the Synoptic date.[3]

Interestingly, while Mark makes it clear that Jesus was crucified on the first day of the Passover, it also states earlier that when, two days before the Passover, the chief priests and the experts in the law were conspiring to kill Jesus, they did not want to kill him "during the festival, or there may be a riot among the people" (Mark 14:2). This passage may belong to a different tradition which could be aligned with the Johannine chronology of the crucifixion.

Unsurprisingly, there have been attempts to harmonize the contradictory Gospel accounts. One popular attempt suggests that John used a different calendar from that used by the other three Evangelists. There is no evidence to support this suggestion and there are strong arguments against it.[4] The one-day difference between John and the other three Gospels has historical implications as well (§3.3).

1.2 Was Jesus' Trial by the Jewish Leaders at Night or in the Morning?

Mark (14:30-53) and Matthew (26:31-57) state that Jesus was arrested and tried by the Jewish leaders in the night and then he was taken to Pilate in the morning (Mark 15:1; Matt. 27:1). John (18:27-1) also implies this, as he states that after the arrest and later interrogation by the second high priest, Jesus was taken to the Roman governor when it was "very early morning" (John 18:28). Luke also implies that Jesus was arrested at night,

---

[3] Sanders, *Historical Figure*, 72.
[4] Theissen and Merz, *The Historical Jesus*, 159.

but he has the trial in the morning, "When day came, the assembly of the elders of the people, both chief priests and scribes, gathered together, and they brought him to their council" (Luke 22:66).

1.3 Was Jesus Questioned by the Sanhedrin or the High Priest?

There is confusion as to whether Jesus was questioned by the high priest or the Sanhedrin. The latter, whose name is derived from the Greek word *synedrion*, which means "council", was a Jewish judicial body of seventy-one members headed by the high priest. It settled religious and legal matters.

According to Mark (14:53-55, 15:1) and Matthew (26:57-59), the Sanhedrin tried Jesus in the house of the high priest, whom Matthew names as Caiaphas. Luke (22:54) states that after his arrest, Jesus was taken to the high priest's house, and in the morning he was tried by "the assembly of the elders of the people, both chief priests and scribes" (Luke 22:66). We can safely presume that he meant the Sanhedrin even though he did not use that term.

John, on the other hand, claims that after his arrest, Jesus was taken to the house of Annas, the father-in-law of Caiaphas who was the "high priest that year" (John 18:12-13). However, during Annas' questioning of Jesus, he is repeatedly described as the "high priest" (John 18:15-22). When Annas finished the interrogation, he sent the accused to Caiaphas, who is again confirmed as the "high priest" (John 18:24)! Surprisingly, no details are given of Caiaphas' interrogation of Jesus.

While Annas is not mentioned in Mark and Matthew, Luke (3:2) states that John the Baptist started his ministry "during the high priesthood of Annas and Caiaphas". However, Annas is never mentioned after that, so he plays no role in the questioning of Jesus.

The Sanhedrin is completely missing from John's account, although he earlier indicates that the Sanhedrin, led by Caiaphas, had been planning to kill Jesus (John 11:47-53). This Evangelist also confusingly describes in one passage Caiaphas as the high priest and Annas as his father-in-law but then calls the latter the high priest in several passages. One way of harmonizing this apparent contradiction is to suggest that while Caiaphas was the high priest that year, Annas was the high priest earlier, which is why he retained the title. But this suggestion has historical problems (§3.7).

1.4 What Charges Were Made against Jesus before the Jews?

According to Mark (14:53–65), many testified against Jesus before the Sanhedrin, but their testimonies disagreed. Some witnesses *falsely* accused him of saying, "I will destroy this temple that is made with hands, and in three days I will build another, not made with hands" (Mark 14:58). When questioned about this charge, Jesus remained inexplicably silent. The high priest, persecuting on behalf of the Sanhedrin, then went on to question Jesus about whether he claimed to be "the Messiah, the Son of the Blessed One" (Mark 14:61). Jesus answered, "I am, you will see the Son of Man seated at the right hand of the Power and coming with the clouds of heaven" (Mark 14:62). This led the high priest to accuse him of blasphemy.

The trial in Matthew is very similar to Mark's. Jesus was first accused of claiming to be "able to destroy the temple of God and to build it in three days" (Matt. 26:61)—a charge that he met with silence. The high priest went on to raise a second accusation, asking him if he was "the Messiah, the Son of God", to which Jesus replied, "You have said so. But I tell you, from now on you will see the Son of Man seated at the right hand of Power and coming on the clouds of heaven" (Matt. 26:63–64). Jesus' reply made the high priest accuse him of blasphemy and declare that no more witnesses were required (Matt. 26:64–65).

One difference between Mark and Matthew is that the latter states that two witnesses testified that Jesus had made the claim about the temple (Matt. 26:60), whereas Mark (14:57-59) says that witnesses disagreed about this accusation. But both Gospels agree that Jesus was first accused of claiming to be able to destroy and rebuild the temple and then of calling himself the Christ, the son of God.

The accusation of destroying the temple is also mentioned in Acts when a Christian called Stephen was put on trial by people from the synagogue:

> Then they secretly instigated some men to say, "We have heard him speak blasphemous words against Moses and God." They stirred up the people as well as the elders and the scribes; then they suddenly confronted him, seized him, and brought him before the council. They

set up false witnesses who said, "This man never stops saying things against this holy place and the law; for we have heard him say that this Jesus of Nazareth will destroy this place and will change the customs that Moses handed on to us." (Acts 6:11-14)

The charge about the temple relates to a Jesus prophecy that is reported in the Synoptic Gospels (Matt. 24:1-2; Luke 21:5-6):

As he came out of the temple, one of his disciples said to him, "Look, Teacher, what large stones and what large buildings!" Then Jesus asked him, "Do you see these great buildings? Not one stone will be left here upon another; all will be thrown down." (Mark 13:1-2)

Actually, none of these accounts has Jesus say that *he* would destroy the building; he is only reported to have pronounced a prophecy about what would happen to the temple. Mark and Matthew must have been implying that Jesus' words were misreported to make the false charge against him. Otherwise, we would have to conclude that both are confused about what Jesus said or meant.

It is often claimed that Jesus' prophecy was fulfilled when the Romans destroyed the temple in 70 CE after the first Jewish revolt. If the walls that presently surround the Islamic site of *al-Ḥaram al-Sharif* are those of the ancient temple and considered part of it, which means that thousands of stones were left intact in their positions, then the alleged prophecy was not completely fulfilled, although Jesus' description of what would happen has been defended as being hyperbolic.[5]

Unlike Mark and Matthew, Luke's (22:66-71) shorter account of the trial has no witnesses. Also, the prophecy of destroying and rebuilding the temple is not presented as a charge even though it is mentioned. This, unlike the narratives in Mark and Matthew, is aligned with the fact that the wording of the prophecy does not attribute to Jesus any part in the destruction or rebuilding of the temple.

Similar to what we find in Mark and Matthew, Luke (22:67-70) states that Jesus was asked whether he was the Christ. In an implied confirmation, Jesus said, "If I tell you, you will not believe; and if I question you, you will not answer. But from now on the Son of Man will be seated at the right hand of the power of God". His reference to the "the Son of Man" triggered an accusatory question about whether he was "the Son of

---

[5] Stein, "Jesus, the Destruction of Jerusalem", 19.

God". Jesus' vague answer "you say that I am" made the prosecutors conclude that they had the evidence they needed. It looks like this evidence was not only Jesus' claim to the sonship of God but also his supposedly linked claim that he was the Christ.

Contrary to Mark and Matthew but similar to Luke, John makes no mention of the accusation of destroying the temple. He has what appears to be a very different version of the Synoptists' report of this incident:

> The Jews then said to him, "What sign can you show us for doing this?" Jesus answered them, "Destroy this temple, and in three days I will raise it up." The Jews then said, "This temple has been under construction for forty-six years, and will you raise it up in three days?" But he was speaking of the temple of his body. After he was raised from the dead, his disciples remembered that he had said this; and they believed the scripture and the word that Jesus had spoken. (John 2:18-22)

As is the case in the Synoptic Gospel, John's version does not talk about Jesus destroying the temple. It differs in making him the one who would rebuild it. John's interpretation of Jesus' challenge to the Jewish leaders, as being about his death and rise, is also problematic. The Jews asked for a sign to make them believe in Jesus, yet he replied with something that they could have only misunderstood!

In this Gospel, Annas questions Jesus about "his disciples and about his teaching" (John 18:19), but no explicit or specific charges are made, hence there is no mention of witnesses. When Jesus was brought before Pilate, the Jewish leaders told the Roman governor that according to their law Jesus had to die because he "claimed to be the Son of God" (John 19:7). John earlier states that, before Jesus' arrest, Caiaphas had sought his death at any cost to repel what he perceived as a danger of Roman aggression against the Jewish nation:

> So the chief priests and the Pharisees called a meeting of the council, and said, "What are we to do? This man is performing many signs. If we let him go on like this, everyone will believe in him, and the Romans will come and destroy both our holy place and our nation." But one of them, Caiaphas, who was high priest that year, said to them, "You know nothing at all! You do not understand that it is better for you to have one man die for the people than to have the whole nation destroyed." He did not say this on his own, but being high priest that year he prophesied that Jesus was about to die for the nation, and not for the

nation only, but to gather into one the dispersed children of God. So from that day on they planned to put him to death. (John 11:47-53)

The four Gospels, thus, give confusing and contradictory accounts of the charges that the Jews made against Jesus.

1.5 Was Jesus Tried or Interrogated by the Jews?

Another disagreement between the Gospels is whether the Sanhedrin and high priest subjected Jesus to a trial or an interrogation.[6] Both Mark (14:64) and Matthew (26:65-66) report a trial that ends with finding Jesus guilty of blasphemy and condemns him to death.

The Gospel of Luke describes more of an interrogation than a trial, although it ends with the Sanhedrin getting the evidence they wanted (Luke 22:71), which implies that they found him guilty. No sentencing is mentioned, however. But this is contradicted later when the Gospel states that the "chief priests and leaders handed him over to be condemned to death and crucified him" (Luke 24:20). Acts, which is believed to have been written by the same author of Luke, has the following to say about the Sanhedrin's questioning of Jesus:

Because the residents of Jerusalem and their leaders did not recognize him or understand the words of the prophets that are read every sabbath, they fulfilled those words by condemning him. Even though they found no cause for a sentence of death, they asked Pilate to have him killed. (Acts 13:27-28)

These contradictory statements by the same author have made some wonder whether "Luke wanted to depict the interrogation as a trial" or it is "a sign that the Lukan interrogation scene goes back to a pre-Lukan tradition which contradicts Luke's view elsewhere".[7] The fact that Luke's account concludes with the council finding the evidence they were after seems to imply that the Evangelist may have still thought of it as a trial, although no sentence was passed.

John's account is one of interrogation, not trial. The questioning was conducted by Annas, no witnesses were called, no evidence was obtained, no verdict was reached, and no sentence was passed (John 18:19-24). Annas then transferred Jesus to Caiaphas, the other high priest, but the

---

[6] Vermes, *The Passion*, 97-98; Theissen and Merz, *The Historical Jesus*, 443.
[7] Theissen and Merz, *The Historical Jesus*, 450.

Evangelist seems to imply that Caiaphas did nothing other than sending Jesus to Pilate (John 18:24-28). Jesus was never brought before the Sanhedrin, although John (11:49-53) had told us earlier that the high priest and the Sanhedrin were seeking Jesus' death well before his arrest.

However, Luke's and John's interrogations are still followed by Jesus being taken to Pilate to be executed.

1.6 What Charges Were Made against Jesus before Pilate?

Having discussed the charges that the Jewish authorities made against Jesus, we will now study the charges he faced before Pilate.

All four Gospels agree that after his trial or interrogation by the Sanhedrin and/or high priest, Jesus was brought before Pilate. According to Mark and Matthew, Pilate asked Jesus whether he was the king of the Jews, to which Jesus vaguely answered, "You say so". Pilate's question implies that the Jewish leaders accused Jesus of claiming to be the king of the Jews, which is how they perceived their awaited Messiah.[8] This highly charged political accusation was bound to raise the interest of the Roman governor. The chief priests and the elders then brought "many" unspecified charges against Jesus, but he did not respond to any of them (Mark 15:2-5; Matt. 27:11-14).

Luke (23:2) elaborates more on the accusation, "We found this man perverting our nation, forbidding us to pay taxes to the emperor, and saying that he himself is the Messiah, a king". He then reports the same question and answer between Pilate and Jesus about the kingship of the Jews that Mark and Matthew report. Jesus was accused of "inciting" (Luke 23:5) and "misleading" people (Luke 23:14).

John's account differs yet further. When Pilate asks the people about Jesus' charge, their reply was simply to stress his guilt, "If this man were not a criminal, we would not have handed him over to you" (John 18:30). Upon the Jews' insistence that Jesus be killed, Pilate asked him whether he was the king of the Jews. Unlike the account in the Synoptic Gospels, Jesus replied by explaining that his kingdom is heavenly, not from this world (John 18:36). This should have allayed Pilate's concerns.

John (19:7) also states that the Jews told Pilate that Jesus had to die

---

[8] Fatoohi, *The Messiah in Islam, Christianity, and Judaism.*

because of his claim to the sonship of God. This *religious* charge could not have been of less interest to Pilate.

Despite their differences about what charges were brought against Jesus before Pilate, all four Gospels agree that the crucified Jesus was mocked by having a titulus with the inscription "the king of the Jews" put on his cross. This agreement highlights the charge that was of significance to the Roman governor, which is the claim to kingship. Since the Jews believed that the Messiah would become their king, this mocking of Jesus ridiculed his claim to messiahship.

The titulus is one instance that shows that even when the Gospels are consistent, they do not completely agree with each other. The inscription according to Mark (15:26) is "the King of the Jews", in Matthew (27:37) it is "this is Jesus, the King of the Jews", but Luke (23:38) has "this is the King of the Jews", and John (19:19) has yet a fourth variant, "Jesus of Nazareth, the King of the Jews".

1.7 Was Jesus Tried by Herod Antipas?

All four Gospels state that Jesus was tried by Pilate, the Roman governor of the province of Judea, as events took place in Jerusalem, Judea's capital. Luke adds a trial by Herod Antipas, one of the three brothers among whom the kingdom of their father, Herod the Great, was split after his death in 4 BCE. This Evangelist claims that after questioning Jesus in Jerusalem, Pilate learned that he was from Galilee, which was under Antipas' jurisdiction, so he sent him to the Galilean governor. Antipas questioned, mocked, and humiliated Jesus before sending him back to Pilate (Luke 23:6-12). This whole episode is missing from Mark, Matthew, and John.

1.8 How Did Judas Iscariot Die?

All four Gospels state that Jesus was betrayed by one of his twelve disciples, Judas Iscariot, who handed him over to the Jewish leaders in return for money (Mark 14:43-46; Matt. 26:47-50; Luke 22:47-54; John 18:2-12). Matthew (26:15) adds that Judas was paid thirty silver coins to betray his master, which he later regretted before committing suicide:

> When Judas, his betrayer, saw that Jesus was condemned, he repented and brought back the thirty pieces of silver to the chief priests and the elders. He said, "I have sinned by betraying innocent blood." But they

said, "What is that to us? See to it yourself." Throwing down the pieces
of silver in the temple, he departed; and he went and hanged himself.
But the chief priests, taking the pieces of silver, said, "It is not lawful to
put them into the treasury, since they are blood money." After
conferring together, they used them to buy the potter's field as a place
to bury foreigners. For this reason that field has been called the Field of
Blood to this day. Then was fulfilled what had been spoken through the
prophet Jeremiah, "And they took the thirty pieces of silver, the price
of the one on whom a price had been set, on whom some of the people
of Israel had set a price, and they gave them for the potter's field, as the
Lord commanded me." (Matt. 27:3-10)

The alleged Jeremiah prophecy that Matthew cites actually does not
exist. If Matthew has not completely made it up, then it could be a garbled
mixture of passages from Zechariah (11:12-13) and Jeremiah (18:2-3), as
explained later in more detail (§2.3).

None of the other three Gospels mentions Judas' suicide, whereas Acts
describes his death as an accident:

(Now this man acquired a field with the reward of his wickedness;
and falling headlong, he burst open in the middle and all his bowels
gushed out. This became known to all the residents of Jerusalem, so that
the field was called in their language Hakeldama, that is, Field of Blood.)
"For it is written in the book of Psalms,
  'Let his homestead become desolate,
    and let there be no one to live in it';
  and
  'Let another take his position of overseer.' (Acts 1:18-20)

This account of Judas' death is supposed to have been known "all the
residents of Jerusalem", but it was not known to Matthew, or at least he
did not believe it, as he gives a different account of events. The two
authors even differ on the origin of the name of the Field of Blood. In
another contradiction with Matthew, Acts links Judas' death to a
completely different passage, which is not a prophecy.

1.9 Who Carried the Cross?

According to Mark, when Jesus was being led to Golgotha to be
crucified, his executioners stopped a passer-by and made him carry the
cross:

They compelled a passer-by, who was coming in from the country, to carry his cross; it was Simon of Cyrene, the father of Alexander and Rufus. (Mark 15:21)

This little detail is also mentioned by both Matthew (27:32) and Luke. The latter clarifies the picture further by adding the following description:

They laid the cross on him, and made him carry it behind Jesus. (Luke 23:26)

John, on the other hand, has Jesus carry his own cross:

So they took Jesus; and carrying the cross by himself, he went out to what is called The Place of the Skull, which in Hebrew is called Golgotha. (John 19:16-17)

1.10 What Time Was Jesus' Crucifixion and Death?
As pointed out earlier, the day of the ancient Jewish lunar calendar was reckoned from sunset to sunset. The night and the daytime consisted of twelve hours each, with the first hour of nighttime starting around 6 p.m. and the first hour of daytime around 6 a.m. In a dialogue with his disciples, Jesus said, "Are there not twelve hours of daylight?" (John 11:9).

According to Mark, Jesus was crucified at the third hour in the daytime (15:25), and at the sixth hour, the land was covered with darkness which lasted until the ninth hour (15:33), at which point Jesus died (15:34-37). These times correspond to 9 a.m., 12 noon, and 3 p.m., respectively. Both Matthew (27:45-50) and Luke (23:44-46) reiterate Mark's statement that the darkness lasted from the sixth to the ninth hour and that Jesus died at the ninth hour.

John (19:14-16) disagrees with the Synoptists, claiming that it was the sixth hour in the daytime, 12 noon, when Pilate handed Jesus over to be crucified. John does not say when Jesus died or specify how long his ordeal lasted so the time of death remains unknown. He does not mention any darkness, either.

To resolve the conflict between John and the Synoptists about when Jesus' crucifixion started, it has been suggested that John followed the Romans in reckoning time from midnight, so his sixth hour corresponds to 6 a.m. In addition to the fact that there is no evidence to support this assumption, this attempt would still require presuming that three more hours passed before the crucifixion started to reconcile John's account with the Synoptists. Furthermore, it is far more likely that John reckoned the time the Jewish way because that would make the crucifixion coincide with the slaughter of the Passover lambs—something that reflects his description of Jesus as "the Lamb of God" (John 1:29, 36).

1.11 What Did the Robbers Say?

Mark (15:32) and Matthew (27:44) briefly state that the two robbers who were crucified with Jesus "taunted him". It is quite a claim that someone suffering the unimaginable torture of crucifixion should have the strength and motivation to abuse another person going through the same ordeal!

Luke has a very different account, though:

> One of the criminals who were hanged there kept deriding him and saying, "Are you not the Messiah? Save yourself and us!" But the other rebuked him, saying, "Do you not fear God, since you are under the same sentence of condemnation? And we indeed have been condemned justly, for we are getting what we deserve for our deeds, but this man has done nothing wrong." Then he said, "Jesus, remember me when you come into your kingdom." He replied, "Truly I tell you, today you will be with me in Paradise." (Luke 23:39-43)

The position of the second robber, whom we are not told how and why he believed in Jesus, is as fanciful as that of the first. In this scene, it must be said, the Synoptists excel in stretching the bounds of credulity even by their own generous standards.

John (19:18) does not cite any dialogue between Jesus and his crucifixion mates whom he mentions only in passing.

1.12 Did Jesus' Followers Witness the Crucifixion?

Mark (15:40) says that women followers of Jesus were present at the crucifixion. Matthew (27:55) gives a further description of the women as being those who "had followed Jesus from Galilee and had provided for him". By mentioning only women, Mark and Matthew imply that none of Jesus' male disciples witnessed the crucifixion. This is in line with Jesus' prediction in Mark (14:27) that his disciples would scatter at the time of the crucifixion.

Luke (23:49) disagrees with Mark and Matthew as he makes "all his acquaintances" present. This must mean not only the disciples but also those who were not as close to Jesus. Indeed, Luke adds that those present included "the women who had followed him from Galilee". John's (19:25-26) account is yet more different, claiming that four women and one of Jesus' disciples were there. The *one whom Jesus loved*, as John describes him, is mentioned by him in two other passages (13:23, 21:7), but he is never mentioned in the Synoptic Gospels.

The four Gospels agree that when faced with the accusation of being one of Jesus' followers, the disciple Peter denied any connection with him (Mark 14:66-71; Matt. 26:69-74; Luke 22:54-60; John 18:16-17, 25-27). John states that another, unnamed disciple was with Peter. Peter's denial and the Synoptists' claim that, after Jesus' arrest, Peter followed him *at a distance* (Mark 14:54; Matt. 26:58; Luke 22:54) suggest that Jesus' disciples could have been prosecuted and had to go into hiding. John's (18:19) claim that Annas questioned Jesus about his disciples is in line with this Synoptic picture, but then the later appearance of one of Jesus' disciples near the crucified Jesus in that Gospel looks contradictory. One explanation is that this disciple was the unnamed one who appears with Peter in John, as that disciple is claimed to have been acquainted with the high priest (John 18:15), in which case it may be argued that he did not need to hide.

1.13 Could Jesus' Followers See Who Was on the Cross?

The presence of followers of Jesus at his crucifixion would be of significance only if they were physically close enough to be eyewitnesses to him being on the cross. Unsurprisingly yet significantly, the Gospels differ.

Both Mark (15:40) and Matthew (27:55) state that their respective women followers were "looking on from a distance". Luke (23:49) claims all those who knew Jesus were present, yet he also makes it clear that they "stood at a distance". The Synoptists, thus, imply that no one of Jesus' followers was close enough to confirm that they saw him crucified.

John, though, introduces eyewitnesses into his narrative:

> When Jesus saw his mother and the disciple whom he loved standing beside her, he said to his mother, "Woman, here is your son." Then he said to the disciple, "Here is your mother." And from that hour the disciple took her into his own home. (John 19:26-27)

John is at pains to depict all five people as direct eyewitnesses to the crucifixion by placing them so close to the cross that they could hear the dying Jesus speak! This unrealistic scene must be fictional. Indeed, Jesus' speech itself makes little sense given that his mother had long disappeared from his life as reported by John himself. That the main characters are Jesus' mother and his closest disciple, i.e. two people who could not fail to recognise Jesus, strongly suggests that this scene was invented to provide reliable characters to witness that it was indeed Jesus who was crucified. This is why, unlike the Synoptists, John did not need to talk about a large number of women or followers watching the crucifixion. In creating this scene, John might even be responding to a rumour he had heard that Jesus was not crucified.

We have to accept the Synoptic consensus that Jesus' crucifixion was not witnessed by any of his followers. It looks like the Synoptists faithfully reported the tradition they inherited that Jesus' crucifixion had no eyewitnesses among his followers. Whether the claim of Mark and Matthew that a few female followers of Jesus watched his crucifixion at a distance is also an old tradition or something that they made up does not change the critical fact that no one of Jesus' companions was able to confirm that it was him on the cross. Luke's claim that everyone who knew Jesus was present at his crucifixion is undoubtedly an exaggeration intended to partly make up for an uncomfortable yet undeniable fact: Jesus' crucifixion was not seen by anyone who could confirm that it was him, not someone else, on the cross.

1.14 Who Were the Women Present at the Crucifixion?

The four Gospels name different women who were supposedly present during or after the crucifixion. The female supporters who were watching the crucifixion *included* "Magdalene, and Mary the mother of James the younger and of Joses, and Salome", according to Mark (15:40), or they *included* "Mary Magdalene, and Mary the mother of James and Joseph, and the mother of the sons of Zebedee", in Matthew (27:56). Luke (23:49) mentions "the women who had followed him from Galilee" but he does not name them.

John names four women and does not imply there were others. The names of these women also differ from Mark's and Matthew's lists: "His mother, and his mother's sister, Mary the wife of Clopas, and Mary Magdalene" (John 19:25). A more significant difference is the mention of Jesus' mother. Mark and Matthew must have implied that Jesus' mother was not present, otherwise, they would certainly have mentioned her, not least because they identified far less significant women. As we have seen, John even invents a scene in which the crucified Jesus talks to his mother.

1.15 Who Buried Jesus?

All four Gospels claim that a good man called Joseph of Arimathea buried Jesus (Mark 15:42-46; Matt. 27:57-60; Luke 23:50-53; John 19:38-42), but this rare agreement then quickly breaks down. Mark and Luke describe this person as a member of the Sanhedrin, which tried Jesus, whereas the other two present him as a disciple of Jesus. Even if we entertain the highly unlikely possibility that Joseph of Arimathea was both a member of the council and a disciple of Jesus, it is difficult to explain why Mark and Luke would not mention the very significant fact that he was one of Jesus' disciples. Both say that he was "looking forward to the kingdom of God", and Luke adds that he was "good and righteous", yet there is no mention of his discipleship. We have to conclude that the two Evangelists imply that he was not a disciple.

It is difficult to understand why a member of the court that tried and indicted Jesus was so keen on burying him. It might be tempting to suggest that he did that to honour the Jewish tradition of not keeping a dead person without burial. But had that been the case, he would surely have done the same with the corpses of the two robbers, which the Gospels say nothing about.

Acts (13:29) challenges the Gospels' consensus that Jesus was buried by Joseph of Arimathea as it states that it was the *people of Jerusalem*, whom it blames along with their rulers for the killing of Jesus, who "took him down from the tree and laid him in a tomb". In yet another contradiction, Luke's (23:51) description of Arimathea as a "Judean town" suggests that it was not in Jerusalem, otherwise, he would have identified it so.

Probably more significant of all, writing before the authors of the Gospels and Acts, Paul shows complete ignorance of the tradition of burying Jesus by Joseph of Arimathea.

The evidence strongly suggests that this tradition, as well as other details surrounding the burial and resurrection of Jesus, developed later.

1.16 Is the Sign of Jonah Relevant to Jesus' Burial and Resurrection?

The Old Testament contains a story of Jonah, who was commissioned by God to go to preach in Nineveh. Jonah disobeyed the divine order and, travelling by sea, tried to escape from God and the mission. While at sea, a powerful wind started to shake the boat dangerously. Jonah confessed to the sailors that this was the result of God's wrath at him and suggested a solution, "Pick me up and throw me into the sea; then the sea will quiet down for you; for I know it is because of me that this great storm has come upon you" (Jon. 1:12). After he was thrown in the sea, "the Lord provided a large fish to swallow up Jonah; and Jonah was in the belly of the fish three days and three nights" (Jon. 1:17). Having repented and prayed to God from inside the fish, "the Lord spoke to the fish, and it spewed Jonah out upon the dry land" (Jon. 2:10).

Mark and John have no mention of Jonah's story, but Matthew and Luke refer to it. Matthew records a prediction in which Jesus likens his burial and resurrection to what happened to Jonah:

> Then some of the scribes and Pharisees said to him, "Teacher, we wish to see a sign from you." But he answered them, "An evil and adulterous generation asks for a sign, but no sign will be given to it except the sign of the prophet Jonah. For just as Jonah was three days and three nights in the belly of the sea monster, so for three days and three nights the Son of Man will be in the heart of the earth. (Matt. 12:38-40)

Apart from disappearing inside something and then emerging again, there is hardly any similarity between the two events. Indeed, there are such clear and fundamental differences that drawing a similarity between the two instances of disappearance and emergence is rather meaningless:

i) Jesus is not simply likening his burial to the disappearance of Jonah in the belly of the fish, but he is also emphasising the duration of his death, making it clear that it is three days and three nights, like Jonah's. The problem is that Jesus did not actually stay that long in the tomb. The Synoptists agree that he died on Friday just after 3 p.m. John does not tell us the time of Jesus' death on the cross, but it must have happened after midday when he was handed over to be executed. All four Gospels also agree that Jesus had already risen from the dead by the early morning of Sunday (Mark 16:1; Matt. 28:1; Luke 24:1; John 20:1). This means that Jesus remained buried for only one day and two nights, which contradicts the prediction in Matthew. The apologetic argument that Jesus' mention of the three days and nights was not intended to refer to an exact time is inadmissible, as it makes the reference to that specific, or indeed any, timeframe meaningless.

Luke has his own version of Jesus' prophecy which, unlike Matthew, he places after the Transfiguration, when Jesus appeared radiant and spoke with Moses and Elijah. This Evangelist avoids the contradiction in Matthew's account by making no mention of the time:

> When the crowds were increasing, he began to say, "This generation is an evil generation; it asks for a sign, but no sign will be given to it except the sign of Jonah. For just as Jonah became a sign to the people of Nineveh, so the Son of Man will be to this generation." (Luke 11:29-30)

But there is another problem with this briefer account. It omits the resemblance that Jesus clearly establishes in Matthew's version between the two temporary disappearances of Jonah and himself, thus leaving the comparison meaningless to his audience.

ii) Jesus' alleged miracle was his resurrection from death. This miracle would not become more impressive if Jesus had stayed, say, ten days in the tomb, nor would it become less impressive if he had stayed in the tomb only one night. The reported miracle is simply one of *resurrection from death*. Conversely, the miraculous aspect of Jonah's experience is his *survival inside the fish for three days and nights*. Inside the tomb, Jesus did not experience any miracle; he was dead like any other dead person.

iii) Jonah's ordeal was a punishment for his failure to obey God. Jesus' miracle happened to fulfil a divine plan that reflected his unique and high status in God's eyes.

iv) Matthew reports a second incident in which Jesus was asked to show a "sign from heaven". He refused to do so, pointing instead to Jonah's miracle:

> The Pharisees and Sadducees came, and to test Jesus they asked him to show them a sign from heaven. He answered them, "When it is

evening, you say, 'It will be fair weather, for the sky is red.' And in the morning, 'It will be stormy today, for the sky is red and threatening.' You know how to interpret the appearance of the sky, but you cannot interpret the signs of the times. An evil and adulterous generation asks for a sign, but no sign will be given to it except the sign of Jonah." Then he left them and went away. (Matt. 16:1-4)

The reply that Matthew attributes to Jesus is completely irrelevant to the challenge. The Evangelist failed to understand what the Pharisees and Sadducees meant by a "sign from heaven", which had nothing to do with a miracle like Jonah's. Indeed, a demand to be shown a "sign from heaven" is reported by Mark (8:11), who attributes it to the Pharisees, and by Luke (11:16), who ascribes it to unidentified people, yet neither links it to Jonah's experience in the belly of the fish. The demand for a "sign from heaven" was, in fact, inspired by a miracle that all Jews were familiar with. The challengers wanted to test whether Jesus could bring food from heaven in the same way that God sent down manna and quails from heaven to the Israelites in the desert of Sinai after fleeing Egypt with Moses:

> The Lord spoke to Moses and said, "I have heard the complaining of the Israelites; say to them, 'At twilight you shall eat meat, and in the morning you shall have your fill of bread; then you shall know that I am the Lord your God.'"
>
> In the evening quails came up and covered the camp; and in the morning there was a layer of dew around the camp. When the layer of dew lifted, there on the surface of the wilderness was a fine flaky substance, as fine as frost on the ground. When the Israelites saw it, they said to one another, "What is it?" For they did not know what it was. Moses said to them, "It is the bread that the Lord has given you to eat." (Exod. 16:11-15)

This miracle is mentioned in a briefer form in the Qur'an as well:

> We made the clouds to give shade over you [O Children of Israel!], and We sent to you manna and quails [saying], "Eat of the good things that We have given you"; and they did not do Us any harm [by their disobedience], but they did wrong themselves. (2.57)

The Qur'an also tells us that Jesus did perform a miracle of bringing down food from heaven:

> When I inspired the companions, "Believe in Me and My messenger".

They said, "We believe. Bear witness that we are Muslims". (111) When the companions said, "O Jesus son of Mary! Can your Lord send down for us a table of food from heaven?" He said, "Fear Allah, if you are true believers". (112) They said, "We wish to eat of it, have our hearts be at ease, know that you have spoken the truth to us, and be witnesses to it [the table]". (113) Jesus son of Mary said, "O Allah our Lord! Send down for us from heaven a table of food, that it may be a feast for the first and the last of us, and a sign from You. Give us sustenance; You are the best of Sustainers". (114) Allah said, "I shall send it down for you, so whoever of you disbelieves afterwards I will punish him with a torment that I do not inflict on anyone among all the nations". (5.111-115)

John has an account that refers to this incident, with the most noticeable difference with the Qur'an being Jesus' refusal to perform the required miracle:

> Then they said to him, "What must we do to perform the works of God?" Jesus answered them, "This is the work of God, that you believe in him whom he has sent." So they said to him, "What sign are you going to give us then, so that we may see it and believe you? What work are you performing? Our ancestors ate the manna in the wilderness; as it is written, 'He gave them bread from heaven to eat.'" Then Jesus said to them, "Very truly, I tell you, it was not Moses who gave you the bread from heaven, but it is my Father who gives you the true bread from heaven. For the bread of God is that which comes down from heaven and gives life to the world." (John 6:28-33)

This account confirms our interpretation of the *sign from heaven* people asked Jesus to show. The demanded sign had nothing to do with Jonah's miracle in the sea.

v) Jesus' alleged likening of his death and resurrection to what happened to Jonah is also contradicted by the Gospel reports of how his disciples and followers behaved after his crucifixion. Their behaviours suggest that they were not aware that he was going to rise from the dead. For instance, the followers who visited his tomb were not expecting an empty tomb. Also, when Jesus appeared to his disciples after rising from the dead, they first did not believe that it was him (Mark 16:11-14; Matt. 28:17; Luke 24:36-43; John 20:25-29).

1.17 Who Discovered the Empty Tomb and when?
Mark says that "when the sun had risen" on Sunday "Mary Magdalene, and

Mary the mother of James, and Salome" (Mark 16:1-2) went to the tomb to anoint the body. These are the same women who watched the crucifixion from a distance (Mark 15:40). Mark also speaks of a "young man, dressed in a white robe" who appeared to the women at the tomb and told them that Jesus had risen and that he was going to appear to the disciples in Galilee, as he had promised them (Mark 16:7).

According to Matthew, the women who went to the tomb when Sunday "was dawning" were "Mary Magdalene and the other Mary". The unidentified Mary is probably the second of the women who witnessed the crucifixion from a distance, "Mary Magdalene, and Mary the mother of James and Joseph, and the mother of the sons of Zebedee" (Matt. 27:56). The scene here is more dramatic. When the two women arrived at the tomb, an "angel" descended from heaven, causing a great earthquake. Presumably, this angel is Matthew's development of Mark's white-dressed young man. He rolled the stone away and told them that Jesus was not in the tomb because he had risen. He invited them to have a look at the empty tomb and instructed them to tell the disciples that they would see Jesus in Galilee (Matt. 28:1-8).

Luke also has a different version. He talks about "women", *including* Mary Magdalene, Joanna, and Mary the mother of James, visiting the tomb "at early dawn" on Sunday. They found that the stone had already been rolled away from the tomb. They suddenly noticed two gloriously dressed men standing beside them. The text seems to imply that these were angels. They informed the women that Jesus had risen. The women rushed to tell the disciples (Luke 24:1-10).

John (20:1-13) ensures that each of the four Gospels gives a different account. He has Mary Magdalene alone visit the tomb on Sunday when "it was still dark". On discovering that the stone had been moved away from the entrance of the tomb, she ran and called Peter and another disciple. The two disciples left the place, unable to make sense of the disappearance of the body. The grief-stricken Mary Magdalene stayed there weeping, thinking that someone had removed Jesus' body to an unknown place. That is when "two angels" enter the scene to tell her about Jesus' resurrection.

Paul (1 Cor. 15:3-4) knew nothing about an empty tomb and the alleged visits. This is what he told a congregation in Antioch of Pisidia:

Even though they found no cause for a sentence of death, they asked Pilate to have him killed. When they had carried out everything that was written about him, they took him down from the tree and laid him in a tomb. But God raised him from the dead; and for many days he appeared to those who came up with him from Galilee to Jerusalem, and they are now his witnesses to the people. (Acts 13:28-31)

Paul passes over a clear opportunity to mention the empty tomb and anyone who witnessed what happened there. He offers only post-crucifixion appearances as evidence of Jesus' rising from death.

1.18 Who Did the Risen Jesus Appear to?

In its oldest surviving manuscripts, the Gospel of Mark ends with 16:8, which describes how the women ran away from the empty tomb in terror and bewilderment and did not talk about it to anyone. But later manuscripts contain three different endings. Scholars have very strong reasons for their agreement that these endings are later additions to Mark. One reason is that early Christian writers show no awareness of any verse after 16:8.[9] Scholars disagree, however, on whether Mark had a different ending that has not survived or whether it really did end with 16:8.[10] The latter case would mean that the oldest Gospel said nothing about Jesus' appearances after his resurrection or his ascension to heaven. For the sake of argument, we will consider the "Longer Ending" (16:9-20) in our discussions of Mark in this book.

The controversial ending states that Jesus appeared first to Mary Magdalene on the first day of the week after his resurrection. Jesus' followers did not believe her, but at some unidentified date he "appeared in another form to two of them, as they were walking into the country". These two, in turn, were disbelieved by other followers. Next, Jesus appeared to his eleven disciples, rebuking them for not believing those who had seen him. After this meeting, Jesus was taken up into heaven, implying that he was not seen by others.

Matthew's (28:6-17) account is very different. After Mary Magdalene and the other Mary left the empty tomb to tell the disciples about what they had seen, as instructed by the angel, they met Jesus, who told them

---

[9] Metzger, *Textual Commentary*, 122-128.

[10] E.g. Stein, "The Ending of Mark".

to inform his brothers to go to Galilee to see him there. Matthew then confirms Jesus' appearance to his eleven disciples in Galilee.

Luke (24:13-51) differs radically from Mark and Matthew, stating that Jesus first appeared to two of his followers, one of whom was named Cleopas, who were on their way to Emmaus. They did not recognize their teacher until later, at which point he vanished. They decided to return to Jerusalem where the other disciples, who are described as *eleven* instead of *nine*, had gathered with other followers of Jesus. The gathering was already aware that Jesus had risen and claimed that he had already appeared to Simon. The two then informed the gathering of their own encounter with Jesus. At this point, Jesus appeared to the whole assembly. He led them as far as Bethany where he was taken up to heaven. Luke differs not only on whom Jesus appeared to, but he also makes his appearance to the disciples in Jerusalem rather than Galilee.

John (20:11-21:14) agrees with Mark that Jesus first appeared to Mary Magdalene, but he places the appearance in her visit to the empty tomb. As instructed by Jesus, she informed the disciples of what happened. In the evening, Jesus appeared to his disciples, except for Thomas who was away, who were hiding from the Jewish authorities. Eight days later, all disciples were together when Jesus appeared to them again. Jesus appeared a third time to the disciples by the Sea of Tiberias. So, one difference John has with the other Gospels is his claim that Jesus appeared to the disciples three times.

In addition to their differences regarding the identities of the followers Jesus appeared to, the four Gospels disagree with each other about the number of appearances, whether they happened in Galilee or Judea, when they happened, and what happened in these appearances.

Paul, writing earlier, differs yet further about Jesus' appearances:

> And that he was buried, and that he was raised on the third day in accordance with the scriptures, and that he appeared to Cephas, then to the twelve. Then he appeared to more than five hundred brothers and sisters at one time, most of whom are still alive, though some have died. Then he appeared to James, then to all the apostles. Last of all, as to one untimely born, he appeared also to me. (1 Cor. 15:4-8)

Jesus' appearance to Paul is also mentioned in Acts (9:3-5). This book reports an earlier appearance in which the first Christian martyr, Stephen, saw Jesus before he was stoned to death by the Jews (Acts 7:55).

Paul's reference to "the twelve" indicates that he was unaware of or did not believe the story of Judas' betrayal which the Gospels later reported.

1.19 Did Jesus' Followers Recognise and Believe in the Risen Jesus?

Mark (16:9) and Matthew (28:9) do not indicate that Mary Magdalene and, according to Matthew, the other Mary doubted Jesus when he appeared to them. Matthew (28:17) says that some of the eleven disciples who saw him later doubted what they saw.

According to Luke (24:15-31), when Jesus appeared to the two disciples on their way to Emmaus, they did not recognise him during his long walk and conversation with them until he revealed his identity to them! Mark's (16:12) Longer Ending seems to try to explain this by saying that "he appeared *in another form* to two of them, as they were walking into the country". When he appeared to the eleven disciples, they thought he was a ghost and they doubted that it was Jesus in the flesh (Luke 24:36-41).

John (20:14-29) disagrees with Mark and Matthew, stating that Mary Magdalene did not recognise Jesus but the eleven disciples did.

1.20 When Was the Ascension?

Mark (16:19) states that after appearing to his eleven disciples while they were eating, Jesus "was taken up into heaven and sat down at the right hand of God". No dating information is given.

Matthew ends with Jesus' appearance to his eleven disciples in Galilee (Matt. 28:16-20). It has no mention of Jesus' ascension to heaven.

Luke says that Jesus' ascension occurred immediately after appearing to his disciples, "Then he led them out as far as Bethany, and, lifting up his hands, he blessed them. While he was blessing them, he withdrew from them and was carried up into heaven" (Luke 24:50-51). It is clear in Luke that this appearance and ascension happened on the same day of the resurrection (Luke 24:1, 13, 21-22).

On the other hand, Acts, which is also attributed to the same author of Luke, states that the ascension happened forty days after the resurrection:

> In the first book, Theophilus, I wrote about all that Jesus did and taught from the beginning until the day when he was taken up to heaven,

after giving instructions through the Holy Spirit to the apostles whom he had chosen. After his suffering he presented himself alive to them by many convincing proofs, appearing to them during forty days and speaking about the kingdom of God. (Acts 1:1-3)

Like Matthew, John (21:1-25) does not make any mention of the ascension, concluding his Gospel with Jesus' third appearance to his disciples by the Sea of Tiberias.

Table 1.1 summarises the differences between the Gospels that we have discussed in this chapter. The New Testament narratives of Jesus' crucifixion and resurrection are inconsistent and contradictory, yet the discussion can be extended further to cover other discrepancies and more details of the story. It is evidently impossible to reconcile the different accounts and come up with one version of the story that accommodates all details.

Table 1.1: Differences between the Gospels

Event	Mark	Matthew	Luke	John
Arrested on the Passover	Yes (15 Nisan)			No (14 Nisan)
Time of trial by Jewish leaders	Night		Morning	Night
Questioned by the Sanhedrin or high priest	High priest and Sanhedrin			Two high priests
Charges in the Jewish trial	Threatening to destroy the temple; claiming to be the Christ; claiming to be the son of God		Claiming to be the Christ; claiming to be the son of God	None
Prosecution witnesses	Many false witnesses; testimonies disagreed	Many false witnesses	None	
Interrogation or trial	Trial		Conflicted	Interrogation

Event	Mark	Matthew	Luke	John
Charges in the Roman trial	Claiming to be the king of the Jews; many unspecified		Claiming to be the king of the Jews; subverting the Jewish people; forbidding paying taxes to the Romans	Claiming to be the king of the Jews; Claiming to be the son of God
Trial by Antipas	None		Yes	None
Judas' death	None	Suicide	None*	None
Carrier of the cross	Simon of Cyrene			Jesus
Crucifixion time	9 a.m.	None		Midday
Darkness	12 noon–3 p.m.			None
Time of death	3 p.m.			None
Robbers' speech	Abusive to Jesus		One abusive and one like a believer	None
Followers present at the crucifixion	Some women		All those who knew Jesus	Four women and one disciple
Followers' position at the crucifixion	At a distance			Beside the cross
Women present at the crucifixion	Include: Mary Magdalene, Mary the mother of James the younger and of Joses, and Salome	Include: Mary Magdalene, Mary the mother of James and Joseph, and the mother of the sons of Zebedee	None named	Jesus' mother, his mother's sister, Mary the wife of Clopas, and Mary Magdalene
Joseph of Arimathea	Member of the Sanhedrin;	Disciple	Member of the Sanhedrin;	Disciple

Event	Mark	Matthew	Luke	John
	awaiting the kingdom of God		awaiting the kingdom of God	
Sign of Jonah	None	Likened to Jesus' time in the tomb	Not likened to Jesus' experience	None
Women who visited the tomb	Mary Magdalene, Mary the mother of James, and Salome	Mary Magdalene and the other Mary	Include: Mary Magdalene, Joanna, and Mary the mother of James	Mary Magdalene
Time women visited the tomb	After sunrise	At dawn	At early dawn	When it was still dark
Others present at the tomb	Young man in a white robe	Angel	Two men/angels	None
First to appear to after resurrection	Mary Magdalene**	Mary Magdalene and the other Mary	Cleopas and another follower	Mary Magdalene
Others appeared to after resurrection***	Two disciples; eleven disciples**	Eleven disciples	Cleopas and unnamed disciple; Simon; eleven disciples; others	All disciples without Thomas; all disciples
Ascension's date	After appearing to eleven disciples**	Ascension not mentioned	After appearing to eleven disciples and others	Ascension not mentioned

* Luke attributes it to an accident in Acts.

** In the Longer Ending of Mark.

*** Paul contradicts the Synoptists by mentioning twelve disciples rather than eleven. He also claims that Jesus appeared to five hundred of his followers and to him.

2

False Old Testament Prophecies

The problems in the arrest, crucifixion, and resurrection narratives in the Gospels are not restricted to inconsistencies within individual Gospels and contradictions with each other. The Evangelists cite seven scriptural prophecies about the Messiah that they link to Jesus' suffering. One problem that *all* of these prophecies share is that *none of them is actually about the Messiah*! Forcibly applied to Jesus' life and used to prove that he was the Messiah, the cited passages have all been taken out of their original contexts. Three of them are not even prophecies in their source texts. Another prophecy found in Matthew does not even exist in the Old Testament!

Matthew, in particular, was interested in citing supposedly scriptural prophecies that he linked to the coming of the Messiah to show that Jesus was the fulfilment of these prophecies. He quotes no less than 16 prophecies (Matt. 1:23, 2:6, 15, 18, 23, 3:3, 4:15-16, 8:17, 11:10, 12:18-21, 13:14-15, 34-35, 15:8-9, 21:4-5, 26:31, 27:9-10). Most of these have the same problems as the prophecies we are studying in this chapter.

Let's examine the seven crucifixion-linked prophecies in their chronological order.

2.1 Stricken Shepherd

Mark and Matthew (26:31) state that Jesus cited an Old Testament prediction to declare that his disciples would scatter after his crucifixion:

> And Jesus said to them, "You will all become deserters; for it is written,
> 'I will strike the shepherd,
>   and the sheep will be scattered.'" (Mark 14:27)

The Biblical prophecy that this passage talks about is Zechariah 13:7. However, the Old Testament prophecy uses the term "sheep" to denote the disobedient Israelites and the "shepherd" for their unbelieving kings! The negative term "shepherd" could not have signified the Messiah. John

(16:32) also mentions that Jesus told the disciples that they would scatter and leave him alone, but the Evangelist does not link this to a prophecy.

2.2 Counted with the Transgressors

In Luke, Jesus tells his disciples the following:

> "For I tell you, this scripture must be fulfilled in me, 'And he was counted among the lawless'; and indeed what is written about me is being fulfilled." (Luke 22:37)

Jesus here cites Isaiah 53:12, but the Old Testament prophecy talks about Israel, not the Messiah. There is no evidence of Jews before Christianity linking this Biblical text to the Messiah.[1]

2.3 Thirty Silver Coins

Matthew states that Judas regretted handing Jesus over, returned the money that he was paid for the treason, which was used to buy the potter's field, and hanged himself. The Evangelist goes on to say:

> Then was fulfilled what had been spoken through the prophet Jeremiah, "And they took the thirty pieces of silver, the price of the one on whom a price had been set, on whom some of the people of Israel had set a price, and they gave them for the potter's field, as the Lord commanded me." (Matt. 27:9-10)

There is no such passage in Jeremiah! There is only a reference to the prophet being commanded to visit a potter (Jer. 18:2-3) and a reference elsewhere to him buying a field from his cousin (Jer. 32:7-9).

The closest passage to this text is found in Zechariah, but the context is completely different and has no relation to the Messiah. The prophet Zechariah here recounts a vision he had:

> I then said to them, "If it seems right to you, give me my wages; but if not, keep them." So they weighed out as my wages thirty shekels of silver. Then the Lord said to me, "Throw it into the treasury"—this lordly price at which I was valued by them. So I took the thirty shekels of silver and threw them into the treasury in the house of the Lord. (Zech. 11:12-13)

---

[1] Dunn, *Jesus Remembered*, 811; Ehrman, *Jesus, Interrupted*, 228-229, 234; Ehrman, *Did Jesus Exist?*, 167; Schürer, *The Jewish People*, II, 549.

While the NRSV, which is used in this book, and some Bible translations, which use the Syriac text, have "treasury", most English translations, which use the Masoretic Text, have "potter" instead.

Matthew's erroneous attribution of the prophecy to Jeremiah has resulted in some scribes changing "Jeremiah" to "Zechariah", in some manuscripts, or omitting the name of the prophet altogether, in others!

2.4 Divided Garments

John has this passage:

> When the soldiers had crucified Jesus, they took his clothes and divided them into four parts, one for each soldier. They also took his tunic; now the tunic was seamless, woven in one piece from the top. So they said to one another, "Let us not tear it, but cast lots for it to see who will get it." This was to fulfill what the scripture says,
> "They divided my clothes among themselves,
> and for my clothing they cast lots." (John 19:23-24)

Psalms 22:18, which this passage references, is not actually a prophecy, but a prayer in which King David complains to God about his enemies.[2]

2.5 Sour Wine

John also has this passage about another alleged scriptural prophecy:

> After this, when Jesus knew that all was now finished, he said (in order to fulfill the scripture), "I am thirsty." A jar full of sour wine was standing there. So they put a sponge full of the wine on a branch of hyssop and held it to his mouth. (John 19:28-29)

This passage seems to cite Psalms 69:21 or 22:15, neither of which is a prophecy nor related to the Messiah.

2.6 No Broken Bone

John relates the following events that took place after Jesus' crucifixion:

> Since it was the day of Preparation, the Jews did not want the bodies left on the cross during the sabbath, especially because that sabbath was a day of great solemnity. So they asked Pilate to have the legs of the crucified men broken and the bodies removed. Then the soldiers came and broke the legs of the first and of the other who had been crucified

---

[2] Ehrman, *Jesus, Interrupted*, 228-229, 234-235.

with him. But when they came to Jesus and saw that he was already dead, they did not break his legs. Instead, one of the soldiers pierced his side with a spear, and at once blood and water came out. (He who saw this has testified so that you also may believe. His testimony is true, and he knows that he tells the truth.) These things occurred so that the scripture might be fulfilled, "None of his bones shall be broken." (John 19:31-36)

This prophecy seems to refer to Exodus 12:46 and Numbers 9:12 in which God states that the Passover lamb must not have any of its bones broken. An unlikely referent is Psalms 34:20, which talks about God's protection of the believer's bones so that none is broken. John is probably linking Jesus' crucifixion to the Passover lamb, as in this Gospel Jesus is crucified at the same time as the slaughter of the Passover lamb. The original text is clearly not a prophecy.

2.7 Pierced One

John follows the account above immediately with this passage:

And again another passage of scripture says, "They will look on the one whom they have pierced." (John 19:37)

This prophecy seems to be a clause from this passage:

And I will pour out a spirit of compassion and supplication on the house of David and the inhabitants of Jerusalem, so that, when they look on the one whom they have pierced, they shall mourn for him, as one mourns for an only child, and weep bitterly over him, as one weeps over a firstborn. (Zech. 12:10)

Like the previous passages, this has been taken completely out of context. It occurs in the Old Testament in the context of describing a war against Israel that ends with its victory (Zech. 12:1-9). The piercing of someone followed by great lamentation by Israel is then mentioned. In addition to the fact that the passage does not talk about the Messiah, the circumstances of Jesus' death bear no resemblance whatsoever to the descriptions given, and the Jews certainly did not cry over Jesus.

Not only do they suffer from serious internal discrepancies, as shown in Chapter 1, but the Gospels also falsely link alleged Old Testament prophecies about the Messiah to the crucifixion of Jesus.

This is the verdict of the Gospels on each other and of the Old Testament on these books; but how does history judge these narratives?

3

Historical Problems in the Gospel Accounts of the Trial

Jewish law and information about first-century Judaism reveal historical problems in the Gospel accounts of Jesus' death. Erroneous statements can be identified by comparing the Gospel narratives of Jesus' trial with the Jewish law governing trials.[1] Commenting on the problems in the Synoptic Gospels in particular, this is the conclusion of the eminent Biblical scholar Géza Vermes, a Jew by birth who was baptised and became a Catholic priest before reverting to Judaism:

> Practically every detail of the Synoptic account conflicts both procedurally and substantively with any known Jewish law.[2]

For reference, this passage from the Mishnah, in which Jewish law is codified, discusses trials involving capital sentences:

> In non-capital cases they hold the trial during the daytime and the verdict may be reached during the night; in capital cases they hold the trial during the daytime and the verdict also must be reached during the daytime. In non-capital cases the verdict, whether of acquittal or of conviction, may be reached the same day; in capital cases a verdict of acquittal may be reached on the same day, but a verdict of conviction not until the following day. Therefore trials may not be held on the eve of a Sabbath or on the eve of a Festival-day.
>
> In non-capital cases concerning uncleanness and cleanness [the judges declare their opinion] beginning from the eldest, but in capital cases they begin from [them that sit at] the side. (Sanh. 4:1-2)[3]

Some New Testament scholars have argued against using the Mishnah for assessing Jesus' trial because of its late redaction date of around 200

---

[1] Winter, *The Trial of Jesus*; Rosenblatt, "The Crucifixion of Jesus".

[2] Vermes, *The Changing Faces of Jesus*, 181.

[3] Mishnah quotations are from Danby, *The Mishnah*.

CE. But there are other first-century sources, such as the Jewish philosopher Philo of Alexandria and the Dead Sea Scrolls, that confirm the laws in this passage. [4] More generally, the teachings and interpretations of a rabbinic literary source, such as the Mishnah, are usually centuries older than the date of their compilation.[5]

We will discuss here the Gospels' ignorance of the Jewish legal system.

3.1 Nocturnal Trial

Mark (14:30-53), Matthew (26:31-57), and John (18:28) claim that Jesus' trial was nocturnal, which violates the law.

3.2 Festival-Day Trial

Mark and Matthew state that Jesus was tried by the Sanhedrin on the Passover night and Luke makes it on the Passover morning. During a festival, trials cannot be held.[6] Even those who argue that it was not illegal to hold a trial on a feast day accept that "the whole day of Passover Eve was devoted to sacred tasks and it was certainly not the right time for a trial or an execution". While not impossible, in first-century Judaism, "it would be an embarrassment that Jewish leaders had chosen this date".[7]

3.3 Same-Day Verdict

Mark and Matthew have the trial conducted and concluded with the guilty verdict on the same day, which contradicts the Mishnah. Luke's account describes a mix of interrogation and trial, and John talks about an interrogation, so it may be argued that these two accounts do not contradict Jewish law. But these two interrogations still led to the Jews asking Pilate to crucify Jesus.

In the Synoptic Gospels, Jesus' trial/interrogation was not only concluded on the same day but lasted for one session only. Only John seems to suggest that more than one session took place, as after questioning Jesus, Annas sent him to the high priest Caiaphas, although there is no report of another interrogation by the latter. John still suggests that all sessions happened on the same day.

---

[4] Vermes, *The Passion*, 20-24.
[5] Vermes, *Jesus in His Jewish Context*, viii.
[6] Vermes, *The Passion*, 100.
[7] Instone-Brewer, "Jesus of Nazareth's Trial", 284.

This is how one scholar described the three historical legal problems in the Gospels that we have discussed so far:

> The Sanhedrin held their sessions every day of the week, except Saturdays and holidays, and on the days preceding them. They never conducted sessions at night. A person who stood trial could be acquitted on the same day, but the law forbade that a conviction should take place on the same day the trial began. Consequently, courts did not hold sessions on the eves of Saturday and holidays. The court could not possess knowledge in advance of the decision that would be reached, whether it would be acquittal or conviction of the offender. If the court should convict the offender, they would have to give the verdict on the morrow.[8]

3.4 No Witnesses

The Mishnah makes the admission of guilt invalid without confirmation by witnesses. Yet Mark (14:63-64) states that after listening to what he considered to be a confession by Jesus, the high priest declared that *no witnesses were needed* and, turning to the Sanhedrin members, he demanded a guilty verdict, "You have heard his blasphemy! What is your decision?" They all obliged and "condemned him as deserving death". The witnesses spoke *before the alleged confession*, and they also disagreed with each other (Mark 14:56-58).

In Matthew (26:59-61) also, false witnesses are called at the beginning of the trial, and Jesus is convicted based on his confession, with no witnesses called to confirm the admission of guilt. Luke does not contain a clear verdict, but the implication is that what Jesus said, again without support by witnesses, proved the case against him. If the Mishnah law on the need for witnesses was in force in Jesus' day, then Jesus' confession could not have been sufficient to convict him. In any case, Biblical law stipulates that court proceedings cannot take place unless reliable prosecution witnesses had confirmed the charge.[9]

3.5 Sentencing by Proclamation

As well as describing a detailed process for examining witnesses and ensuring that the court is satisfied with their testimony, which the Gospels say did not happen in Jesus' trial, the Mishnah also states that each

---

[8] Zeitlin, *Who Crucified Jesus?*, 71-72.

[9] Vermes, *The Passion*, 18.

judge had to cast his vote for the verdict he reached individually, one judge after another. Announcing a capital sentence by common proclamation, as we see in the Gospels, is unhistorical.[10]

3.6 Trial in the Abode of the High Priest

The Gospels place Jesus' trial in the house of the high priest. There is no reference in the writings of the first-century Jewish Roman historian Flavius Josephus or rabbinic literature to the Sanhedrin ever convening in the house of the high priest.[11] The usual place of assembly is the hall of cut stone within the temple.[12] The temple gates were closed at night. Like the other Gospels, Luke states that after his arrest, Jesus was taken to the house of the high priest. Yet he later suggests that the trial was held in the official place:

> When day came, the assembly of the elders of the people, both chief priests and scribes, gathered together, and they brought him to their council. (Luke 22:66)

3.7 Two High Priests

Mark and Matthew talk about one high priest, Caiaphas. Luke (3:2), however, dates God's revelation to John the Baptist to a period "during the high priesthood of Annas and Caiaphas". This implies that the office of the high priest was jointly held. Later in the story, the high priest is mentioned indirectly and only twice. When they came to arrest Jesus, one of Jesus' disciples struck with his sword "the slave of the high priest" (Luke 22:50), and after the arrest, Jesus was brought to the "high priest's house" (Luke 22:54). The implication seems to be that there was only one high priest.

John also calls both Annas and Caiaphas high priests. In addition to calling Caiaphas "high priest" (John 18:24, 26), John describes Caiaphas three times as the "high priest that year" (John 11:49, 51, 18:13), implying that this position was rotated annually. He also, directly and indirectly, calls Annas, Caiaphas' father-in-law, the high priest (John 18:15-16, 19).

Annas was appointed as the high priest in 6 CE by Quirinius the

---

[10] Ibid., 23.

[11] Winter, *The Trial of Jesus*, 20.

[12] Vermes, *The Passion*, 22; Theissen and Merz, *The Historical Jesus*, 461.

governor of Syria, but he remained an influential figure even after his removal in 15 CE by Valerius Gratus, the new Roman prefect of Judea. He managed to have his son-in-law Caiaphas, five of his sons, and one of his grandsons appointed to the high priesthood in succession.[13] Acts (4:6) reports that Annas the high priest was involved with Caiaphas and other members of the high priest's family in the Sanhedrin's investigation of Peter and John in Jerusalem. This continuing influence could explain why Annas got involved in interrogating Jesus even though Caiaphas was the high priest at the time, occupying this position in 18-37 CE.

The Gospels still contain two historical errors. First, the Old Testament, the writings of Josephus and Philo, and rabbinic literature unanimously testify that the office of high priest could be occupied by one person only. Luke's claim that Annas and Caiaphas held the high priesthood jointly is unhistorical. Second, John's claim that the high priesthood was rotated annually is untrue.[14]

3.8 Accusation of Blasphemy

The Gospels state that Jesus was accused of claiming to be the Messiah and the son of God and was therefore convicted of blasphemy:

> But he was silent and did not answer. Again the high priest asked him, "Are you the Messiah, the Son of the Blessed One?" Jesus said, "I am; and
> 'you will see the Son of Man
> seated at the right hand of the Power,'
> and 'coming with the clouds of heaven.'"
> Then the high priest tore his clothes and said, "Why do we still need witnesses? You have heard his blasphemy! What is your decision?" All of them condemned him as deserving death. (Mark 14:61-64)
> But Jesus was silent. Then the high priest said to him, "I put you under oath before the living God, tell us if you are the Messiah, the Son of God." Jesus said to him, "You have said so. But I tell you,
> From now on you will see the Son of Man
> seated at the right hand of Power
> and coming on the clouds of heaven."
> Then the high priest tore his clothes and said, "He has blasphemed! Why do we still need witnesses? You have now heard his blasphemy.

---

[13] Vermes, *The Passion*, 98-99.

[14] Ibid., 43.

(Matt. 26:63-65)

All of them asked, "Are you, then, the Son of God?" He said to them, "You say that I am." Then they said, "What further testimony do we need? We have heard it ourselves from his own lips!" (Luke 22:70-71)

The Jews answered him, "We have a law, and according to that law he ought to die because he has claimed to be the Son of God." (John 19:7)

The rending of one's garment is a Jewish legal requirement for hearing the name of God blasphemed directly or for hearing the blasphemy from the person who heard it first (Sanh. 7:5).

While claiming divine dignity was blasphemous, the claim to messiahship or sonship of God was not an act of blasphemy or a religious crime in Judaism.[15] This proclamation could not have been considered a capital offence. The title "son of God" is used in the Old Testament itself for certain non-human beings (Gen. 6:1-4), King David (2 Sam. 7:14; Ps. 2:7), and all of Israel (Exod. 4:22-23). In post-Biblical periods, this title started to be applied only to pious Jews (Jub. 1:21-24). In all four Jewish uses, the title "son of God" is always used as a figure of speech. A son of God is someone close to God; he does not share the divinity of God. The sonship of God does not mean that the person is divine.[16]

Pronouncing the four-letter divine name YHVH or speaking disrespectfully about God is blasphemous. This is an instance of pronouncing and abusing the sacrosanct Tetragram from Moses' time:

A man whose mother was an Israelite and whose father was an Egyptian came out among the people of Israel; and the Israelite woman's son and a certain Israelite began fighting in the camp. The Israelite woman's son blasphemed the Name in a curse. And they brought him to Moses—now his mother's name was Shelomith, daughter of Dibri, of the tribe of Dan—and they put him in custody, until the decision of the Lord should be made clear to them.

The Lord said to Moses, saying: Take the blasphemer outside the camp; and let all who were within hearing lay their hands on his head, and let the whole congregation stone him. And speak to the people of Israel, saying: Anyone who curses God shall bear the sin. One who blasphemes the name of the Lord shall be put to death; the whole congregation shall stone the blasphemer. Aliens as well as citizens, when

---

[15] Sanders, *Jewish Law*, 64-65, 92; Vermes, *The Passion*, 101-103; Rosenblatt, "The Crucifixion of Jesus", 319; Theissen and Merz, *The Historical Jesus*, 464.
[16] Fatoohi, *Jesus the Muslim Prophet*, 35-37.

they blaspheme the Name, shall be put to death. (Lev. 24:10-16)

By the start of the first century CE, blasphemy became specifically linked to pronouncing the divine name YHVH.[17] Rabbinic literature states categorically that "'the blasphemer' is not culpable unless he pronounces the Name itself" (Sanh. 7:5).

The Gospels were written decades after Jesus' time when Christians had already developed the term "son of God" to mean sharing divine attributes.[18] The four Evangelists attribute to Jesus' Jewish accusers their own, late understanding of "son of God", which was never known to the Jews, including at the time of Jesus. These are anachronistic errors by the Evangelists.[19] As noted by one scholar, "The exchange between the high priest and Jesus (messiah, Son of God, blasphemy) is probably a Christian composition which has Jesus die for holding the church's christology".[20]

3.9 Threat to Destroy the Temple
Mark and Matthew included in their charges of Jesus his prophecy of destroying the temple and rebuilding it in three days. Critics of the temple did attract hostility but not the death penalty. Most of those who criticized the temple survived.[21]

3.10 Release of a Prisoner on the Passover
Three of the Gospels claim that it was a custom during the Passover for one prisoner to be released to the people:

Now at the festival he used to release a prisoner for them, anyone for whom they asked. (Mark 15:6)
Now at the festival the governor was accustomed to release a prisoner for the crowd, anyone whom they wanted. (Matt. 27:15)
But you have a custom that I release someone for you at the Passover. Do you want me to release for you the King of the Jews?" (John 18:39)

Mark (15:8) implies that the Passover amnesty was a custom of Pilate's, while Matthew states this explicitly. John contradicts them by making it

---

[17] Vermes, *The Passion*, 101.

[18] Fatoohi, *Jesus the Muslim Prophet*, 39-55.

[19] Vermes, *The Passion*, 103.

[20] Sanders, *Jewish Law*, 92.

[21] Theissen and Merz, *The Historical Jesus*, 463.

a Jewish custom! Bizarrely, the Roman governor is seen reminding the Jews of their own custom!

Luke (23:18) also hints at this practice. When Pilate told the Jews that he was going to flog Jesus and release him, they asked for another prisoner to be released instead. This alleged custom, though, has no historical basis.[22]

Josephus[23] reports that the high priest asked Judea's Roman procurator Albinus (62-64 CE) to release ten prisoners, which was the price that was asked for the freedom of his kidnapped son. Albinus granted the high priest his wish, but that was a one-off event and not a custom in any way.

Mark (15:7), Luke (23:25), and John (18:40) all state that the freed prisoner, Barabbas, had been imprisoned for involvement in an insurrection. This is an extremely serious crime, to which Mark and Luke add murder. The claim that this dangerous political prisoner was freed, when there must have been other prisoners with much less serious crimes who posed less danger to the state, further suggests that the story of the Passover amnesty is fictional.

Additionally, the very suggestion that the Roman governor let the Jews decide which prisoner he should release is rather absurd. This is another product of the narrative atmosphere in which the Roman ruler unrealistically and unjustifiably delegates to the Jews important legal and official decisions and shows inexplicable flexibility, weakness, and indecision.

In conclusion, the Gospel narratives do not only contradict each other and use false scriptural prophecies, as we saw in the first two chapters, but they are also at odds with historical facts. This is how one scholar summarised the trial accounts in the Gospels:

> If such a trial did take place, and if it were possible to reconstruct its proceedings from the discrepant, and often contradictory reports of the Gospels, the only justifiable conclusion would be that in a single session the Sanhedrin managed to break every rule in the book: it would, in other words, have been an illegal trial.[24]

---

[22] Ibid., 465; Vermes, *The Passion*, 95; Winter, *The Trial of Jesus*, 93-94.

[23] Josephus, *Antiquities*, 20.9.3.

[24] Vermes, *Jesus the Jew*, 36.

4

The Unhistorical Theological "Suffering Messiah"

The crucifixion and resurrection of Jesus underlie what is arguably the most important doctrine in Christian theology: "substitutionary atonement". Paul considered this doctrine so fundamental to Christianity that he told fellow Christians, "If Christ has not been raised, your faith is futile and you are still in your sins" (1 Cor. 15:17).

In brief, atonement denotes the reconciliation between God and man that is brought about by the death and subsequent resurrection of Jesus. Adam sinned and all people inherited his sin, which signifies death. To save people from His wrath and give them eternal life after death, God caused His son, Jesus, to die and raised him from the dead. Jesus' resurrection signifies the hope to be freed from sin and to attain eternal life, "for as all die in Adam, so all will be made alive in Christ" (1 Cor. 15:22). Those who believed in Jesus as their saviour would be redeemed and rewarded with salvation. This is one passage from Paul in which he explains the significance of the Easter experience and its role in the salvation of man:

> For while we were still weak, at the right time Christ died for the ungodly. Indeed, rarely will anyone die for a righteous person—though perhaps for a good person someone might actually dare to die. But God proves his love for us in that while we still were sinners Christ died for us. Much more surely then, now that we have been justified by his blood, will we be saved through him from the wrath of God. For if while we were enemies, we were reconciled to God through the death of his Son, much more surely, having been reconciled, will we be saved by his life. But more than that, we even boast in God through our Lord Jesus Christ, through whom we have now received reconciliation. (Rom. 5:6-11)

Because of Jesus' sacrifice, following the law is no longer necessary for attaining salvation. Paul says that Jesus' death and resurrection "nullified" the law (Eph. 2:15), although he does not advocate a complete abolishment of it.

Jesus' vicarious function as the suffering Messiah who saves people from their sins and God's wrath permeates Paul's writings. While Jesus' soteriological role is found in the Gospels, Paul's link of his suffering to the forgiveness of sins is not. A detailed discussion of the differences between the New Testament authors about the atonement is not of much relevance here because our focus is on history, not theology. But I would like to give two examples to illustrate the inconsistency.

Mark (10:45) has Jesus tell his disciples that "For the Son of Man came not to be served but to serve, and to give his life a *ransom for many*". Jesus' description of himself as a "ransom for many", which also appears in Matthew's (20:28) version, is seen as the most explicit reference by Jesus to the atonement in the Gospels. Yet the report in Luke (22:27) of the same speech has no trace of this particular phrase! Even if Mark's and Matthew's passages are more authentic, the absence of that particular phrase from Luke's account means that it could not have signified as important and fundamental a doctrine as the atonement, whether Luke or his sources dropped it deliberately or did not realize its supposed meaning.

Bart Ehrman, a leading authority on early Christianity, notes that in Acts also, Luke's author recounts apostolic speeches that stress the importance of Jesus' death as a means to drive people to repent and seek forgiveness from God, but nowhere does he consider Jesus' death as an atonement for sins. Ehrman also makes the interesting observation that in some manuscripts of Luke, Jesus' speech during the Last Supper misses the words "which is given for you" (Luke 22:19) about his body, which may be seen as a reference to the atonement. He concludes that these were added later by copyists.[1] This suffices here to point out the serious problems with the significance of the doctrine of atonement in the New Testament.

What is of more interest, though, is the historical genesis of atonement, namely how it relates to Judaism and, ultimately and more importantly, the Jewish concept of the Messiah. The main point here is that Paul's cross-centred theology is foreign to the Old Testament. The latter does not speak of the salvation of man through the death of one

---

[1] Ehrman, *Misquoting Jesus*, 166-167.

person acting as a vicarious sacrifice. In the many centuries that the Old Testament spans, neither God nor any Patriarch or prophet taught that sins could be forgiven through the death and resurrection of a man, let alone someone who would come many centuries later, so his role as a saviour is irrelevant to the generations before him.

Even theologians who try to show that Christian substitutionary atonement is not a complete innovation but an extension of an earlier Jewish version have to admit that it "is unique primarily because it has to do with Jesus Christ as the Son of God and the Messiah, and because of the extent of the atoning efficacy of his death".[2] The reason is that "rabbinic traditions did not envision the Messiah's death as the atoning sacrifice".[3]

More fundamentally, Paul's foundational concept of the suffering Messiah, and subsequently his resurrection, is unhistorical:

> Neither the authors of the Old Testament nor postbiblical Jewish writers inferred that either the death or resurrection of Israel's Messiah was expected in any way.[4]

The Messiah was supposed to come to redeem Israel and reinstate its long-gone kingdom. He was not supposed to be tortured and put to death, let alone by crucifixion. Crucifixion was seen by the Jews, like the Romans, as the most shameful and humiliating form of punishment. This view of the crucifixion is confirmed in the New Testament and by the early church Fathers.[5] In fact, while good and pious people would be honoured after their execution, there is no instance in Jewish history before Jesus of this posthumous positivity being applied to victims of crucifixion. This absolutely negative attitude seems to stem from the following Old Testament text that describes those who are crucified as *cursed by God*:[6]

> When someone is convicted of a crime punishable by death and is executed, and you hang him on a tree, his corpse must not remain all night upon the tree; you shall bury him that same day, for anyone hung

---

[2] Kim, "The Concept of Atonement", 135.
[3] Ibid., 126.
[4] Vermes, *The Changing Faces of Jesus*, 183.
[5] Chapman, *Perceptions of Crucifixion*, 252-253.
[6] Holmén, "Crucifixion Hermeneutics".

on a tree is under God's curse. You must not defile the land that the Lord your God is giving you for possession. (Deut. 21:22-23)

The fact that Jesus' crucifixion is in contradiction to the Jewish concept of the Messiah is easily read from Paul's acknowledgement that a "Christ crucified" is a "stumbling block to Jews" as it is "foolishness to Gentiles" (1 Cor. 1:23). Convincing a Jew that the crucified Jesus was the long-awaited victorious national saviour was at least as hard as getting a wisdom-seeking Greek to welcome the weakness and humiliation of the crucifixion as a sign of divinity or even support by a god:

> The gospels clearly show that nobody associated with Jesus anticipated for him a career that would end in death. The primitive Christians had too much difficulty in defending their faith in a suffering Messiah to allow us to believe that they found the idea current in Judaism or even that the heathen notion of a dying and rising divinity was recognized as having any essential similarity with their preaching about "Jesus Christ and him crucified".[7]

Jesus' empty tomb and later appearances seem to have astonished his followers as much as they would have stunned anyone else. This fact is unambiguously borne out by the behaviour of Jesus' disciples in the relevant episodes in the Gospels:

> It seems clear that the disciples did not entertain any hope of any impending resurrection, judging from their behaviour after Jesus' arrest— they all fled—and their original disbelief on Easter day. Neither did the women who set out for the tomb to anoint the body of Jesus. But this lack of expectation potently conflicts with the claim repeated no less than five times in the Synoptic Gospels that Jesus distinctly predicted not only his death, but also his resurrection on precisely the third day (Mark 8:31; 9:9, 9:31; 10:33-34; 14:28). This most significant prophecy of Jesus appears to have fallen on deaf ears or to have sunk straight into oblivion, with not a single apostle or disciple recalling it during the crucial hours between Friday and Sunday, or even later when the resurrection became the central topic of the preaching of the primitive church. Luke alone realized this internal contradiction and tried to overcome it by suggesting that the women were reminded of Jesus' prediction by the two men they had met in the empty tomb (Luke 24:7-8).

If all his close companions had known exactly what was going to happen, despite their instinctive anxiety they would have comforted themselves with the thought that on the third day all would be well. As this manifestly was

[7] Case, "The Historicity of Jesus", 30.

not the case, one is inclined to conclude that the announcements concerning the resurrection of Jesus are later editorial interpolations. They are often accompanied by clumsy explanations, namely that Peter was unwilling to believe the words of Jesus and began to rebuke him (Mark 8:32-33; Matt. 16:22-23), and that the apostles were dim-witted and could not comprehend what resurrection from the dead meant (Mark 9:10; 9:32; Matt. 17:23; Luke 18:34).[8]

How, then, did the concept of the "suffering Messiah" come about? It was an ingenious way to reconcile the belief that Jesus was the Messiah with the counterintuitive belief that he suffered and died. Packaging this suffering with resurrection, the pair was turned into a theological doctrine. The New Testament authors repositioned the cross experience and the following resurrection as a fulfilment of messianic expectations.[9] What was *never supposed to happen* to the Messiah yet did happen was recast as what *had to happen*. The historical fact that Jesus did not liberate the Jews or rebuild their kingdom could not be changed or disputed. His perceived mission, therefore, had to be changed to accommodate and reflect that unfulfilled expectation.

---

[8] Vermes, *The Changing Faces of Jesus*, 183-184.
[9] Theissen and Merz, *The Historical Jesus*, 553.

5

The Jewish and Roman Roles in the Crucifixion

The Gospels differ on what the high priest and Jewish leaders charged Jesus with (§1.4), and they also give contradictory accounts on the different charges that were examined by Pilate (§1.6). But the Evangelists agree on the identity of Jesus' killers, making the Jewish leaders and crowd responsible for his execution. The Roman governor is the one who ordered the crucifixion of Jesus, but he is presented as an unwilling partner.

This Christian image has come under increased questioning, with scholars suggesting that it was the Romans who killed Jesus and that the Jews were made scapegoats by the Christians. While this book argues that Jesus was not crucified and that someone else was killed in his stead, the questions of who wanted to crucify him and who had the power to do it are critical to understanding what exactly happened.

5.1 The Gospels' Indictment of the Jews

According to Mark, Pilate knew that the Jewish chief priests handed Jesus over to him because of jealousy. After questioning the accused, the Roman prefect could not find anything wrong done by the man, and he wanted to let him go as the prisoner to release for the Passover. But that was not what the Jewish leaders and the crowd wanted, so the governor granted them their request:

> So the crowd came and began to ask Pilate to do for them according to his custom. Then he answered them, "Do you want me to release for you the King of the Jews?" For he realized that it was out of jealousy that the chief priests had handed him over. But the chief priests stirred up the crowd to have him release Barabbas for them instead. Pilate spoke to them again, "Then what do you wish me to do with the man you call the King of the Jews?" They shouted back, "Crucify him!" Pilate asked them, "Why, what evil has he done?" But they shouted all the more,

"Crucify him!" So Pilate, wishing to satisfy the crowd, released Barabbas for them; and after flogging Jesus, he handed him over to be crucified. (Mark 15:8-15)

In Matthew, this story is further developed in a way that emphasizes Pilate's innocence and the Jews' *full* and *perpetual* responsibility for the crucifixion. This Gospel introduces Pilate's wife in the plot to stress her husband's innocence, makes Pilate declare that he is innocent of Jesus' blood and, catastrophically, makes *the Jews* accept *with their children* the responsibility for his execution:

> So after they had gathered, Pilate said to them, "Whom do you want me to release for you, Jesus Barabbas or Jesus who is called the Messiah?" For he realized that it was out of jealousy that they had handed him over. While he was sitting on the judgment seat, his wife sent word to him, "Have nothing to do with that innocent man, for today I have suffered a great deal because of a dream about him." Now the chief priests and the elders persuaded the *crowds* to ask for Barabbas and to have Jesus killed. The governor again said to them, "Which of the two do you want me to release for you?" And they said, "Barabbas." Pilate said to them, "Then what should I do with Jesus who is called the Messiah?" All of them said, "Let him be crucified!" Then he asked, "Why, what evil has he done?" But they shouted all the more, "Let him be crucified!"
> So when Pilate saw that he could do nothing, but rather that a riot was beginning, he took some water and washed his hands before the crowd, saying, "I am innocent of this man's blood; see to it yourselves." Then *the people as a whole* answered, "His blood be *on us and on our children!*" So he released Barabbas for them; and after flogging Jesus, he handed him over to be crucified. (Matt. 27:17-26)

It is not difficult to see why Matthew's version of Pilate's trial of Jesus has seen this Evangelist be accused of anti-Semitism. In another passage (Matt. 27:9), he cites a non-existent Jeremiah prophecy that suggests that the price of thirty silver coins that Judas Iscariot sold Jesus for was set by the Israelites (§2.3). The guilt of the whole of the Jewish people is stressed over and over.

Luke (23:4) also has Pilate say that he could "find no basis for an accusation against this man". To avoid being involved in killing Jesus, Pilate even sent him to Herod Antipas because the accused was Galilean, so the case fell under Antipas' jurisdiction. Luke then goes on to exonerate Antipas also, thus laying the blame mainly on the Jewish accusers:

> Pilate then called together the chief priests, the leaders, and the people, and said to them, "You brought me this man as one who was perverting the people; and here I have examined him in your presence and have not found this man guilty of any of your charges against him. Neither has Herod, for he sent him back to us. Indeed, he has done nothing to deserve death. I will therefore have him flogged and release him."
>
> Then they all shouted out together, "Away with this fellow! Release Barabbas for us!" (This was a man who had been put in prison for an insurrection that had taken place in the city, and for murder.) Pilate, wanting to release Jesus, addressed them again; but they kept shouting, "Crucify, crucify him!" A third time he said to them, "Why, what evil has he done? I have found in him no ground for the sentence of death; I will therefore have him flogged and then release him." But they kept urgently demanding with loud shouts that he should be crucified; and their voices prevailed. So Pilate gave his verdict that their demand should be granted. (Luke 23:13-24)

Luke stresses Pilate's innocence of Jesus' blood by having him declare three times his belief that Jesus was innocent. This Evangelist later makes two of Jesus' disciples say that their "chief priests and leaders handed him over to be condemned to death and crucified him" (Luke 24:20).

The same picture is found in John. Pilate told the Jews that he could "find no case against him" (John 18:38). John's account then goes on as follows:

> Pilate went out again and said to them, "Look, I am bringing him out to you to let you know that I find no case against him." So Jesus came out, wearing the crown of thorns and the purple robe. Pilate said to them, "Here is the man!" When the chief priests and the police saw him, they shouted, "Crucify him! Crucify him!" Pilate said to them, "Take him yourselves and crucify him; I find no case against him." The Jews answered him, "We have a law, and according to that law he ought to die because he has claimed to be the Son of God."
>
> Now when Pilate heard this, he was more afraid than ever. He entered his headquarters again and asked Jesus, "Where are you from?" But Jesus gave him no answer. Pilate therefore said to him, "Do you refuse to speak to me? Do you not know that I have power to release you, and power to crucify you?" Jesus answered him, "You would have

no power over me unless it had been given you from above; therefore the one who handed me over to you is guilty of a greater sin." From then on Pilate tried to release him, but the Jews cried out, "If you release this man, you are no friend of the emperor. Everyone who claims to be a king sets himself against the emperor."

When Pilate heard these words, he brought Jesus outside and sat on the judge's bench at a place called The Stone Pavement, or in Hebrew Gabbatha. Now it was the day of Preparation for the Passover; and it was about noon. He said to the Jews, "Here is your King!" They cried out, "Away with him! Away with him! Crucify him!" Pilate asked them, "Shall I crucify your King?" The chief priests answered, "We have no king but the emperor." Then he handed him over to them to be crucified. (John 19:4-16)

John has Pilate end the trial by handing Jesus over to *the Jews*, rather than to his soldiers, to crucify him, possibly to further incriminate the Jews.

Let's summarise the Gospels' narrative. The Jews indicted Jesus, wanted him killed, and asked Pilate to do the dirty work for them. The implication, which John (18:31) explicitly confirms, is that the Jews did not have the power to execute Jesus. This is likely to have been the case, as we shall see. Although not convinced by the case against Jesus and not finding him to have done anything that deserved death, the Roman governor is said to have bowed to pressure from the Jews and granted them their wish, crucifying Jesus. It was the priestly authorities who initiated Jesus' prosecution, but it ended up being a popular cause that involved the Jewish public.

It has been suggested that the Christian accounts deliberately tried to absolve the Roman governor and blame the Jews to curry favour with Rome.[1] At the time of the writing of the Gospels, the Jews had become very unpopular with the Romans,[2] having had their first rebellion put down by the Romans in 66-70 CE. The Gospels' narrative, it is claimed, would have then helped to show that Christianity was never at odds with Rome. One fundamental problem with this reasoning is that while the Gospels mainly blame the Jews for Jesus' death, they still unambiguously attribute to the Roman ruler the major role of carrying out the Jewish

---

[1] Dunn, *Jesus Remembered*, 774-777.
[2] Vermes, *The Passion*, 121.

sentence. The Gospel authors wouldn't have ascribed any role to Pilate at all had they wanted to completely avoid any suggestion that the Romans held a negative view of their teacher.

Some later Christian writings went further in stressing the sole responsibility of the Jews for the execution of Jesus. For instance, *The Gospel of Peter*, which is dated to the early second century, starts as follows:

> ...but none of the Jews washed his hands, nor did Herod or any of his judges. Since they did not wish to wash, Pilate stood up. The king Herod ordered the Lord to be taken away and said to them, "Do everything that I ordered you to do to him".[3]

The surviving text suggests that the missing text talked about Pilate washing his hands of Jesus' blood. Indeed, towards the end of this gospel, agitated by the news of the miracle of the resurrection of Jesus, Pilate is made to say, "I am clean of the blood of the Son of God; you decided to do this".[4] This book also repeats Matthew's claim that none of the Jews, including Antipas, washed their hands of the blood of Jesus. This seems to suggest that it was Antipas, rather than Pilate, who ordered the execution of Jesus and that the sentence was carried out by the Jews.

The later book of the *Acts of Pilate*, which is also known as the *Gospel of Nicodemus*, shows Pilate repeatedly trying to convince the Jews that Jesus had done nothing wrong and that he should not be killed. Ultimately, he had to sentence Jesus to death.[5] The enthusiasm of some Christian circles to acquit Pilate went even further, as he was turned into a saint in the Coptic and Ethiopian Church.[6] This is in further acknowledgement of his supposed reluctance to partake in the crime.

The motive behind this increasing exoneration of Pilate could not be clearer: the more innocent Pilate is, the more guilty the Jews are. The agenda of these authors is too naked to credit their claims with any historical credibility. Some have argued that this post-Gospels increasing criminalisation of the Jews and exoneration of the Romans with time can also be found in the Gospels themselves. They argue that a similar

---

[3] Ehrman, *Lost Scriptures*, 32.

[4] Ibid., 34.

[5] James, *The Apocryphal New Testament*, 96-108.

[6] Van den Broek, *Pseudo-Cyril of Jerusalem*, 34.

development in the narrative can be seen from the earliest Gospel, Mark, through Luke and Matthew, to become clearer in the latest Gospel, John. Yet any such development in the Gospels over time cannot hide the fact that even the earliest Gospel makes it abundantly clear that it was the Jewish authorities who prosecuted and indicted Jesus and handed him over to Pilate to carry out their sentence. It also states that having Jesus executed became a popular demand, with a crowd of Jews joining their leaders in asking for Jesus' blood. This Evangelist claims that Pilate even pleaded with the crowds, saying that he could not find Jesus to have done anything wrong, before confirming that the Roman governor finally *reluctantly* acceded to the demand to have Jesus crucified "wishing to satisfy the crowd" (Mark 15:15).

True, unlike later sources, Mark does not completely exonerate Pilate by making Antipas the executioner or go further and declare him a saint. But his account still lays the blame on the Jews, both the leaders and the people. Mark's Pilate is portrayed as a reluctant accomplice who felt he had to grant the Jewish crowd their demand. This account alone already had enough ammunition for the vicious persecution of the Jews over centuries for their role in the crucifixion of Jesus, which is why developing it further was not necessary for the case for persecution.

Post-Gospels sources that further magnified the guilt of the Jews did not start, even if they further strengthened, anti-Jew sentiments. They were already firmly grounded in the Gospels. Later writings simply reflected that already-established hostility towards the Jews and elaborated on it. Over time, the canonical Gospels of Mark, Matthew, Luke, and John became by far the most read, most revered, and most influential Christian books on Jesus' life. Other apocryphal gospels cannot be credibly claimed to have played any significant role in the historical Christian hostility towards the Jews.

For almost two millennia, Christians accepted the Gospels' image of Pilate as an unwilling participant in the execution of Jesus and of the Jews as the culprits who solely shoulder the blame for what happened to him. In modern times, this portrayal has gradually come under question. This is partly due to the general gradual change, which started after the Enlightenment, from treating Scriptures as infallible revelations to subjecting them to critical analysis. More specifically and influentially, this questioning is in response to the realisation of the devastating role this image has played in fuelling the long and bloody history of Christian persecution of the Jews.

Even a selective reading and highly liberal interpretation of the Gospels cannot dispute that they portray the Jews as Jesus' main killers, let alone claim that they present them as a non-player in his murder. Attempts to exonerate the Jews, thus, had to focus on showing that the Gospel accounts are historically inaccurate and wrong rather than misread and misinterpreted. There is no denying that these narratives are riddled with inconsistencies, contradictions, and irredeemable errors, as we have already discussed. But there is a limit to how much change to a narrative is possible before the integrity of a text is seriously damaged. For instance, holding all Jewish generations from Jesus' day responsible for his execution makes no sense and, tragically, brings no good. Rejecting this illogical and dangerous sweeping generalisation is reasonable and does not undermine the entirety of the Gospels' narrative.

But coming up with a Gospels-based scenario that exonerates the Jews of Jesus' death and criminalises Pilate is simply impossible. A dismissive statement such as "the high-priest and his staff played only a minor role in bringing Jesus to trial before Pilate" is absurd.[7] The tightly connected claims that the Jews sought the death penalty for Jesus and Pilate only reluctantly signed it off are part of the very fabric of the Gospels' narrative of the crucifixion and permeate all of its episodes. Changing this image to one where Pilate becomes mainly, let alone solely, responsible for Jesus' death amounts effectively to a rewrite of just about every step of the story from the Jewish authorities' plan to arrest him to his crucifixion. In an attempt to fully exonerate the Jews from the crucifixion of Jesus, this is what one scholar has noted:

> Everything about the crucifixion of Jesus, from the indictment and the trial to the execution of sentence was contrary to Pharisaic law and could not by the furthest stretch of the imagination have been plotted or planned and carried out by the official and responsible spokesmen of Pharisaic Jewry.[8]

But a complete revision of the Gospel accounts would require changing Jesus' earlier history as well. He is reported to have had frequent confrontations with Jewish teachers and leaders and was very critical of

---

[7] Winter, *The Trial of Jesus*, 125.
[8] Rosenblatt, "The Crucifixion of Jesus", 321.

them in his speeches, yet there is complete silence on any tension or even encounter he had with the Romans. History revisionists ignore the serious implications that their efforts have for the integrity and reliability of the Gospels as historical sources.

There are good reasons to accept the historicity of the Gospels' specific apportioning of responsibility for the crucifixion of Jesus between the Jews and the Romans:

- Jesus was never popular with the Jewish public.
- He provoked the ire of the religious establishment to the point of them seeking his death.
- He did nothing to upset the Roman authorities.
- The Jews did not have the power to enact capital punishment, so they had to ask the Roman prefect to kill Jesus for them.

I shall deal with these points in the next four sections, respectively.

5.2 Jesus' Limited Popularity with the Jewish Public

The account of Jesus' arrest, trial, and execution reflects an inexplicably sudden and fundamental change to how the Jewish public viewed him. The supposedly popular healer and teacher suddenly became a detested blasphemer and a hate figure that the mob was adamant must be killed. The people who loved Jesus so much were suddenly asking for his head:

> The Gospel account of Jesus' first two or three days in Jerusalem further attests indirectly that large groups were listening to his teaching in the Temple and that his patent popularity is given as the cause of why the priestly authorities abstained from immediately taking steps against him. In short, until his arrest Jesus seems to have been the darling of the Galilean country folk and even warmly welcomed by the Jewish crowd in Jerusalem.
>
> Yet, if we are to believe the same evangelists, on the last day of the life of Jesus a sea-change suddenly occurred. Jesus became the object of hatred not only for the leaders of Judaism, the chief priests and the Sanhedrin, but also for the Jewish people at large. No one had a good word to say in his favour. Many witnesses testified against him, but none for him. The crowd abominated him. All the people, "the Jews", asked for his death and egged on the Roman governor to crucify him. Luke, it is true, attempts to diminish the contrast by reporting that the previously hostile crowd present at the crucifixion beat their breasts after the death of Jesus, but this mitigating

circumstance seems to be of the evangelist's own making, unsupported by Mark, Matthew or John.[9]

The Jewish leaders first hesitated to arrest Jesus because they feared that the crowds would turn against them (Matt. 26:5). Such was his popularity, it is claimed.

Yet the Gospels repeatedly mention that Jesus' teaching was rejected by most of the Jews he preached to, not only those in power who ultimately plotted to kill him.[10] At one point, he said that the whole world hated him (John 15:18). He was even rejected in his own hometown of Nazareth, leading him to complain, "Prophets are not without honor, except in their hometown, and among their own kin, and in their own house" (Mark 6:4). Indeed, early in his ministry, his family members are said to have been so unhappy with his teaching that they tried to stop him and accused him of losing his mind (Mark 3:21). John (7:5) states that "not even his brothers believed in him", and Paul (1 Cor. 15:7) seems to imply that Jesus' brother James believed in him only after he appeared to him after his resurrection. It seems most reasonable to conclude that "the general impression given by the Gospels is that Jesus had a small band of actual followers".[11]

Acts (1:14-15) states that, several months after the crucifixion, when Peter addressed the Christian community, they consisted of only 120 believers. One estimate by a sociologist puts the number of Christians in the year 40 CE at 1,000 and at the turn of the first century at 7,500;[12] another study by a historian has the respective figures of 1,000 and 7,400;[13] whereas one New Testament scholar suggests that at the time of Jesus there were only twenty Christians and they had grown to 1,000-1,500 by the year 60 CE.[14] These figures are not exact but they are indicative of the fact that even well after Jesus was gone, the Christians were still a tiny minority.

This is confirmed by the Jewish trial of Jesus being completely focused

---

[9] Vermes, *The Passion*, 7.

[10] Ehrman, *Apocalyptic Prophet*, 200-202.

[11] Sanders, *Jesus and Judaism*, 303.

[12] Stark, *The Rise of Christianity*, 7.

[13] Hopkins, "Christian Number and its Implications", 441–442.

[14] Ehrman, *The Triumph of Christianity*, 170.

on him, showing no interest whatsoever in his followers. Indeed, those who arrested him did not arrest any of his disciples who were present with him. This was a hostile action against a single charismatic teacher, not the mass persecution of a recognised movement. Reports in Acts of the Jewish persecution of known Christian figures, such as Peter and John, happened years after Jesus as his following, contrary to Jewish expectations, survived his death and continued to grow. In the case of these two disciples, they were released after their arrest and trial (Acts 4:1-23). The targeting of certain individuals indicates that their persecution was not merely because they were Christian.

Further evidence that Jesus left a very small following and that it grew slowly, albeit steadily, comes from outside the New Testament. In the first two centuries, Christians are mentioned in only a handful of historical sources. For instance, writing in the first half of the third century his history of the Roman empire in the period 180-238 CE, the historian Herodian did not mention the Christians a single time. One stark consequence of the small number of early Christians is that "the development and maintenance of Christian religious ideology in the first century after Jesus' death was at any one time the intellectual property of only a few dozen men, scattered throughout the Mediterranean basin".[15] This confirms the high likelihood that Jesus' original teaching was significantly altered and explains how a post-Jesus convert, Paul, became the most influential person in shaping Christian theology.

Leaving the question of why the Jewish authorities wanted to eliminate Jesus to the next section, we must ask here why he was not popular with the public. It looks like there were four reasons. **First**, the public rejected Jesus' claim that he was the Messiah. His portrayal of the Messiah as a peaceful spiritual teacher was completely at odds with the military figure that the Jews were expecting and hoping would come to liberate them. Instead of fulfilling the centuries-long Jewish dream, Jesus declared that this hope was misguided and effectively proclaimed its demise instead of its realisation. The Jews expected to benefit in this world, there and then, yet Jesus' message preached an otherworldly kingdom.

This also means that, contrary to the implicit and explicit claims

---

[15] Hopkins, "Christian Number and its Implications", 479.

attributed to him in the Gospels, Jesus did not envisage or present himself as an eschatological figure. It was the misguided popular image of the Messiah at the time that positioned his coming at the end of time. Jesus' messiahship was not about a final and lasting earthly victory. Broadly speaking, it was another divinely driven mission to call people to God, just like that of Noah, Abraham, Jacob, and others. As we shall see later, this is how the Qur'an portrays Jesus' mission.

Also, the Messiah was largely expected to be a descendant of King David, which Jesus wasn't.[16] Both Matthew (1:18-25) and Luke (1:26-39) state that while still a virgin, Mary miraculously conceived Jesus. With Mary having had no relationship with a man, Jesus had no paternal link to David. Yet each of the two Evangelists introduced a genealogy that linked Jesus to David through Joseph (Matt. 1:1-16; Luke 3:23-38), Mary's fiancé and future husband, even though he was not Jesus' father. These unconvincing genealogies are the Evangelists' response to the Jewish objection to Jesus' messiahship because he was not a Davidic descendant.

Second, Jesus had a relatively relaxed attitude towards the law and held a reformist interpretation of it. His teaching at times even contradicted the views of the religious establishment. Having preached what he believed in, regardless of how unpopular it was, he did not win over many people with his message.

The **third** reason for Jesus' limited appeal was that he did not belong to any of the Jewish religious groups in Palestine in his day. As an *independent radical reformist teacher*, he was not endorsed by one of those groups. Furthermore, he portrayed himself as being anti-establishment. We will discuss this in more detail in the next section.

Fourth, as I explain later in detail (§23.3), I believe Jesus started teaching to the public when he was a teenager. His young age would have worked against his acceptance by the public. As he grew older, his credibility in the eyes of people also grew. A few years into his mission, probably when he was around eighteen, his success with the public started to become visible and alarming to the Jewish authorities, which was when they moved to kill him. He would have become far more successful had he been allowed more time. Nevertheless, by the time his

---

[16] Fredriksen, *Jesus of Nazareth*, 124.

mission was cut short by the extreme animosity of the Jewish leadership, he had developed enough of a following to ensure its continuation after him.

These four reasons explain why Jesus was unpopular. Accepting that Jesus had only a small following when his mission ended and that his following started to grow significantly only many decades after he was gone also helps to explain these historical certainties:

- Christianity grew outside mainstream Judaism.
- Christianity took a long time to grow into a significant movement.
- Substantial changes were made to Jesus' teaching, not least by Paul.
- The persecution of Christians did not become a policy of the Roman empire until over two centuries after Jesus.

But what about Jesus' impressive miracles? How could these wonders not convince the public that he was the Messiah? They certainly supported his claim in the eyes of some, but those who rejected his teaching saw them as evidence that he was a false teacher. Let's explore this in some detail.

Judaism always believed in supernatural feats, considering those that are good "miracles" and evil ones "magic". This labelling reflects how the person who performed such feats was seen. If he was perceived to be righteous, his supernatural works were considered to be miracles. But if he was considered evil or a false claimant to piety, then the same wonders would be treated as magic.

Moses, for instance, was a miracle worker, whereas one "who practices divination, or is a soothsayer, or an augur, or a sorcerer, or one who casts spells, or who consults ghosts or spirits, or who seeks oracles from the dead" was condemned as being "abhorrent to the Lord" (Deut. 18:10-12). This Old Testament distinction is mirrored in rabbinic teachings, as we find in the Talmud. Whether a supernatural feat is considered miraculous or magical depends mainly on how the performer was seen:

> In the Rabbinic view, an unusual event is "magic"—and culpable—or "miracle"—and laudable—depending upon who does it, in what context, and for what purpose. Exactly what is accomplished is rarely at issue at all.
>
> For the rabbis, miracles are distinguished from magic primarily by the fact

that the former are performed by a sage whose power derives from the merit earned through knowledge of Torah and a life of piety.[17]

One first-century BCE Jew was known for his ability to draw a circle, stand inside it, and then pray and cause rain to fall. Honi the circle-drawer, as he was consequently called, was also able to affect other related weather elements. He was considered righteous (b. Ta'an. 23a).[18]

Another famous miracle worker is Hanina ben Dosa, who lived a generation or two after Jesus in Galilee, the city where Jesus is said to have lived. Hanina is reported to have performed many miracles, some of which are similar to those worked by Jesus. His wonders included healings (b. Ber. 34b), clairvoyance (b. Yev. 121b), and others (b. Ber. 33a; b. Ta'an. 25a). Hanina was considered a good person and was even called a rabbi later, so his wonders were seen as miracles.

Jewish law did not concern itself with trickery and illusions, but it criminalised real supernatural acts of magic. The Mishnah states that the "sorcerer" who performs a real act is culpable but not the one who only deceives the eyes (Sanh. 7:11). Elsewhere, it makes stoning the punishment for the person "who has a familiar spirit", the "soothsayer", the person who "leads [a whole town] astray", and the "sorcerer" (Sanh. 7:4).

Accusing Jesus of practising magic was a natural consequence of rejecting his claim to be the Messiah and to have been sent by God. A false Messiah can only perform magic, not miracles. This is why Jesus' miracles were used against him instead of in his favour. For instance, his ability to heal the possessed was said to have been facilitated by Beelzebul, the ruler of the devils (Mark 3:22).

Jesus achieved little acceptance among the Jews. Killing him would no doubt have upset his small number of followers, but Matthew's (26:5) assertion that the Jewish authorities were concerned that eliminating Jesus could trigger "a riot among the people" is false. The Gospel narratives of the arrest, trial, and crucifixion confirm that Jesus had very limited success with the Jewish public.

---

[17] Avery-Peck, *Magic in Rabbinic Judaism*, III, 1614.
[18] Babylonian Talmud quotations are from Epstein, *The Babylonian Talmud.*

5.3 The Jewish Leaders' Intolerance of Jesus

Jesus' failure to convince more than a small number of Jews to follow him early in his mission meant that the Jewish authorities could afford to ignore him. His limited popularity meant that he was not in a position to cause any public disorder or anything that would seriously alarm the establishment. As he grew older and became more credible and, accordingly, more successful, the Jewish authorities decided that they could not tolerate him any longer. But what provoked them against him to the point of seeking his death? Before I offer my answer to this question, I would like to discuss what most scholars think and explain why I disagree with them. But we first need to quickly review the religious scene in Palestine at the time of Jesus.

There were four Jewish religious groups, the main two of which are mentioned in the New Testament. The largest group, the Pharisees, which is also the one that features the most in the Gospels and Acts, was concerned with the interpretation and observance of the Torah. The Pharisees did not get involved in politics and they tolerated any government as long as it did not interfere with their observance of the law.

Much less information has survived about the Sadducees. They were aristocrats and associated with the priesthood. The high-priestly families belonged to them. At the time of Jesus, they were in charge of the temple. Unlike the Pharisees, the Sadducees were closely associated with those who ruled the Jewish state.[19]

The third group is the Essenes. They are not mentioned in the New Testament. Most of the information about this group came from Josephus, until the discovery of the Dead Sea Scrolls in 1946. These writings, which represent the library of the Essenes, provide detailed information about their way of life and beliefs. Believing that the other Jews had lost their way, the Essenes were withdrawn from the rest of society and lived as ascetics. They disappeared after the ransacking and destruction of Jerusalem by the Romans in 70 CE.

The fourth and last group is the Zealots, whom Josephus refers to as the "fourth sect of Jewish philosophy".[20] These were concerned with

---

[19] Schürer, *The Jewish People*, II, 388-414.

[20] Josephus, *Antiquities*, 18.1.6.

liberating the holy land from foreign occupiers.

Jesus did not belong to any of these sects. He had his own teaching and interpretation of the Torah, he was not connected to the temple, he did not live in seclusion from other Jews, and he did not aspire to liberate the Jews from Roman rule. He considered himself to have been commissioned and given authority by God and did not need the approval of anyone else. There is no mention in the Gospels of Jesus receiving any schooling, nor of how he developed his religious education in addition to the default self-study.

For over a century now, most scholars have argued that Jesus was an apocalyptic teacher who predicted the end of the world as being in his own time.[21] Jesus spoke about a cosmic judge called the "Son of Man" (Dan. 7:13-14) who was going to descend to establish the kingdom of God on the earth. The Gospels have passages in which Jesus unambiguously identifies himself as the Son of Man:

> Then he began to teach them that the Son of Man must undergo great suffering, and be rejected by the elders, the chief priests, and the scribes, and be killed, and after three days rise again. (Mark 8:31)

The coming of the Son of Man was imminent, with Jesus telling his audiences that some of them "will not taste death before they see the Son of Man coming in his kingdom" (Matt. 16:28). In this new world order, the righteous will be rewarded but the evil will suffer. Anyone who opposed the new kingdom of God would be destroyed, whether they were strict keepers of the law like the Pharisees, or revered the temple, or were even its guardians, like the Sadducees. Such teachings were, obviously, revolutionary and anti-establishment. They would have been seen as a threat by the Jewish authorities even if Jesus was not a popular teacher. They might have feared, for instance, that such a theme could be picked up by other, more successful crowd-wooers.

While I agree that Jesus' message included teachings about the Final Judgment and the need to prepare for the coming life, I do not believe that he thought that this was imminent, that the earth was its theatre, or that he was the main actor in this cosmic play. Following as he did in the footsteps of the Patriarchs and previous prophets of Israel, he would not

---

[21] Ehrman, *Jesus, Interrupted*, 156-171; Schweitzer, *The Quest of the Historical Jesus*, 313-376.

have taught an imminent end of the world. His teachings would have focused on mending the individual and society spiritually to lead the life that God demanded of them. There was a kingdom to come at some unknown point in the future, but that had nothing to do with this world. This, after all, is aligned with the centuries-old Jewish beliefs that scholars now accept Jesus upheld and tried to reform rather than revolted against.

I should also point out that while an apocalyptic message would have angered and alarmed Jewish leaders, it would not have bothered the Romans in the slightest. For them, this would have been yet another Jewish theological concept that made no sense and would have no impact on the empire. They would have cared only if Jesus was calling for any political or violent action, which he was not. Therefore, it is a contradiction to consider Jesus' apocalyptic message as having led to his death while at the same time accusing the Romans, rather than the Jews, of seeking his death, as most scholars do.

There are two specific events that scholars agree directly led to Jesus' crucifixion. First, he supposedly claimed that he would destroy the temple (Mark 13:1-2; Matt. 24:1-2; Luke 21:5-6), which would have alarmed the Sadducees, the priestly aristocrats in charge of the temple. Indeed, this was to later become one of the charges levelled at him during his Jewish trial (Mark 14:58; Matt. 26:61). Yet, as we have already seen (§1.4), the Gospels offer no evidence that Jesus made that threat. He is only reported to have pronounced a prophecy about a future destruction of the temple that had nothing to do with him. The accusation was false, so it could not have been a reason for his prosecution, let alone for sentencing him to death.

Second, Jesus is said to have followed his offensive reference to the destruction of the temple by causing a major disturbance there, which most scholars think was the immediate cause of his arrest and condemnation to death.[22] This is the account of Jesus' attack on the traders in the temple:

> Then they came to Jerusalem. And he entered the temple and began to drive out those who were selling and those who were buying in the temple, and he overturned the tables of the money changers and the seats of those who sold doves; and he would not allow anyone to carry

---

[22] Sanders, *Historical Figure*, 265; Sanders, *Jewish Law*, 66-67.

anything through the temple. He was teaching and saying, "Is it not written,

'My house shall be called a house of prayer for all the nations'?
But you have made it a den of robbers."

And when the chief priests and the scribes heard it, they kept looking for a way to kill him; for they were afraid of him, because the whole crowd was spellbound by his teaching. (Mark 11:15-18)

This narrative, which is reported by all four Evangelists (Matt. 12:12-17; Luke: 19:45-48; John 2:12-21), suffers from serious credibility problems. For instance, Jesus' actions would have stopped the temple from operating as a place for offering sacrifice. The temple covered a huge area and was protected by armed guards who would immediately arrest anyone causing a disturbance. [23] If the event could not have occurred, then it could not have been the cause of his arrest, prosecution, and death either.

Contrary to what most scholars now think, Jesus was not a deluded teacher who dreamed up an imminent kingdom of God on the earth, whether the Son of Man was himself, someone else, or even a collective title, as some argue.[24] Similarly, he was not so naïve as to not realise that creating a disturbance in the temple was not only completely futile but would also result in nothing less than his arrest and severe punishment. These unhistorical claims could not have caused his historical prosecution. What, then, did?

I see in the Gospels four causes that are likely to have combined to make the Jewish leaders see Jesus as an intolerable danger. It is too speculative, though, to take a view on the relative contribution of each factor to that hostility.

First, Jesus was very critical of the Pharisees and Sadducees and never shied away from admonishing them severely. But, contrary to general belief, this was not because of differences over the importance of the Mosaic law. The Gospels document a long list of complaints that the Pharisees had about Jesus, accusing him of repeatedly failing to follow the law. They objected to him and/or his disciples eating without washing their hands first (Mark 7:1-9; Matt. 15:1-20), eating with the sinners and

---

[23] Ehrman, *Apocalyptic Prophet*, 212.
[24] Kazen, "The Coming Son of Man Revisited".

tax collectors (Mark 2:13-17), not fasting with the Pharisees and other Jews (Mark 2:18-20), not observing the Sabbath (Mark 2:23-28; Matt. 12:1-8; Luke 6:6-11, 3:11-17; John 5:5-18, 9:13-18), and casting out devils by what they considered to be evil power (Matt. 12:22-28).

Christian scholarship, as is the case with Christians in general, believes that Jesus spoke against the law of Moses and deliberately broke it. No doubt, this view is mainly a product of Paul's emphasis that salvation is achieved through faith in Jesus, not the law (e.g. Gal. 2:16). But a careful reading of the Gospels does not *necessarily* indicate that Jesus broke the laws governing the relations between humans and God or between humans and humans. This is one of the most direct statements by Jesus on the importance of keeping the law:

> Do not think that I have come to abolish the law or the prophets; I have come not to abolish but to fulfill. For truly I tell you, until heaven and earth pass away, not one letter, not one stroke of a letter, will pass from the law until all is accomplished. Therefore, whoever breaks one of the least of these commandments, and teaches others to do the same, will be called least in the kingdom of heaven; but whoever does them and teaches them will be called great in the kingdom of heaven. (Matt. 5.17-19)

What the Gospels instead show, many maintain, is that Jesus had his own interpretations of the law.[25] No doubt, though, what looks to some like interpretation may be seen by others as a breach of the letter and spirit of the text. In the third part of this book (§18.4), we will see that the Qur'an confirms that Jesus' mission involved abolishing some unidentified proscriptions but, otherwise, he honoured the Torah.

This is how one scholar summarised Jesus' attitude towards the law and the establishment's narrow interpretation of it:

> Jesus did not think that what really mattered before God was the scrupulous observance of the laws in all their details. Going out of one's way to avoid doing anything questionable on the Sabbath or to tithe all produce, whether bought or sold, was of very little importance to him. Unlike some Sadducees, Jesus did not think that it was of the utmost importance to adhere strictly to the rules for worship in the Temple through the divinely ordained

---

[25] Sanders, *Jesus and Judaism*, 245-269, 272-281; Sanders, "Jesus and the First Table"; Vermes, *Jesus in His Jewish Context*, 40-43.

THE JEWISH AND ROMAN ROLES IN THE CRUCIFIXION

sacrifices. Unlike some Essenes, he did not think that people should seek to maintain their own ritual purity in isolation from others in order to find God's ultimate approval. For Jesus—as for some other Jews from his time about whom we are less well informed (see, e.g., Mark 12:32-34)—what really mattered were the commandments of God that formed, in his opinion, the very heart of the Law, the commandments to love God above all else and to love one's neighbor as oneself.[26]

I think the theme of "love" in Jesus' teaching has been overemphasised, but he certainly looks to have been forgiving of sinners and more concerned about the purity of one's heart and spiritual wellbeing than outward behaviours.

Jesus' criticism of the Jewish leaders and teachers was not because of differences over the status of the law; he honoured the law as much as anyone else. But he thought that they had placed the letter of the law ahead of its spirit. More troubling for them was his accusing them of hypocrisy and of ignoring the core values of Judaism in favour of rituals and formalities. Instead of being genuine spiritual teachers, according to Jesus, they used Judaism as a profession for worldly gain. This is what he had to say about the experts in the Mosaic law:

> Beware of the scribes, who like to walk around in long robes, and to be greeted with respect in the marketplaces, and to have the best seats in the synagogues and places of honor at banquets! They devour widows' houses and for the sake of appearance say long prayers. They will receive the greater condemnation. (Mark 12:38-40)

The Gospels report several incidents in which Jesus criticised those self-appointed guardians of religion, including the two dominant groups of the Pharisees and Sadducees. What is more, he did not mince his words when castigating them for their failings. When he was told of criticism of one of his sayings by the Pharisees, he replied:

> Every plant that my heavenly Father has not planted will be uprooted. Let them alone; they are blind guides of the blind. And if one blind person guides another, both will fall into a pit. (Matt. 15:13-14).

He warned his audiences of the two largest religious groups:

> When the disciples reached the other side, they had forgotten to

---

[26] Ehrman, *Apocalyptic Prophet*, 166.

bring any bread. Jesus said to them, "Watch out, and beware of the yeast of the Pharisees and Sadducees." (Matt. 16:5-6)

He attacked the Pharisees and Sadducees for their self-worthiness and self-entitlement (also Matt. 16:1-4):

> You brood of vipers! Who warned you to flee from the wrath to come? Bear fruit worthy of repentance. Do not presume to say to yourselves, "We have Abraham as our ancestor"; for I tell you, God is able from these stones to raise up children to Abraham. Even now the ax is lying at the root of the trees; every tree therefore that does not bear good fruit is cut down and thrown into the fire. (Matt. 3:7-10)

There is a critical conclusion that must be reached here: Jesus' popular image of a completely meek figure is only partially correct. This incomplete image comes mainly from two portrayals of him in the Gospels: his forgiveness and tolerance of sinners and his submission to his crucifixion. Yet these same sources portray another Jesus who is angry and, at times, even provocative and aggressive towards the religious authorities. This is particularly stressed in the unhistorical scene of Jesus singlehandedly setting out to cleanse the temple of its abusers, but more realistic reports about his relentless criticism of the religious teachers reflect the same image. Here, for instance, he accuses religious teachers of hypocrisy and using religion for worldly privileges:

> The scribes and the Pharisees sit on Moses' seat; therefore, do whatever they teach you and follow it; but do not do as they do, for they do not practice what they teach. They tie up heavy burdens, hard to bear, and lay them on the shoulders of others; but they themselves are unwilling to lift a finger to move them. They do all their deeds to be seen by others; for they make their phylacteries broad and their fringes long. They love to have the place of honor at banquets and the best seats in the synagogues, and to be greeted with respect in the marketplaces, and to have people call them rabbi. (Matt. 23:2-7)

Jesus was very concerned about the spiritual wellbeing of the Jews and saw them as victims of the misguidance of religious teachers who abused their authority. As forgiving and accommodating as he was of the unsuspecting misled laypeople, he was uncompromisingly critical of their unscrupulous misleaders. With Jesus voicing his disapproval loudly and in stinging language, it is not difficult to see why the Jewish leaders would have lost patience with him and sought to silence him once and for all.

Second, the religious leaders were becoming more alarmed by this *freelancing* teacher's ability to attract a growing number of highly loyal followers. These committed believers preferred this independent teacher to establishment figures. The Jewish authorities had to move and stop him from growing his small but loyal anti-establishment following.

Third, another possibility that could have mobilised the Jewish authorities against Jesus is if he moved his preaching activity to Jerusalem, the power base of the priestly authorities. While the Gospels tell us that Jesus went to Jerusalem for the Passover, this may also be read to mean that he went there for a longer visit or even to relocate. Such a move would have been seen by the Sadducees as a direct and serious challenge that led them to take extreme action.

Fourth, reports of Jesus' impressive miracles might well have made other religious teachers envious of him. Such a mundane factor could have played as big a role as any of the other three in the enmity that the Jewish leaders harboured for him. Indeed, both Mark (15:10) and Matthew (27:18) state that Pilate knew all too well that the Jewish authorities handed Jesus over to him "out of jealousy".

In this historical reconstruction of what led the Jewish authorities to see Jesus as an intolerable enemy, all of these four causes are realistic and credible. It would add unjustified speculation to take a view on how big a role each played in the unfolding of the events leading to the attempt to put Jesus on trial and crucify him. This would require intimate knowledge of the specific events of the plot and their timeline, which we do not possess.

5.4 The Romans' Indifference to Jesus

Conversely, the Gospels record virtually nothing that Jesus said or did that could have drawn the attention of the Romans, let alone alarm them, much less make them execute him. Contrary to the case with his strong criticism of the Jewish religious elite, no criticism of the Roman authorities is attributed to him. He had no political activity, his teaching did not advocate any form of violence against anyone, and he was little known. The fact that Jesus was a peaceful Messiah meant that the Romans had no reason to see him as a troublemaker and that the Jewish public did not like his teaching.

While considering Jesus' offensive prophecy about the temple and the disturbance he caused there as the direct reason for his prosecution by the Jewish authorities, scholars think that people's reception of Jesus as a king is what made Pilate see him as a threat. The clearest manifestation of his royal status in the eyes of the public, it is said, was his entry to Jerusalem (also Matt. 21:8-11; Luke 19:36-38):

> Many people spread their cloaks on the road, and others spread leafy branches that they had cut in the fields. Then those who went ahead and those who followed were shouting,
>   "Hosanna!
>   Blessed is the one who comes in the name of the Lord!
>   Blessed is the coming kingdom of our ancestor David!
>   Hosanna in the highest heaven!"
> Then he entered Jerusalem and went into the temple; and when he had looked around at everything, as it was already late, he went out to Bethany with the twelve. (Mark 11:8-11)

This is supposed to explain why Pilate also wanted Jesus dead and is used to shift the blame for his execution from the Jews to the Romans. This cinematic scene is unhistorical, not least because Jesus had achieved little popularity in his own hometown, let alone in Jerusalem, which he would have visited at most a few times for short stays.

Another fundamental flaw with portraying Jesus as a political threat is that, according to the same sources that report the episode of his entry to Jerusalem, he had no political ambitions. He was indeed the Messiah, but not the military Messiah that the Jews had conjured up and expected. He was a spiritual Messiah who resisted any attempt to drag him into secular politics. He did not give the Romans any reason to become aware of him, let alone perceive him as a threat. He advocated giving "to the emperor the things that are the emperor's, and to God the things that are God's." (Mark 12:17; Matt. 22:21; Luke 20:25). The accusation of the Jews against Jesus that he claimed to be the king of the Jews was based on their image of the awaited Messiah, not on the peaceful Messiah that Jesus was. The Gospels do not record any action by Jesus that could have credibly alarmed the Romans in the slightest. This observation is borne out in Pilate's questioning of Jesus.

The Synoptists agree that when Pilate asked Jesus whether he claimed to be the king of the Jews, Jesus answered "you say so" (Mark 15:2; Matt.

27:11; Luke 23:3). John gives a different, more detailed answer in which Jesus makes the critical declaration that his kingdom was not of this world:

> Then Pilate entered the headquarters again, summoned Jesus, and asked him, "Are you the King of the Jews?" Jesus answered, "Do you ask this on your own, or did others tell you about me?" Pilate replied, "I am not a Jew, am I? Your own nation and the chief priests have handed you over to me. What have you done?" Jesus answered, "My kingdom is not from this world. If my kingdom were from this world, my followers would be fighting to keep me from being handed over to the Jews. But as it is, my kingdom is not from here." Pilate asked him, "So you are a king?" Jesus answered, "You say that I am a king. For this I was born, and for this I came into the world, to testify to the truth. Everyone who belongs to the truth listens to my voice." Pilate asked him, "What is truth?" After he had said this, he went out to the Jews again and told them, "I find no case against him. (John 18:33-38)

Jesus told Pilate that kings on the earth are appointed by people, but his appointment came from God, so his kingdom was not earthly. His kingdom was heavenly, not the kind of earthly kingdom that the Jews were expecting the Messiah to establish. The Gospels attribute to Jesus many sayings in which he talks about the "kingdom of heaven". It is a kingdom that can be entered into only by those who "change and become like children" (Matt. 18:3; also Mark 10:15 and Luke 18:17). This kingdom, which Jesus also calls the "kingdom of God", is obviously spiritual. This is how Pilate also understood Jesus and, accordingly, concluded that there was no basis for the charges against him. This is probably also why the earliest Gospel has Pilate, speaking to the Jews, refer to Jesus as the "the man you call the King of the Jews" (Mark 15:12). Indeed, nothing in what the Gospels recorded of Jesus' sayings or works indicates in any way that he tried to establish or was interested in establishing an earthly kingdom or had any political ambitions. Making the Romans responsible for Jesus' execution contradicts much of his history in the Gospels, not just the account of his last days.

I fully agree that "contrary to the claim of some contemporary New Testament interpreters, the general context of the portrait of Jesus in the Synoptic Gospels and in the rest of the New Testament shows that he was not a pretender to the throne of David, or a would-be leader of a revolt against Rome".[27] Even though Luke (1:32) claims that Gabriel told Mary, about Jesus, that "the Lord God will give to him the throne of his ancestor David", Jesus was not only never given that throne, but he also never sought it. Jewish sources also do not provide any evidence that Jesus claimed to be the king of the Jews. The Christian concept of Jesus being a king is inherited from Jewish tradition where the Messiah is an earthly military king who would liberate the Israelites and re-establish their lost kingdom. But Christianity changed this earthly kingship to a spiritual one, in line with Jesus' life and teaching.[28]

The Gospels' assertion that the Jews had to alert Pilate to Jesus' danger is another confirmation that he did not do anything to draw the attention of the Roman authorities. Pilate entered the story of Jesus only after the Jews contacted him. In John (18:35), when Jesus asked Pilate about the source of the accusation that he claimed to be the king of the Jews, the Roman governor replied, "I am not a Jew, am I? Your own nation and the chief priests have handed you over to me. What have you done?". Pilate had no clue who Jesus was before he was brought before him.

It is perplexing that the overwhelming majority of scholars think that Pilate crucified Jesus because of his reputation as the king of the Jews despite an obvious contradiction in this view:

> We are apparently faced with a contradiction. On the one hand, the events and legal procedures leading up to Jesus' death can be established with reasonable certainty as implications of the bare statement that he was crucified; and the charge upon which he was crucified is given by a report which, again, seems highly reliable: King of the Jews. On the other hand, it seems incredible that the person condemned on this charge was Jesus of Nazareth. Either we have a totally distorted picture of Jesus, or the charge was unfounded and conviction unjust.[29]

Another prominent scholar who adopts the popular position that "Jesus was executed by the Romans as would-be 'king of the Jews'" accepts that it is at odds with the indisputable fact that "his disciples subsequently formed a messianic movement which was not based on the hope of military victory". He goes on to admit the difficulty to reconcile

---

[27] Vermes, *The Changing Faces of Jesus*, 194.

[28] Fatoohi, *The Messiah in Islam, Christianity, and Judaism.*

[29] Harvey, *Jesus on Trial*, 3-4.

these two "facts" because "everything we know about Jesus indicates that he sought no secular kingship".[30]

I could not agree more with this conclusion. Of these two mutually exclusive *facts*, I choose to consider the charge against Jesus to be false. This requires rejecting much less of the Gospels' narrative. The alternative, as pointed out in the above quotation, is to disregard so much of the Gospel accounts that we have to redraw a new image of Jesus. Preferring this option over the former is unjustified. Yet many do not make a choice and instead live with the contradiction! This is one price to pay for insisting on making the Romans responsible for Jesus' execution.

But the fact that Jesus did not claim to be the king of the Jews would have been immaterial if the Jewish leaders succeeded in misleading Pilate. If the latter accepted any false political accusation that the Jews levelled at Jesus, then that would have been a sufficient reason for him to eliminate Jesus. In addition to the Gospel narratives, there is good reason to believe that Pilate did not take the claims about Jesus seriously, but he granted the Jews their request to execute the man they presented to him only as a gesture of goodwill and possibly as a good opportunity to send out another reminder about what awaits anyone who opposes the Romans. The Romans' indifference to Jesus is confirmed by the fact that Christians were allowed to continue to practise their religion for decades after the execution of their master.

The Book of Acts reports Jewish but no Roman persecution of Christians after Jesus. Peter and John were arrested, jailed, and put on trial (Acts 4:1-21); Peter and other apostles were jailed, tried, beaten up, and only the intervention of a Pharisee spared them execution (Acts 5:18-40); and Stephen was stoned (Acts 7:58-60). All persecution of Christians in Acts was Jewish, with not a single incident involving the Romans. This as much shows that Jesus was never seen as a political threat as it confirms that it was the Jews who persecuted Jesus and appealed to the Roman prefect to kill him.[31]

If Jesus was perceived to be a political threat or even a nuisance, his followers would have been rounded up by the Romans and his movement

---

[30] Sanders, *Jesus and Judaism*, 294.

[31] Ibid., 285-286.

would have been banned. Yet contrary to common belief, historical sources indicate that, for a long time, it was not illegal to be Christian, to worship the Jewish God or Jesus, or even to try to convert others to Christianity.[32] This is also partly because the Christians were negligibly small in number.[33] The earliest documented case of official Roman persecution of Christians is linked to the Roman emperor Nero who accused Christians of the Great Fire in 64 CE that he started in order to burn Rome. Paradoxically, this event, which happened three decades after the crucifixion and was first reported another half a century later by the Roman historian Tacitus, neither indicates that Christianity was illegal nor that Christians were living in hiding. In another account, also from the second decade of the second century, Pliny the Younger, who was a Roman governor in Asia Minor and a friend of Tacitus, consulted the Roman emperor Trajan on how to punish Christians, implying there were no such laws in place. Interestingly, Trajan instructed Pliny to not go out of his way to look for Christians. Only if they were brought before him and their guilt was proven were they to be punished.[34]

Early Roman persecution of Christians was sporadic and localized, rather than organized and centrally driven by Rome. That did not change until 250 CE when Emperor Decius made the persecution of Christianity an imperial policy.[35] If the Romans killed the man they thought to be Jesus because they truly saw him as a danger, then his religion would have immediately been banned and his followers persecuted, yet there is no evidence that this happened.

A reply to this argument would be that as the Christians were a very small sect, Pilate thought that killing their leader was enough to destroy the sect; he and later Roman governors did not need to launch a persecution campaign against the Christians. I do not find this argument convincing. If Jesus was seen as dangerous, his religion and followers would have surely been seen in the same way. After all, the power of any leader is exercised through his followers. The Romans would have tried to eradicate Jesus' followers as well rather than taking an unnecessary risk.

---

[32] Ehrman, *Misquoting Jesus*, 196.

[33] Hopkins, "Christian Number and its Implications", 445-447.

[34] Pliny, *The Letters*, II, 10.97-98.

[35] Peper and DelCogliano, "The Pliny and Trajan Correspondence", 368.

Yet they did not persecute even the main Christian leaders in Jerusalem. These were targeted by Jewish leaders, not Roman officials, just as was the case with Jesus himself.

One detailed study has concluded that the persecution of the early Christians that Christian tradition has propagated over the centuries is nothing more than a myth. The author even doubts Tacitus' claim that Nero used the Christians as scapegoats for the fire he started. She argues that Tacitus, writing half a century after the event, used the term "Christians" somehow anachronistically:

> It's highly unlikely that, at the time the Great Fire occurred, anyone recognized Jesus followers as a distinct and separate group. Jesus followers themselves do not appear to have begun using the name "Christian" until, at the earliest, the very end of the first century.[36]

Acts (11:26) claims that the disciples were first called "Christians" in Antioch when Barnabas and Paul were teaching the new faith. This is supposed to have happened towards the end of the first half of the century. But there are only two other uses of this term in the whole of the New Testament (Acts 26:28; 1 Peter 4:16). Significantly, the term does not occur in Paul's letters or the Gospels. The earliest use of it in non-Christian sources is by the Roman Jewish historian Josephus from the last decade of the first century. But this account is almost certainly a late forgery (§10.2). Moss' argument seems to be supported by the Roman historian Suetonius who, writing a few years after Tacitus and Pliny, seems to describe the followers of Jesus as "Jews". We will review all these Roman accounts in detail later (§11).

In summary, every piece of evidence suggests that Pilate could not have crucified Jesus for claiming the kingship of the Jews.

5.5 Jewish Indictment and Roman Execution

As we have already seen, had Jewish leaders not decided to kill Jesus, the Romans would have had no interest in him, that is, if they would even have heard of him in the first place. Once the priestly authorities indicted Jesus, they had to ask the Roman prefect to carry out their sentence.

---

[36] Moss, *The Myth of Persecution*, 139.

Outside Christian sources, Josephus[37] and Tacitus[38] confirm that it was Pilate who executed Jesus. But the former is a Christian forgery and the latter is unlikely to be independent of Christian sources, as we shall see later (§10 and §11.2). There are other reasons, though, to believe that the Roman prefect would have had direct involvement in the killing of Jesus.

Crucifixion was a Roman, not Jewish, punishment. It was used for several centuries until it was abolished in 337 CE by the first Christian emperor Constantine in veneration of Jesus. Capital punishment in Jewish law is performed by one of four methods. The Old Testament mentions stoning (e.g., Deut. 17:5) and burning (e.g., Lev. 20:14), and the Mishnah adds slaying by the sword and strangulation (Sanh. 7:1). Crucifixion is mentioned in the Old Testament in that stoning to death is followed by hanging the executed person on a tree (Deut. 21:21-23). It was a way of displaying the corpse of the executed person, not a method of execution as the Romans used it.

I should quickly mention here scholarly debate on the uncertainty of the meaning of "crucifixion" in the ancient world, including its use by the Romans. One scholar has argued that the popular image of Jesus nailed on a cross formed by a horizontal beam affixed at a right angle to an upright post is a Christian interpretation of the sparse descriptions in the Gospels of Jesus' execution by suspension, various forms of which existed in antiquity.[39] This claim of ambiguity, however, is rejected by others. One study concludes, "In the Greco-Roman texts that mention crucifixion, there are many similarities with the Gospel narratives of the crucifixion of Jesus, although the Gospel accounts are the most extensive of any that have survived antiquity".[40] A third approach that falls between these two extremes points to the "likelihood that crucifixion on a cross was simply one specific form within the broader category of human bodily suspension". The author argues that "this dynamic goes a long way to explain how general references in the Hebrew Bible to suspended bodies could later be associated more specifically with crucifixion

---

[37] Josephus, *Antiquities*, 18.3.3.

[38] Tacitus, *The Annals*, 15.44.

[39] Samuelsson, *Crucifixion in Antiquity*.

[40] Cook, *Crucifixion in the Mediterranean World*, 452. See also Evans, "Hanging and Crucifixion".

terminology".[41]

Killing by crucifixion is rare in Jewish history. One notable instance, reported by Josephus,[42] is when the Maccabean king and high priest Alexander Janneus (103–76 BCE) crucified 800 rebellious Pharisees while they were alive and had the throats of their wives and children cut before their eyes. The crucifixion "was no longer attested as part of Jewish legal practice in the Herodian age, that is, from 37 BC onwards".[43]

The titulus on the cross was written from a Roman not Jewish perspective.[44] All four Gospel versions mock Jesus as the "king of the Jews", whereas the Jews would speak of the "king of Israel" (Mark 15:32). This further confirms that it was the Romans who killed Jesus.

On the other hand, the Gospels' claim that the Roman governor executed Jesus because of the pressure of Jewish mobs is absurd. It must have been his decision. Jewish historians Philo, who was contemporary to Pilate, and Josephus show Pilate as an extremely violent and merciless ruler who executed numerous people without trial. He was also insensitive to Jewish religious tradition. For instance, he introduced standards of effigies of Caesar into Jerusalem, offending its Jewish inhabitants whose law forbids making images.[45] This strong and determined ruler is unrecognisable in the indecisive and weak Pilate of the Gospels. Pilate's brutality is actually referred to once in the Gospels, not in relation to Jesus' execution. In this sole reference, which fits with the Pilate of history but contradicts that of the Gospels, Luke (13:1) describes the Roman governor as someone who mixed the blood of Galileans with their sacrifices.

The supposed influence that the Jewish high priest had on Pilate is further undermined by other historical facts. In 6-41 CE, the government of Judea was transferred from the Jews to Roman prefects appointed by the emperor. The Roman prefect had the power to appoint and dismiss the Jewish high priest.[46] When Emperor Tiberius removed Pilate in 36

---

[41] Chapman, *Perceptions of Crucifixion*, 32.

[42] Josephus, *Antiquities*, 13.14.2.

[43] Vermes, *The Passion*, 26.

[44] Theissen and Merz, *The Historical Jesus*, 458.

[45] Josephus, *Antiquities*, 18.3.1.

[46] Vermes, *Searching for the Real Jesus*, 12.

CE because of a massacre he committed, Caiaphas was also demoted from the position of high priest. This may suggest that Caiaphas was close to Pilate and could have influenced him to crucify Jesus, but this would still disagree with the Gospels' portrayal of the balance of power in their exchanges.

This element of absurdity in the Gospels' versions of events can be replaced with more realistic alternatives. For instance, the Jews may have succeeded in misleading Pilate about Jesus' real intent. This would have been facilitated by the fact that Pilate had not heard of Jesus and he may not have felt the need to bother checking the veracity of the accusations. In this alternative scenario, the Jewish leaders *petitioned rather than egged on* Pilate to take Jesus out. He obliged because they depicted Jesus as a potential insurgent. This possibility is significantly weakened by the fact that Pilate did not persecute Jesus' followers. It is also contrary to the Gospels' assertion that Pilate did not find the accusation credible.

The Gospel narratives can be reconciled with the more likely alternative that Pilate killed Jesus as both a good gesture and a warning to the Jews. For Pilate, this was an easy and inconsequential decision. He might have done it as a favour for Caiaphas if he was indeed on particularly good terms with him. He might have also used the crucifixion of Jesus as a useful reminder to the Jews of what awaited anyone who dared to challenge the authority of Rome. In conclusion, there are credible scenarios for why Pilate could have killed Jesus at the request of Jewish leaders even though he did not believe the charges against him.

Let's finally consider whether the Jews had the power to execute Jesus according to the Gospels and historical sources.

Mark and Matthew indicate that the Sanhedrin had the power to pass the death penalty as the Jewish body condemned Jesus to death at the end of his trial. Luke (24:20; Acts 13:27) makes the same claim, although he seems to contradict that elsewhere in his Gospel where no verdict is passed. The Synoptists still say that the Jews took Jesus to Pilate to crucify him, which seems to imply they did not have the power to implement death sentences and had to ask the Roman governor to carry them out. This would make the pronouncement of any capital sentence by the priestly authorities more of a recommendation to the Roman authorities than a final sentence.

John (18:31) explicitly states that when Pilate told the Jews to take Jesus and punish him according to their law, the Jewish leaders, who were seeking Jesus' death, told the Roman governor, "We are not permitted to put anyone to death". The Roman prefect, who had been governing the Jews for at least 3-4 years at the time of Jesus' supposed crucifixion, is somehow portrayed to be ignorant of the fact that the Sanhedrin did not have the power to impose capital punishment. The same Evangelist has another scene in which the Jewish leaders considered stoning Jesus:

> The Jews took up stones again to stone him. Jesus replied, "I have shown you many good works from the Father. For which of these are you going to stone me?" The Jews answered, "It is not for a good work that we are going to stone you, but for blasphemy, because you, though only a human being, are making yourself God." (John 10:31-33)

This does not contradict John's denial of the Jews having the power of execution. The context of the threat of stoning looks more like a threat of extrajudicial mob killing than execution under the power of the law.

Whether or not the Jews at around 30 CE had the power to carry out capital punishment remains a point of disagreement between scholars.[47] There is a vague and late Talmudic reference stating that the Sanhedrin lost its capital jurisdiction 40 years before the destruction of the temple by the Romans in 70 CE. This is taken to have happened before the crucifixion and is interpreted as meaning that the Jews could not execute Jesus. On the other hand, there is evidence that the Sanhedrin kept its right to impose capital punishment. For instance, the Alexandrian Jewish philosopher Philo said that any Jew, including priests, and even a Roman would be put to death if he entered the innermost sanctuary of the temple, known as the Holy of Holies. After confirming that only the high priest is allowed to enter the Holy of Holies on any one specific day of the year, Philo goes on to explain:

> And if any priest, to say nothing of the other Jews, and not merely one of the lowest priests but of those who are ranked directly below the chief, goes in either by himself or with the High Priest, and further even if the High Priest enters on two days in the year or thrice or four times on the same day death without appeal is his doom. So greatly careful was the law-giver to guard the inmost sanctuary, the one and only place which he wished to keep

---

[47] Theissen and Merz, *The Historical Jesus*, 455-456.

preserved untrodden and untouched.[48]

That the Romans had allowed the Jews to execute those who entered the sanctuary or second court of the temple is confirmed by Josephus. This confirmation comes in a speech to the Jews by the Roman general Titus during his siege of Jerusalem in 70 CE, after a Jewish revolt that started four years earlier:

> Have not you, vile wretches that you are, by our permission, put up this partition-wall before your sanctuary? Have not you been allowed to put up the pillars thereto belonging, at due distances, and on it to engrave in Greek, and in your own letters, this prohibition, that no foreigner should go beyond that wall. Have not we given you leave to kill such as go beyond it, though he were a Roman?[49]

Josephus also mentioned that when Herod the Great renovated the temple there was an inscription that warned any foreigner from going inside its sanctuary "under pain of death".[50] He confirms that the warning that "no foreigner should go within that sanctuary" was inscribed on pillars in both Greek and Latin.[51]

Another report from Josephus[52] is the sentencing by the high priest Ananus of James, Jesus' alleged brother, and others to death by stoning, having accused them of breaking the law. The complaint against Ananus that led king Herod Agrippa (41-44 CE) of Judea to remove him as the high priest was not the execution of those victims but his assembly of the Sanhedrin for the trial without the consent of the Roman governor of Judea. It sounds unlikely that the Sanhedrin could not be assembled without the permission of the Roman governor yet had the power of execution.

The stoning of the Christian Stephen (Acts 7:58) is also seen as another piece of evidence that the Jews had the power of capital punishment, although some view this incident as more of a mob execution; there are other pieces of evidence.[53]

---

[48] Philo, *The Embassy to Gaius,* X, 307-308.

[49] Josephus, *Wars,* 6.2.4.

[50] Josephus, *Antiquities,* 15.11.5.

[51] Josephus, *Wars,* 5.5.2.

[52] Josephus, *Antiquities,* 20.9.1.

[53] Vermes, *The Passion,* 103-108.

The Romans used to keep the power of execution in the provinces they conquered in their own hands, so it seems unlikely that they would have delegated that power in Palestine to the Jews. But the Romans might have given the Jews very limited power to carry out capital punishment, probably restricted to cases of defiling the Holy of Holies, in acknowledgement of this specific religious sensitivity. If the Jews had unrestricted or even more rights to execution, Titus would not have highlighted in his speech only one specific case. I join the majority of scholars in accepting the Gospels' claim that the Jews had to refer Jesus to the Romans and could not kill him themselves.

For many, whether the Jews had the power to impose capital punishment at the time of Jesus remains an open question. If the agreement of the four Gospels that the Jews took Jesus to Pilate to crucify him is largely historical, then it must be concluded that they did not have the power to carry out capital punishment. This conclusion is necessary to explain why although they tried Jesus and condemned him to death, or at least wanted him dead, they took him to the Roman governor rather than killing him themselves.

This, anyway, is what Christian tradition says. But those same early sources, i.e. the Gospels, are unequivocal that it was the Jewish leader who instigated the whole conspiracy to kill Jesus. Whether it was the Jews who carried out the sentence or they had to ask Pilate to pull the trigger is actually a moot point. Indeed, when boasting about killing Jesus, Jewish sources do not mention any non-Jewish involvement (§12). Similarly, the Qur'an only accuses the Jews of the plot to kill Jesus (§19.1). The now popular scholarly view that it was the Romans, not the Jews, who wanted Jesus dead is effectively *alternative history* as far as the Gospels are concerned. Furthermore, this view requires a complete restructuring of the last episodes of Jesus' life in the Gospels and even his overall image. It requires changing his image from that of a non-political spiritual teacher who consciously avoided raising the concerns of the Romans to someone whom they suspected of insurrection or disorder. This would effectively mean accepting the historicity of the Gospels' claim that Jesus was crucified but rejecting almost all other details!

6

The Date of the Crucifixion

All four Gospels agree that Jesus was killed during Pontius Pilate's prefectship of Judea, which lasted from 26 to 36 CE. Mark does not give any other information. Matthew and John state that Caiaphas was the high priest at the time. Caiaphas was in office in 18-36 CE, so this claim is congruent with the dating of Jesus' crucifixion to Pilate's rule, but it does not help in narrowing down the wide range of 26-36 CE. The other priest that John mentions, Annas, was the high priest in 6-15 CE, but these dates are rather irrelevant, as Annas was not the high priest at the time of the crucifixion.

Unlike the other Evangelists, Luke (23:6-7) claims that because Jesus was a Galilean, Pilate sent him to be tried by Herod Antipas, who had jurisdiction over Galilee. Emperor Augustus made Antipas tetrarch of Galilee and Perea, east of the Jordan River, after the death of his father, Herod the Great, in 4 BCE. He kept this position until 39 CE when he was dismissed and exiled by Emperor Caligula. Again, this reference does not help in reducing the range of 26-36 CE.

Luke has other information that can help with more specific dating. First, he states that John the Baptist started preaching "in the fifteenth year of the reign of Emperor Tiberius" (Luke 3:1). This corresponds to the year 29 CE. Second, he seems to imply that Jesus' baptism happened shortly afterwards, so we can presume that it was in the same year. Third, he also suggests that Jesus' public ministry lasted for around one year before he was crucified. There is, for example, one Passover mentioned in that period. The other two Synoptists also talk about one Passover and imply that Jesus preached for one year or so. Luke, therefore, dates the crucifixion in the year 30 CE.

But then Luke gives other information that contradicts this dating. First, he states that Jesus was "about thirty years old" when he was baptised by John (Luke 3:23). Second, we have already seen that he implies that Jesus' ministry lasted only one year, so he was 31 years old when he was executed. Third, he claims that Jesus was born during a Roman census that was ordered by the emperor Augustus which took place when Quirinius was the governor of Syria (Luke 2:1-2). Now, we know that Quirinius was appointed legate of Syria in 6 CE. Immediately after that, he travelled to Judea, which was added to the province of Syria, and undertook a census there.[1] This set of information indicates that Jesus' crucifixion would have happened in the year 37 CE. This is not only seven years later than the date suggested by the earlier set of information in Luke, but it also places Jesus' trial and execution one year after Pilate's dismissal as prefect of Judea.

Luke's (2:1) description of Quirinius' census as having included "all the world", meaning the whole of the Roman empire, is unrealistic and unhistorical. Furthermore, this census took place over a decade after the death of King Herod the Great, in whose reign Matthew claims Jesus was born.

Another relevant contradiction is between John and the Synoptists. Unlike the latter, who mention one Passover and imply that Jesus' ministry lasted for only one year, John talks about three Passovers, which could extend Jesus' ministry to up to three years. He mentions two Passovers in addition to the one just before the crucifixion. Jesus spent the first one in Jerusalem in the south (John 2:13, 23) and the second in Galilee in the north (John 6:4). Scholars differ on the length of Jesus' ministry, but it has been suggested that John might have extended Jesus' public ministry to "accommodate his numerous and lengthy, almost certainly fictional speeches".[2] The differences between the Gospels have led the early Church Fathers to also disagree on the length of Jesus' ministry.[3] Some early Christians advocated a much longer duration. For instance, the second-century bishop of Lyon Irenaeus suggested that Jesus lived past his fifties and that one of his disciples was in Asia:

> They, however, that they may establish their false opinion regarding that which is written, "to proclaim the acceptable year of the Lord", maintain that He preached for one year only, and then suffered in the twelfth month. [In speaking thus], they are forgetful to their own disadvantage, destroying His

---

[1] Josephus, *Antiquities*, 17.13.5–18.1.1.

[2] Vermes, *The Passion*, 15.

[3] Zeitlin, "The Duration of Jesus' Ministry".

whole work, and robbing Him of that age which is both more necessary and more honourable than any other; that more advanced age, I mean, during which also as a teacher He excelled all others. For how could He have had disciples, if He did not teach? And how could He have taught, unless He had reached the age of a Master? For when He came to be baptized, He had not yet completed His thirtieth year, but was beginning to be about thirty years of age (for thus Luke, who has mentioned His years, has expressed it: "Now Jesus was, as it were, beginning to be thirty years old", when He came to receive baptism); and, [according to these men,] He preached only one year reckoning from His baptism. On completing His thirtieth year He suffered, being in fact still a young man, and who had by no means attained to advanced age.

Now, that the first stage of early life embraces thirty years, and that this extends onwards to the fortieth year, everyone will admit; but from the fortieth and fiftieth year a man begins to decline towards old age, which our Lord possessed while He still fulfilled the office of a Teacher, even as the Gospel and all the elders testify; those who were conversant in Asia with John, the disciple of the Lord, [affirming] that John conveyed to them that information. And he remained among them up to the times of Trajan. Some of them, moreover, saw not only John, but the other apostles also, and heard the very same account from them, and bear testimony as to the [validity of] the statement.

The reign of the Roman emperor Trajan began in 98 CE, seven decades after the accepted date of the crucifixion. John is believed to have lived until he was a hundred years old.

Irenaeus' discussion is centred on a passage in John that seems to imply that, at the time of his death, Jesus was much older than is suggested by Luke. In a heated debate with Judeans, Jesus told them, "Your ancestor Abraham rejoiced that he would see my day; he saw it and was glad" (John 8:56). Pointing out that he was too young to have lived in Abraham's time, Jesus' opponents fired back, "You are not yet fifty years old, and have you seen Abraham?" (John 8:57). If Jesus was indeed in his early thirties, Irenaeus argues, his opponents would have naturally said that he was not yet *forty*, rather than *fifty*, years old. He concludes from the debate in John that Jesus seemed to be in his forties.[4]

Some scholars have tried to use the darkness that happened when Jesus

---

[4] Irenaeus, *Against Heresies*, 2.22.5-6.

was crucified, which is reported by all three Synoptists (Mark 15:33; Matt. 27:45; Luke 23:44) (§1.10), to date the crucifixion, or to show that the darkness could not have happened.[5] Presuming that the darkness was a solar eclipse, they have tried to look for total solar eclipses that were visible in Jerusalem in the years surrounding 30 CE. Such attempts have to consider two descriptions of the darkness as being completely wrong. First, the darkness is said to have happened at a full moon, whereas a solar eclipse takes place at a new moon. Second, a total solar eclipse cannot last more than about seven and a half minutes, so the darkness could not have lasted for three hours. To accommodate the claim that the darkness happened at a full moon, there has been the suggestion that the event was, in fact, a lunar eclipse.[6]

A fundamental flaw in these attempts is that the Evangelists present the darkness as supernatural, not natural. The supernaturality is confirmed by the report that the temple curtain was then torn (Mark 15:38; Luke 23:45) and, in the case of Matthew, the report that the following even more fantastic events occurred:

> The curtain of the temple was torn in two, from top to bottom. The earth shook, and the rocks were split. The tombs also were opened, and many bodies of the saints who had fallen asleep were raised. After his resurrection they came out of the tombs and entered the holy city and appeared to many. (Matt. 27:51-53)

Such a miraculous event would have been witnessed by many, if not all, Jerusalemites. Yet history does not know of such an occurrence.

In conclusion, the Gospels imply that Jesus was killed sometime when Pilate was prefect of Judea between 26 and 36 CE. They are too imprecise and contradictory to narrow down this range. Furthermore, Luke has information that breaks even this agreement, placing Jesus' death after Pilate had been removed from office. On a broader note, such dating attempts, whether confirmatory or refutative, look rather hollow given the numerous problems that blight the crucifixion accounts in the Gospels. For easy reference, I have compiled in Table 6.1 the main information in the Gospels that is of relevance to dating Jesus' birth and death.

---

[5] Allen, "Thallus and Phlegon".
[6] Fotheringham, "The Evidence of Astronomy", 160-162.

Table 6.1: Dating information in the Gospels

Claim about Jesus	Dating	Source
Born under Herod the Great	Before 4 BCE	Matthew
Born during Quirinius' census	6 CE	Luke
Started preaching in year 15 of Tiberius	29 CE	Luke
Baptised by John	When thirty years old	Luke
Length of ministry	One year	All Synoptists
Length of ministry	Up to three years	John
Caiaphas was high priest at crucifixion	18–36 CE	Matthew, John
Tried by Herod Antipas in Galilee	4 BCE–39 CE	Luke
Crucified by Pilate	26–36 CE	All Gospels

We shall revisit the question of Jesus' age later (§23.3). I will argue that Jesus was much younger, probably no older than eighteen years, at the time of the crucifixion. This impacts the potential dates of his birth and alleged crucifixion.

7

The Historical Unreliability of the Gospels and Paul's Writings

Of the twenty-seven books of the New Testament, Paul's letters and the Gospels have the most relevant content for studying the crucifixion. While Paul's writings are the earliest of the two sets of books, I will start with the Gospels because they are the main sources of Jesus' history in the New Testament.

7.1 The Gospels

The Gospels are of very limited historical value in general, and their reports of the crucifixion are no exception. There are four major problems with the Gospels as historical documents. **First**, they have irreconcilable internal discrepancies. **Second**, they have historical errors. We saw many instances of these two kinds of flaws when we examined the Gospels' accounts of the crucifixion.

The Gospels contain so many internal inconsistencies and unhistorical claims that some scholars have even argued that history did not mean to those ancient authors what it means to us today. Historical accuracy, it is claimed, did not matter then as it does today. The continued influence of this tendency is attributed to the famous dictum of the German scholar Rudolf Bultmann, who stated in 1926 that "we can now know almost nothing concerning the life and personality of Jesus, since the early Christian sources show no interest in either". He also attributed the impossibility of this knowledge to the "fragmentary and often legendary" nature of those writings, as well as the absence of other sources.[1] But this attempt to explain the failings of the Gospels as historical documents has been convincingly rejected. This is what one prominent authority on the historical Jesus has had to say:

---

[1] Bultmann, *Jesus and the Word*, 8-9.

This view is inspired, I fear, more by a learned Christian believer's disinclination to face up to the real Jesus than by the nature of the Gospel evidence itself. If the evangelists had intended to report, as Bultmann and his followers claim, not the life, ideas and aspirations of Jesus, but the doctrinal message corresponding to the spiritual and organizational needs of the primitive church, they would have been better advised to adopt the more suitable literary form of letters, tracts, or sermons than to write a fake biography.[2]

The above two problems with the reliability of the Gospels are only to be expected in light of the **third** problem they have. They were written decades after Jesus' time. The earliest, Mark, is believed to have been written around 65-70 CE, that is, over three decades after the events. Matthew and Luke are believed to have been written about two decades later and John even later, possibly by more than two decades. This means that none of the Gospels can be an eyewitness account. This is implicitly confirmed by the Gospels themselves, as all four are written in a way that suggests that their respective authors did not witness the events they reported. If any of the authors was an eyewitness, he surely would not have missed the opportunity to highlight this fact to secure as much credibility and acceptability as possible. Relevant to this is the fact that the Gospel authors are anonymous. They acquired their traditional names and attributions by the end of the second century.

Not being written by eyewitnesses to the events, the Gospels used earlier sources. Luke makes it clear that he relied on previous sources when putting together his Gospel. This is how he starts his Gospel, which he has compiled for a certain Theophilus:

> Since many have undertaken to set down an orderly account of the events that have been fulfilled among us, just as they were handed on to us by those who from the beginning were eyewitnesses and servants of the word, I too decided, after investigating everything carefully from the very first, to write an orderly account for you, most excellent Theophilus, so that you may know the truth concerning the things about which you have been instructed. (Luke 1:1-4)

A gap of at least three decades between a source and the events it reports is likely to be too long to ensure high accuracy of the reported

---

[2] Vermes, *The Changing Faces of Jesus*, 158.

details. This would be true today, let alone in ancient times.

Fourth, the fact that we hardly know anything about the sources of the Gospel authors, in the same way that we are ignorant of who the Evangelists were, further exacerbates the problem of reliability. While John differs from the other three and does not share their sources, the Synoptic Gospels are not completely independent of each other. Scholars believe that Matthew and Luke used Mark as one of their sources, which explains the significant similarities between them. They changed those stories, which is why they are not identical. These three Gospels have significantly less independent material than it appears.

Most of Mark is found in Matthew and Luke, but the latter two share mainly sayings of Jesus that are not found in Mark. This prompted German scholars around the beginning of the twentieth century to theorise that Matthew and Luke must have had a second source. This hypothetical document is called "Q", from the German word "Quelle" for "source". Luke, as we have seen, has indicated that he derived his material from earlier sources.

But each of Matthew and Luke has non-Markan material that is not found in the other, so this cannot be attributed to Q. Matthew and Luke, therefore, must each have had a third oral or written source, which are referred to as "M" and "L", respectively. The need to hypothesise the existence of Q, M, and L, none of which we have access to or know who wrote or transmitted, shows how difficult it is to assign much reliability to the Synoptic Gospels. John is significantly later than Mark, which shows in its advanced theology that must have developed over time after Jesus, which makes it even less reliable. This is how one eminent scholar summarised the situation:

> The sources of the Gospels are riddled with just the same problems that we found in the Gospels themselves: they, too, represent traditions that were passed down by word of mouth, year after year, among Christians who sometimes changed the stories—indeed, sometimes invented the stories—as they retold them.[3]

The problems in the Gospels that we have highlighted in the first three chapters of the book, in which we focused on the accounts of the crucifixion, are partly due to the limitedness and unreliability of the

---

[3] Ehrman, *Apocalyptic Prophet*, 83.

information available to their authors. This situation was exacerbated by each of them portraying Jesus in a way that reflected his belief. There is an element of the Gospel authors recounting the story as they thought it *must have happened* rather than reporting what they learned to *have actually happened*:

> The survey of the redactional tendencies in the Easter stories shows that each Gospel has reshaped the Easter stories with motifs from its own theology. These stories comprise not just an account of the Easter experience but also further experiences of Easter down to the time of the evangelists.[4]

If the Gospels' version of the trial of Jesus is broadly accepted, it is difficult to see how those details could have reached Jesus' followers. There is not even a hint that someone could have leaked proceedings. This already serious problem is made worse by the additional layer of ambiguity about how those details were transmitted until they were finally documented in the Gospels.

The Gospels, however, are not the earliest books of the New Testament. These are Paul's letters.

7.2 Paul's Letters

Paul died around 67 CE, about the time Mark wrote his Gospel. The New Testament contains thirteen letters attributed to him, although only seven are considered to be genuine: Romans, Philippians, Galatians, Philemon, First Corinthians, Second Corinthians, and First Thessalonians. Of the remaining six letters, Colossians and Second Thessalonians have divided the opinions of scholars, whereas the remaining four—Ephesians, First Timothy, Second Timothy, and Titus—most accept were not written by Paul. Their real authors are unknown.

Paul's epistles were written over about ten years. The earliest letter, First Thessalonians, is dated to around 50 CE, which is about 15-20 years earlier than the earliest Gospel. While being closer to the time of Jesus, Paul's letters are even less useful as historical sources on the life of Jesus than the Gospels for three reasons.

First, Paul shows almost complete disinterest in the historical Jesus, focusing only on the spiritual Messiah. He says that Jesus was crucified and buried without giving any details. He also states that Jesus was raised

---

[4] Theissen and Merz, *The Historical Jesus*, 495.

without any elaboration on what happened and how; he does not even mention the empty tomb (§1.17). He mentions the post-resurrection appearances (1 Cor. 15:5-7). Apart from these, he briefly reports four other pieces of historical information:

- Jesus was "born of a woman, born under the law" (Gal. 4:4), which is not much to say about anyone's birth. Having been given birth to by a woman may be an indirect reference to Jesus' virginal conception, i.e. not having a father. Being born under the law simply means that Jesus was born a Jew.
- Jesus had more than one brother (1 Cor. 9:5), one of whom is called "James" (Gal. 1:19).
- In addition to Jesus' brother James, Paul names Cephas, who is also called Peter, and John as two of his disciples (Gal. 2:9).
- Jesus' Last Supper with his disciples (1 Cor. 11:23-27).

That is all! Paul does not talk, for instance, about Jesus' birth, miracles, upbringing, or encounters with Jewish leaders. Even his crucifixion and resurrection are cited mainly in the context of talking about their spiritual and theological significance; their historical details are never mentioned. He has nothing to say, for instance, about Jesus' arrest, trial, or even how he was crucified. Not even the headlines of the when, where, and how of these most important events are reported.

This becomes completely understandable given the **second** problem with Paul's usability for studying Jesus' history, which is the fact that he never met Jesus. Paul was first involved in the persecution of Christians. His conversion happened a few years after the crucifixion after experiencing the spiritual Jesus when he was on his way to Damascus to bring Christian prisoners to Jerusalem:

> Now as he was going along and approaching Damascus, suddenly a light from heaven flashed around him. He fell to the ground and heard a voice saying to him, "Saul, Saul, why do you persecute me?" He asked, "Who are you, Lord?" The reply came, "I am Jesus, whom you are persecuting. But get up and enter the city, and you will be told what you are to do." The men who were traveling with him stood speechless because they heard the voice but saw no one. Saul got up from the ground, and though his eyes were open, he could see nothing; so they led him by the hand and brought him into Damascus. For three days he was without sight, and neither ate nor drank. (Acts 9:3-9)

Paul was proud that what he reported about Jesus came not through a normal channel of communication but via direct revelation:

> For I want you to know, brothers and sisters, that the gospel that was proclaimed by me is not of human origin; for I did not receive it from a human source, nor was I taught it, but I received it through a revelation of Jesus Christ. (Gal. 1:11-12)

One problem is that while Paul narrates more than once his spiritual encounter with Jesus (Acts 22:6-10, 26:13-18), he does not explain anywhere how his knowledge of Jesus' teachings was communicated to him. Even when he has to defend the authenticity of his teachings, he fails to tell his sceptical audiences how he got them from Jesus to dispel their doubts. It is reasonable to conclude that had Paul experienced any distinct spiritual experiences in which he was informed of Jesus' true teachings, he would have mentioned them as he detailed his visionary encounter with Jesus.

We also know from Paul himself that *his* Jesus was not the same Jesus that was being preached by *unnamed distinguished* apostles:

> I feel a divine jealousy for you, for I promised you in marriage to one husband, to present you as a chaste virgin to Christ. But I am afraid that as the serpent deceived Eve by its cunning, your thoughts will be led astray from a sincere and pure devotion to Christ. For if someone comes and proclaims *another Jesus than the one we proclaimed*, or if you receive a different spirit from the one you received, or a *different gospel from the one you accepted*, you submit to it readily enough. I think that I am not in the least inferior to these super-apostles. I may be untrained in speech, but not in knowledge; certainly in every way and in all things we have made this evident to you. (2 Cor. 11:2-6)

Paul's criticism is unambiguous that the other apostles proclaimed a *different Jesus and gospel* from what he taught. Unfortunately, he does not explain the differences between his teachings and those of his competitors.

Equally significant is Paul's description of his adversaries as "super-apostles". Continuing to assert his credibility, he goes on to tell his audience how he matched certain qualifications of those apostles:

> But whatever anyone dares to boast of—I am speaking as a fool—I also dare to boast of that. Are they Hebrews? So am I. Are they Israelites? So am I. Are they descendants of Abraham? So am I. Are they ministers

of Christ? I am talking like a madman—I am a better one: with far greater labors, far more imprisonments, with countless floggings, and often near death. (2 Cor. 11:21-23)

Paul does not clarify what attribute gave the other apostles the status of superiority. It must be something that he did not possess, which also explains the angry tone of his rhetoric and his need to assert his equal status. Significantly, he does that by stressing that he also was an Israelite, a Hebrew, a descendant of Abraham, and a servant of Christ and that he suffered more. Yet these personal attributes only serve to highlight his lacking credibility as a historical source on Jesus. They do not endow his teachings on Jesus with more credibility than his teachings on any other figure he could have become excited about. In all likelihood, the superiority of those apostles denoted their direct knowledge of Jesus and that they might have even seen, listened to, and accompanied their master. It is difficult, otherwise, to explain why Paul took seriously their claim of superiority and refuted it in highly emotional language. The special status of those apostles, which Paul's dismissal of suggests that he lacked, did not stop him from vilifying them completely:

And what I do I will also continue to do, in order to deny an opportunity to those who want an opportunity to be recognized as our equals in what they boast about. For such boasters are false apostles, deceitful workers, disguising themselves as apostles of Christ. And no wonder! Even Satan disguises himself as an angel of light. So it is not strange if his ministers also disguise themselves as ministers of righteousness. (2 Cor. 11:12-14)

This is what one scholar had to say:

Paul never questions the historical reality of Jesus' life and ministry. There is no evidence, however, that Paul had ever seen or heard the earthly Jesus, let alone that he had ever met or conversed with him. What the apostle emphasizes is the vision that he had been granted of the resurrected Jesus, revealed as God's Son. Whatever Paul had known about Jesus before then, whether firsthand or secondhand, was of lesser importance to him. The vision was decisive.[5]

There is no questioning the significance of Paul's contribution to Christian theology. In fact, his is arguably the biggest contribution. This,

---

[5] Furnish, *Jesus According to Paul*, 18.

in turn, takes us to the **third** reason why his writings cannot be used to study the historical Jesus: he was a theologian, not a historian. The focus of his writings is the spiritual Messiah and the theological meanings and significance of this concept. This is also a prominent feature in John, which has a far more developed theology than is found in the Synoptic Gospels. The crucifixion and resurrection of Jesus underlie Paul's theology, but they are treated more as theological requirements than historical events.

In summary, Paul is of no use at all for studying the historical Jesus. The Gospels, on the other hand, offer considerable information about the historical Jesus. But these books report manifestly contradictory and verifiably inaccurate and erroneous information, so their accounts cannot be treated as reliable sources on Jesus' life.

This has encouraged some scholars, albeit a tiny minority, to go as far as denying the existence of one historical figure that inspired the confusing picture of Jesus in the available sources. The historical Jesus, according to this view, never existed! This theory can be traced back to as early as the eighteenth century. A 1926 book by the German historian Arthur Drews names thirty-five mythicists, as they are usually known, over one hundred and fifty years. Mythicism survives today in few writers, probably most known among them are Robert Price, a former Baptist minister who wrote several books that deny the historicity of the Gospel accounts, and Earl Doherty. This is the latter's definition of mythicism:

> No historical Jesus worthy of the name existed, that Christianity began with a belief in a spiritual, mythical figure, that the Gospels are essentially allegory and fiction, and that no single identifiable person lay at the root of the Galilean preaching tradition.[6]

Mythicism is seen as such a preposterous proposition that it is dismissed out of hand by other scholars. They often critically point out the rarity of scholars trained in relevant fields among mythicists.[7] I do not find the lack of specialisation among mythicists more damaging to the merit of their position than the biases of *real* specialists, Christian and non-Christian, to their respective strongly held views.

---

[6] Doherty, *Neither God Nor Man*, vii-viii.
[7] Ehrman, *Did Jesus Exist?*, 17-20.

I consider mythicism an extreme view that fails to give a convincing reconstruction of history. It makes many assumptions to show that the history of Jesus was made up of bits and pieces borrowed from a variety of sources and myths. It has considerably bigger problems than the historical claims it denies. It is poor judgment to dismiss all references to Jesus in ancient writings as incapable of even proving that he one day existed. I do not agree either that the Gospels are devoid of any factual information about Jesus. But given the nature of these narratives, they cannot be considered to be historically accurate without independent confirmatory evidence. As for the Gospels' accounts of the crucifixion and related events, we have seen that they are beset by historically false claims and inaccurate information, in addition to internal discrepancies.

8

Criteria of Authenticity

To help them in their search for history in the inconsistent and contradictory Gospel accounts, scholars have had to come up with methodological criteria. These are expected to help to identify authentic deeds and words of Jesus in sources whose reliability is highly questionable. Naturally, they have been used with the crucifixion accounts as well.

Several sets of authenticity criteria have been proposed. Criteria proposed by different scholars may overlap, and at times one criterion may be called differently by different scholars. For instance, John Meier has proposed a set of ten criteria, equally split into primary and secondary subsets, E. P. Sanders has four criteria, whereas Bart Ehrman's system has only three.[1] Within any one system, the more criteria a reported action or saying meets, the more likely it is that it is historical. The most important and widely used criteria are the criteria of multiple attestation, dissimilarity, and embarrassment.

The criterion of multiple attestation presumes that a saying or deed of Jesus that is mentioned in multiple sources that are independent of each other has a bigger claim to authenticity than one that is found in a single source. For instance, a saying or deed that is reported in Q, Mark, Paul, and John, which are considered to be independent of each other, is more likely to be authentic than another that is found only in John. One example of this is Jesus' description of bread as his body and wine as his blood at the Last Supper, which is found in Paul (1 Cor. 11:23-26), Mark (14:22-25), and in a different context in John (6:51-58).

The criterion of dissimilarity states that Jesus' sayings and deeds that can be derived from neither the Judaism of his time nor the early Church have a claim to authenticity. This criterion is also called the criterion of

---

[1] Meier, *A Marginal Jew*, 1, 167-184; Sanders and Davies, *The Synoptic Gospels*, 304-334; Ehrman, *Did Jesus Exist?*, 288-293.

"double dissimilarity". Meier and Sanders call it the criterion of "discontinuity" and "uniqueness", respectively. A typical example of this is Jesus' objection to the voluntary fasting of his disciples (Mark 2:18-20).

The criterion of embarrassment asserts that sayings or actions by Jesus that would have embarrassed the early Christians or landed them in trouble have a claim to historicity. Sanders calls this criterion "against the grain". In Ehrman's system, the criterion of dissimilarity covers the criterion of embarrassment as well, which makes his definition of the criterion of dissimilarity rather confusing. Its popularity and distinction make the criterion of embarrassment more appropriate to consider separately, as Meier does. One application of this criterion is to Jesus' rejection in his hometown. It is not something that the Evangelists would have made up because it is embarrassing that Jesus' teachings did not appeal even to people who knew him. Similarly, the claim that one of Jesus' personally selected disciples, Judas, betrayed him is seen as scandalous. It shows Jesus' lack of sound judgment when selecting those special twelve disciples and his lack of authority even over his closest followers. The significance of this betrayal is seen in the description of Judas as "one of the twelve" by all four Evangelists (Mark 14:10; Matt. 26:14; Luke 22:3; John 6:71). This very description of Judas, in turn, leads to the identification of another saying that is likely to be authentic. Luke (22:30) has Jesus telling his *disciples* that they will judge the twelve tribes of Israel, but in Matthew (19:28) it is his *twelve disciples* who will be the judges. In Matthew's version of the saying, Jesus counts Judas with the twelve, which proved to be incorrect, as Judas betrayed Jesus later. This, then, is taken to mean that Matthew's version of the saying is more likely to be authentic than Luke's.

Bart Ehrman's system has also the criterion of "contextual credibility". This mirrors the "criterion of Palestinian environment" in Meier's set of secondary criteria. This criterion stipulates that a tradition that looks out of place in first-century Palestine is almost certainly inauthentic. For instance, an anachronistic claim is clearly something that was added after the event. Unlike the other criteria, this criterion can only be used to reject a tradition rather than confirm its authenticity.

Another criterion that is used by some is "coherence". This is a second-level criterion. Basically, once the main criteria have been used to identify authentic historical material, others of Jesus' sayings and deeds that fit in well with that material are also considered authentic.[2]

There are general observations that should be made before we discuss the application of these criteria to the crucifixion and related episodes in Paul and the Gospels.

Having well-thought-out criteria for assessing the likelihood of Jesus traditions being historical is necessary, not least to ensure method consistency and clarity. But there are limitations as to what such criteria can achieve. They could give a disproportionate, or even false, sense of confidence, and they are not immune to the use of convenience to confirm a user's presumptions. This is attested by the fact that these *objective* criteria have done nothing to even tone down the *subjectivity* of scholarly findings:

> Whether or not one shares my misgivings about dissimilarity, coherence, and embarrassment, it is certain that they and other criteria have not led us into the promised land of scholarly consensus. If our tools were designed to overcome subjectivity and bring order to our discipline, then they have failed.[3]

A fundamental fact is that the perception of the effectiveness of any set of criteria is itself reflective of the view of the reliability of the sources to which the criteria are applied:

> The more unreliable the sources are deemed, the greater demands are placed on the criteria and the less persuasive they will appear. The more reliable the sources are deemed, again, the more cogency the authenticity criteria can be invested with.[4]

Bad sources would frustrate any criteria. There is only so much that any set of criteria can do to effectively interrogate sources that are inconsistent, contradictory, and of unknown genesis. This is the case with the Gospels. The authenticity criteria can easily be operated as a bias confirmation tool.

The criteria of multiple attestation and embarrassment/dissimilarity, which are used positively to confirm the likelihood of historicity, have their specific problems. One problem with the particularly popular

---

[2] Meier, *A Marginal Jew*, 1, 176; Bock, "The Words of Jesus", 93.

[3] Allison, *Jesus of Nazareth*, 6.

[4] Holmén, "Seven Theses", 349.

criterion of embarrassment is that what may be seen as embarrassing
today may not have embarrassed people in the past. Indeed, what is
presumed today to have been scandalous to the early Christians may, on
the contrary, have been beneficial. This may be applied, for instance, to
one of the most used incidents for the criterion of embarrassment.
Scholars claim that the baptism of Jesus by John would have embarrassed
Christians because it portrayed him as having a lower status than his
baptiser, not least because this ritual was supposed to be a "baptism of
repentance".[5] Yet it could be equally argued that even if this narrative
became embarrassing later, for the early Christians "the association of the
lesser-known Jesus with the prestigious prophetic figure, John, enhanced
the former's reputation".[6] Furthermore, later Christians did not find it
difficult to find theological arguments to make the whole episode serve
their faith. This is borne by the fact that Christians over the centuries
always saw in Jesus' baptism by John a confirmation of his unique
elevated status. There is always a way to explain things away.

Also, while it is presumed that an apparently embarrassing saying or
deed would have its claim to authenticity further strengthened by being
attested in multiple independent sources, it could be equally argued that
multiple attestation weakens the embarrassment argument:

> I can't help thinking that one cancels out the other. If everyone, Q, an
> independent Thomas, Mark, Matthew, Luke all have this same material, who
> is embarrassed about it? The multiple attestation is itself an argument against
> embarrassment.[7]

The operation of these criteria is inherently subjective.

Similarly, the pair of the criterion of dissimilarity and any criterion
that uses the environment at Jesus' time as a reference, such as contextual
credibility, may be used to support or weaken each other. If a Jesus saying
could not be derived from the Judaism of his time and the early Church,
it is considered more likely to be authentic by the criterion of double
dissimilarity. Yet it can be equally argued that the saying's departure from
its historical setting should make it less likely to be authentic, which is
how the criterion of contextual credibility is operated.

---

[5] Dunn, *Jesus Remembered*, 350-352.
[6] Rodríguez, "The Embarrassing Truth", 143.
[7] Lyons, "A Prophet is Rejected", 79.

Other criticisms have been made of authenticity criteria.[8] But our main interest here is the application of these criteria to the crucifixion and the related claims of the empty tomb and the suffering Messiah.

The criterion of embarrassment is often used to argue for the authenticity of the empty tomb story. More specifically, the Gospels' claim that the empty tomb was discovered by women followers of Jesus is considered to be historical because of "the low status of women in Jewish society and their lack of qualification to serve as legal witnesses".[9] Had the authors of the Gospels made up the story of the empty tomb, the argument goes, they would have chosen men as witnesses, in particular the disciples.[10] A survey spanning thirty years, up to 2005, of scholarly publications in English, French, and German has found that 75% of the authors accepted the empty tomb narrative. The author of this meta-study notes that "by far the most popular argument favoring the Gospel testimony on this subject is that, in all four texts, women are listed as the initial witnesses".[11] The fact that the four Gospels contradict each other on the identities of these women (§1.17) and other details involving them did very little to undermine the confidence in the likelihood of the historicity of the claim. In other cases, this level of contradiction by all sources would have made most historians dismiss the historicity of the reported event or at least label it as unlikely, even without considering its paranormal background. Not in this case, though, thanks to the criterion of embarrassment, or so it is claimed.

The claim that the Evangelists would have chosen men as witnesses to the empty tomb because women were not seen as credible seems to be contradicted by a story in John. The testimony of a woman who witnessed Jesus' miracles was so effective that it convinced many to become believers:

> Many Samaritans from that city believed in him because of the woman's testimony, "He told me everything I have ever done". (John 4:39)

---

[8] Crossan, *The Birth of Christianity*, 144-146.

[9] Craig, *Assessing the New Testament*, 366. See also Evans, "The Silence of Burial", 40; Craig, "Closing Response", 170.

[10] Craig, "Did Jesus Rise From the Dead?", 162.

[11] Habermas, "Resurrection Research", 141.

Additionally, naming the women witnesses reflects their critical role in the story; they were not just any women. Naming them means that their role as witnesses is seen as adding more credibility to the story.[12] There is no indication of any embarrassment. Also, women were widely accepted in Judaism as Jewish heroines. In Mark, the three women that visit the empty tomb are the same three that witnessed the crucifixion while the disciples fled.[13]

Furthermore, I find the overemphasis on women being the *first* who discovered the empty tomb to be misguided. The Synoptic Gospels make females *the first of Jesus' followers* to see the empty tomb but not the *first witnesses ever*. In Mark, the empty tomb was first seen by a young man. In Matthew's account, the first witness was an angel. Luke's narrative has two angels instead. These, in their respective Gospels, told the women followers of Jesus that he was raised. In none of the Synoptic Gospels were women the first or only witnesses.

It is only in the latest of the four Gospels, John, that we find a woman truly being the first witness to the empty tomb, ensuring that the four Gospels give completely discrepant accounts. Given that the earliest Gospel, Mark, makes it clear that the first witness was a young man, we have here another problem for the embarrassment argument. The criterion of embarrassment would predict that the earliest account would have had a woman discovering the empty tomb first, and that later accounts would have replaced her with a male to protect the narrative from being questioned based on the incompetence of women as legal witnesses. Yet we have the exact opposite scenario, with Mark having a male witness first and John having a female instead. Surely, this can only mean that there was no perceived embarrassment to start with. The development of the different accounts of the empty tomb has nothing to do with any sense of embarrassment.

Even if we ignore the non-disciple male witnesses and go with the unjustified emphasis on women being the only witnesses to the empty tomb, the argument from embarrassment remains untenable. The fact that *all four* Gospels have women discovering the empty tomb indicates that this detail was not particularly, if at all, embarrassing to the

[12] Bauckham, "The Eyewitnesses", 52, 54.

[13] Casey, *Jesus of Nazareth*, 475.

Evangelists.

Paul does not mention the empty tomb at all. This is a serious problem for the belief that Jesus rose from the dead. It is so much so that some have tried to argue that Paul theologically implied that the tomb was empty.[14] But the standard explanation of Paul's notable failure to mention the empty tomb has been to attribute it to the fact that it was first discovered by females who were not fully qualified as witnesses in Jewish law.[15] This explanation is counterintuitive. Presuming that Paul was aware of the story of the empty tomb, he would certainly have mentioned it because it is supportive of his theology, which is based on the risen Jesus. Surely, its convenience for his theology would have been more than worth the embarrassment. Even if only a small number of people would believe the report, that would still be better than not reporting it at all! Isn't this what the four supposedly *embarrassed* Evangelists concluded?

But to further expose the absurdity of the argument from embarrassment, let's presume that Paul was, for some unknown reason, particularly bothered by the presence of only female witnesses. He could have simply introduced one or more male witnesses to the account to remedy it as a source of embarrassment and stop any question of its credibility. This would have been a much smaller manipulation than erasing it from history. It makes little sense for him to have decided to suppress it instead of fixing it!

That the Gospels have four different accounts of male-female witnesses of the empty tomb confirms our conclusion about Paul. Had he been aware of an empty tomb narrative in which the first witness was a female, and had he felt uncomfortable about reporting it as is, he would have introduced an earlier role for a male. Indeed, it has been suggested that this is what Mark did, introducing a man into his story to "add weight to the witness".[16] But Paul had no embarrassment to remedy; he knew of no empty tomb narrative.

The criterion of embarrassment cannot be used to explain the absence

---

[14] Mánek, "The Apostle Paul and the Empty Tomb".

[15] Craig, "Did Jesus Rise From the Dead?", 155; Vermes, *Nativity, Passion, Resurrection*, 415, 434; Theissen and Merz, *The Historical Jesus*, 497.

[16] Crossley, "Against the Historical Plausibility", 185.

of the empty tomb from Paul's account. This is an example of how easy it is to misuse this criterion. The argument from embarrassment in support of the historicity of the empty tomb is completely eclipsed by the argument of its non-historicity from Paul's complete unawareness of this event. The criterion that is supposed to test for authenticity is here more of a vehicle to override stronger counterevidence and confer authenticity.

My conclusion is that the empty tomb narrative is empty of any historical substance, so to speak.

Unsurprisingly, the crucifixion has also been claimed to be likely historical using both the criteria of dissimilarity and embarrassment.[17] As I have already explained (§4), Judaism never knew of a crucified Messiah. Paul even singles it out as the main barrier for Jews accepting Jesus as the Messiah (1 Cor. 1:23). This example works with the first part of the criterion of double dissimilarity, which requires divergence from the Judaism of the time, but not with its second part, which requires its distinction from the teachings of the early Church after Jesus. The early Church always had Jesus as the suffering Messiah at the foundation of its theology. This concept is, obviously, fully built on the crucifixion of Jesus.

The early Christians would have also been embarrassed by their leader being put to the humiliation of crucifixion, a punishment that was reserved for the lowest of the low in society. The crucifixion of Jesus meets the criterion of embarrassment as well. It is, again, concluded that it is highly likely to have happened.

Yet despite all of that, early Christians succeeded in turning the crucifixion from a potentially fatal blow to their new faith to its cornerstone. We find this in the earliest sources, Paul's letters. This is one illustration of this amazing deed:

> For the message about the cross is foolishness to those who are perishing, but to us who are being saved it is the power of God. For it is written,
> "I will destroy the wisdom of the wise,
>   and the discernment of the discerning I will thwart."
> Where is the one who is wise? Where is the scribe? Where is the

---

[17] Ehrman, *Apocalyptic Prophet*, 93.

debater of this age? Has not God made foolish the wisdom of the world? For since, in the wisdom of God, the world did not know God through wisdom, God decided, through the foolishness of our proclamation, to save those who believe. For Jews demand signs and Greeks desire wisdom, but we proclaim Christ crucified, a stumbling block to Jews and foolishness to Gentiles, but to those who are the called, both Jews and Greeks, Christ the power of God and the wisdom of God. For God's foolishness is wiser than human wisdom, and God's weakness is stronger than human strength. (1 Cor. 1:18-25)

Paul acknowledges that a crucified Messiah is a foolish idea and that rejecting it is only rational. He ingeniously and clumsily gets around the problem by labelling that foolishness as "divine" and the counter wisdom as "human", so that he can claim that the foolishness of the crucifixion of the Messiah rather than the wisdom of rejecting it represents the truth! Far from feeling embarrassed, "Paul revels in the scandal of the crucifixion... and elevates the cross of Christ to a central place in his theologizing".[18] Instead of being a source of enormous embarrassment, the counterintuitive crucifixion is seen as a source of pride and brag.

This highly creative yet surprisingly successful repositioning of the crucifixion from a devastating weakness in the new faith to a unique strength and advantage exposes the intrinsic uselessness of the criterion of embarrassment. Rather than being a probe to discover history proper, it is a tool in the hands of its user to choose the version of history they prefer:

> Nothing was so difficult for early Christian theology as the crucifixion of Israel's messiah. But nothing was so fruitful for early Christian theology as the crucifixion of Israel's messiah. We intended the criterion of embarrassment to strain out the historical gnats (Jesus' baptism, the underwhelming faith of the disciples, etc.), but we find that with it we swallow even the camel of Jesus' crucifixion! This seems an awfully messy way to do history.[19]

Whether an episode was embarrassing or not is determined by how the assessor's reading places it in the overall narrative. It is not possible to describe an event as embarrassing without this judgment being

---

[18] Rodríguez, "The Embarrassing Truth", 147.

[19] Ibid., 147-148.

influenced by a particular interpretation of related events.

Let's look more closely at the application of the authenticity criteria to the concept of the suffering Messiah, which did not exist before Christianity, and how it is forced to confirm the historicity of the crucifixion. Bart Ehrman has this to say:

> The idea of a suffering messiah cannot be found there. It had to be created. And the reason it had to be created is that Jesus—the one Christians considered to be the messiah—was known by everyone everywhere to have been crucified.[20]

While Paul's letters and the Gospels show that their authors believed that Jesus was crucified, they certainly do not tell us that his crucifixion "was known by everyone everywhere". This belief of the New Testament authors is being presented here as global common knowledge. When the same scholar elsewhere applies the criterion of dissimilarity, he concludes the following:

> Christians who wanted to proclaim Jesus as Messiah would not have invented the notion that he was crucified, because his crucifixion created such a scandal. Indeed, the apostle Paul calls it the chief "stumbling block" for Jews (1 Cor. 1:23). Where, then, did the tradition come from? It must have actually happened.[21]

Here, using one of the criteria of authenticity, the belief of Paul and the Evangelists that Jesus was crucified is effectively turned into firm history, that he was indeed crucified! Ehrman also ignores the fact that even the writers of the earliest sources were not eyewitnesses to the crucifixion.

We know that the concept of a suffering Messiah is unhistorical, so we must conclude that it was created by someone at some point for some purpose, even though we do not know the details. The concept was then adopted by Paul, if he was not its creator, and the Evangelists, proving their ability to accept and promote unhistorical beliefs. They did not stop to argue with whoever passed on this challenging notion to them that even if the Messiah was crucified, the idea of a suffering Messiah had no roots in history. No, they wholly embraced this self-contradictory

---

[20] Ehrman, *Did Jesus Exist?*, 173.

[21] Ehrman, *Apocalyptic Prophet*, 93.

concept that made no sense to the Jews of the time. They inherited a tradition that packaged the *historically possible* crucifixion of Jesus with the *verifiably unhistorical* suffering Messiah. The Gospel authors even made the concept of the suffering Messiah an intrinsic and unique aspect of Jesus' mission. How confident can we be that the nonhistorical belief is based on a historical event?

The historicisation of the suffering Messiah by early Christians highlights a fundamental problem with the criteria of authenticity, in addition to the already discussed concerns that scholars have raised. Simply put, these criteria can effectively equate faith with historical truth. Let me explain.

Each New Testament author wrote a history that reflected his knowledge of Jesus. No one doubts that some aspects of the early tradition that those authors faithfully reported are inaccurate or wrong. Scholars are also certain that, at times, authors manipulated what they reported to reflect their own views and expectations. While the Evangelists were far more interested in reporting history than Paul, they were not news reporters or dispassionate historians. Every Gospel, then, is a mix of three types of historical claims:

- Faithfully reported accurate history from tradition
- Faithfully reported inaccurate and erroneous history from tradition
- Deliberately manipulated or made-up history driven by faith

To add considerable complexity to an already confusing situation, one critical unknown is the percentage of each of these three ingredients in the recipe that makes up each book. This inevitably directly impacts the effectiveness of any criteria of authenticity used in finding true history in this mix. For instance, what if fake history makes up most of the text? Can any textual analysis tools truly allow us to sift through the mix to find the randomly scattered history? Indeed, everyone knows that the Gospels are more books of faith than history.

The only truth that we can be certain of is that a Gospel represents the beliefs of its writer, but we cannot tell how close that faith is to history. Yet the criteria of authenticity are based on the assumption that they can help us navigate from faith to history, even though just about every piece of text can potentially be history, inaccurate history, or fake history.

Let me use Paul's conversion to further explain the insurmountable difficulty that the criteria of authenticity face in bridging the gap between faith and history and, consequently, their intrinsic limitation in confirming the historicity of the crucifixion. Paul reported a spiritual experience in which Jesus spoke to him that completely changed him from a sworn enemy of Christianity to one of its most committed believers. Paul's new belief thoroughly contradicted his long-held view about Christianity, in the same way that the concept of the suffering Messiah contradicted the centuries-old image of the Messiah. Now, does this mean that Paul's experience happened exactly as he reported it because it was utterly unexpected and had such an impact on him? A nonconfessional answer would point out that numerous personal experiences happened and will happen that are both unexpected and life-changing, but it would be unjustified to declare the details of these experiences historical without further investigation. Let's accept the argument that *something must have happened* to Paul, but this is not the same as saying that the reported event was *historical in all of its details*. He may have, for instance, experienced some form of hallucination, which is not the same as actually hearing Jesus. In this case, something did happen, but it was not exactly what Paul reported. Significantly, in this alternative scenario, Jesus' appearance is unhistorical!

The case is the same with Paul's and the Evangelists' belief in the crucifixion. That belief might well have been triggered by a real event, but that event does not have to be the crucifixion of Jesus. A failed attempt on Jesus' life that mistakenly led to another man being crucified could have been that event, which is what I argue happened. Given the design of the criteria of authenticity and the nature of the historical sources they have been introduced for, these tools can never confirm that Jesus was crucified.

II

The Crucifixion in Classical and Early Jewish Sources

9

Overview of the Early Non-Christian Sources

The crucifixion is said to be attested in non-Christian historical sources, not only in the New Testament. I have compiled in this part of the book all sources in the first two centuries that mention Jesus' execution. That might sound like a mammoth task, given that there are numerous historical, philosophical, and other writings from that period. Yet the reality is that this is a rather easy undertaking because there are only a few sources that mention Jesus' crucifixion! To be precise, there are four such sources, one each from the Roman-Jewish historian Josephus, the Roman historian and governor Tacitus, the Greek writer Lucian, and the Greek philosopher Celsus. The earliest of these, Josephus' reference, comes from the last decade of the first century CE, that is, sixty years after Jesus' time.

If we narrow down the period to the first century following the crucifixion, we have only two sources that mention Jesus' crucifixion. The earliest is Josephus and the second, Tacitus, is from the second decade of the second century. Still, this two-item list is probably one too long, as Josephus' passage is almost certainly a Christian forgery!

There are another two sources that are usually considered among the early references to the crucifixion of Jesus, one by the Greek historian Thallus and a second by an unknown writer called Mara Bar Serapion. Yet these do not explicitly mention Jesus. Linking the ambiguous references in them to his crucifixion is highly speculative.

The Jewish Talmud also contains a reference to the crucifixion. While there is the suggestion from some that this passage may be from the second century, this is not possible to confirm. The Talmud itself was not compiled until around the sixth century, so the report we have could be that late. As we shall see, there are problems with this passage that are too serious for it to be of any historical value.

I will discuss these sources in order of significance and likely date of writing. I will dedicate one chapter to Josephus, another to classical sources, and a third to Jewish rabbinic writings. The fourth and last chapter of this part of the book will evaluate these writings as historical sources on the crucifixion.

10

Flavius Josephus

Josephus was born as Yosef ben Matityahu in 37 CE to a Jewish priestly family in Jerusalem, Judea, which was under Roman rule. In 66 CE, when the first Jewish-Roman war broke out, he was charged with commanding the Jewish forces in Galilee. After the Jewish resistance collapsed and he surrendered, he told Vespasian, who led the Roman forces, that he would become emperor. The latter did not kill him but kept him as a slave. When the prediction was fulfilled three years later, the now-emperor Vespasian granted the Jewish slave his freedom. Josephus fully defected to the Romans and became a friend of the emperor's son, Titus. He acted as an interpreter for the latter during his siege of Jerusalem in 70 CE. After the fall of the city, Josephus settled down in Rome and was granted Roman citizenship. He also became a client and pensioner of the emperor, thus becoming known as Flavius Josephus after the emperor's family name. He put this comfortable living to good use by writing extensively on Jewish history.

Writing in Greek, Josephus mentioned Jesus in a famous passage known as the "Testimonium Flavianum", which means the "witness of Flavius (to Jesus)". The Testimonium is generally considered, for good reason, as the most remarkable early non-Christian reference to Jesus. First, the passage occurs in Josephus' book *Antiquities of the Jews*, which he wrote in 93-94 CE. As such, the Testimonium is the earliest non-Christian source that mentions Jesus. Second, Josephus is a highly regarded historian. Third, while short, the passage has significant information about Jesus, including his crucifixion, which is why it is particularly interesting to us here.

The Testimonium has probably also been the most debated passage of Josephus' voluminous writings. The controversy about it stems from what it says about Jesus and the question of its authenticity. This is why we will study the Testimonium before the other early non-Christian sources and dedicate a chapter to discussing it in detail, rather than including it in the chapter on the other Roman or Jewish sources.

This is the text of the Testimonium:

> Now there was about this time Jesus, a wise man, if it be lawful to call
> him a man; for he was a doer of wonderful works, a teacher of such men as
> receive the truth with pleasure. He drew over to him both many of the Jews
> and many of the Gentiles. He was [the] Christ. And when Pilate, at the
> suggestion of the principal men amongst us, had condemned him to the cross,
> those that loved him at the first did not forsake him; for he appeared to them
> alive again the third day; as the divine prophets had foretold these and ten
> thousand other wonderful things concerning him. And the tribe of
> Christians, so named from him, are not extinct at this day.[1]

The authenticity of the Testimonium was unquestioned until the rise
of historical criticism in the sixteenth century when doubts were first
voiced. Today, few scholars argue for the authenticity of the entire
passage. It is almost universally accepted that this passage is either genuine
Josephan writing that has been subjected to significant Christian
redaction, as the majority of scholars argue, or a Christian forgery that
was introduced in its entirety into Josephus' work, as some, including
myself, contend.

The Testimonium is not the only passage in a Josephus work that has
been written or edited by a Christian hand. An Old Russian translation
of the *Wars of the Jews*, known as Slavonic Josephus, contains a longer
version of the Testimonium, in addition to three passages that mention
Jesus and three on John the Baptist scattered in the book. Scholars agree
that these passages, which are not found in the Greek version, could not
have been written by Josephus and are Christian forgeries.

We will now review the arguments supporting the views that the
Testimonium was a partial or total forgery.

10.1 Arguments That the Testimonium Is Partially Authentic

If some parts of the surviving passage were written by Josephus, what
would have been his sources? This is how one scholar tried to answer this
question:

> If this passage is not drawn from oral or written Christian sources, neither

---

[1] Josephus, *Antiquities*, 18.3.3.

does it seem to be drawn from official Roman documents or other Roman historians. For example, Josephus's use of "Jesus" as a personal name and use of "Christ" as a title runs directly counter to the Roman usage that has survived.

A more plausible hypothesis is that Josephus gained his knowledge of Christianity when he lived in Palestine. He supplemented it in Rome, as the words "to this day" may imply, where there was a significant Christian presence. Whether Josephus acquired his data by direct encounter with Christians, indirect information from others about their movement, or some combination of both, we cannot tell... None of these potential sources is verifiable, yet the evidence points to the last option as the more commendable. The same Josephus who followed Christianity in Rome, knowing that it persisted as a movement and merited some short treatment in his book, likely followed it earlier with some interest.[2]

In other words, it is likely that if Josephus is indeed responsible for parts of the surviving passage, it would have been influenced by Christian tradition. The author was himself a Jew but his information might well have come from Christians, directly or indirectly. This disqualifies it as independent historical information.

Nevertheless, let's discuss the main arguments made in support of the partial authenticity view of the passage.

1) **Josephus' style**: A substantial part of the Testimonium reflects the language and style of Josephus. This point is further enforced by contrasting the coherence of the language and style of the Testimonium with those of the New Testament, which the Christian interpolators of the inauthentic text were supposedly familiar with:

> The vocabulary and grammar of the passage (after the clearly Christian material is removed) cohere well with Josephus' style and language; the same cannot be said when the text's vocabulary and grammar are compared with that of the NT. Indeed, many key words and phrases in the Testimonium are either absent from the NT or are used there in an entirely different sense; in contrast, almost every word in the core of the Testimonium is found elsewhere in Josephus—in fact, most of the vocabulary turns out to be characteristic of Josephus.[3]

This is probably one of the more subjective arguments. For instance,

---

[2] Van Voorst, *Jesus Outside the New Testament*, 103.

[3] Meier, "Jesus in Josephus", 90.

another scholar who analysed the language and style of the Testimonium reached a completely different conclusion:

> Comparison of the Testimonium with the writings of Josephus and Eusebius thus reveals that while much of the content is unlikely to have originated with Josephus, none of it is inconsistent with Eusebius' beliefs. Further, except for two phrases peculiar to Josephus, the language is entirely consistent with Eusebius' normal usage. The three phrases "maker of miraculous works", "tribe of Christians", and "to this day" occur several times elsewhere in Eusebius, and never, elsewhere, in Josephus.
>
> Far from being overwhelmingly Josephan, then, the Testimonium (as it appears in *A.J.* 18.3.3 §§63-64) has only two phrases more typical of Josephus than of Eusebius: "receive with pleasure" and "first[4] men". These phrases are conspicuous in their absence from Eusebius' earliest citation of the Testimonium in *Dem. evang.* 3.5 §124, where Eusebius instead uses the words … "to revere" and … "leaders.[5]"

He then goes on to conclude:

> The entire passage was taken from a single source, the *Historia Ecclesiastica*, by Christian scribes who accepted it on Eusebius' authority and inserted it into Josephus' account of Pilate's administration, breaking the continuity of the text, and placing the passage before, not after, Josephus' account of John the Baptist. This had at least one unintended consequence: it almost certainly inspired Christian copyists to preserve Josephus' works for us.[6]

As we shall see later in the chapter, there is a strong case for the suggestion that Eusebius (c.260-before 341 CE), bishop of Caesarea in Palestine, forged, totally or in part, the Testimonium. Another critic has argued that textual and structural similarities between the Testimonium and the dialogue between Jesus and his two followers in the Emmaus passage (Luke 24:19-27) indicate that both had a common Christian source.[7]

Analysis of the language and style of the Testimonium does not represent a strong argument, to say the least, in support of the partial

---

[4] This word appears as "principal" in the translation we are using of the Testimonium.

[5] Olson, "Eusebius and the "Testimonium Flavianum"", 313.

[6] Ibid., 322.

[7] Goldberg, "Coincidences".

authenticity view.

2) **The James passage**: Josephus makes another, albeit passing, mention of Jesus in *Antiquities of the Jews* when talking about a James he identifies as "the brother of Jesus, who was called Christ". After the sudden death of Festus, the procurator of Judea, and before the arrival of his successor Albinus, the high priest Ananus took advantage of the ruler's absence to kill James:

> Ananus was of this disposition, he thought he had now a proper opportunity [to exercise his authority]. Festus was now dead, and Albinus was but upon the road; so he assembled the Sanhedrin of judges, and brought before them *the brother of Jesus, who was called Christ*, whose name was James, and some others [or, some of his companions]; and when he had formed an accusation against them as breakers of the law, he delivered them to be stoned.[8]

It is argued that Josephus was mainly writing to Gentiles, so his audience would not have known what "Christ" meant or who Jesus was unless he had already introduced this title and name earlier.[9] Only one passage, the Testimonium, can be that introduction.

This supposed defence is rather counterproductive as it exposes a serious flaw in the attribution of the two passages to Josephus. Outside those two passages, Josephus nowhere mentions the term "Messiah" or "Christ" in his voluminous writings. Yet neither of these passages provides any information to the Roman reader about what a "Messiah" meant in Judaism. It is unreasonable to expect Josephus to have mentioned a title that is completely alien to Roman culture without explaining it, regardless of whether the claimant he refers to was genuine or false.[10]

A second problem is that the strength of this argument depends on the authenticity of the James passage, which scholars accept. This acceptance, in turn, rests on the view that the wording does not reflect Christian beliefs, such as the noncommittal description of Jesus as one "who was called Christ".[11] I have argued elsewhere that there are strong reasons to

---

[8] Josephus, *Antiquities*, 20.9.1.
[9] Meier, "Jesus in Josephus", 89-90.
[10] Doherty, *Neither God Nor Man*, 545-547.
[11] Schürer, *The Jewish People*, I, 431.

reject the authenticity of the reference to Jesus and Christ in the James passage.[12] I would like to mention one particular argument here.

The James passage in its current form contains a major contradiction that Josephus could not have made. If James was really Jesus' brother, then the accusation must have been related to his embracement of the religion of his brother. In fact, introducing Jesus first before James' name, or mentioning Jesus at all, could be seen as implying that James was killed because he followed his brother. Yet the keepers of the religious law, whom Josephus describes as the "most equitable of the citizens" and "most uneasy at the breach of the laws", considered the high priest's ruling as "unjustified", which means that they did not view James as a lawbreaker. Josephus also thought that James was unfairly accused of breaking the law. The contradiction in this combination of statements is that conversion from Judaism to the new faith, Christianity, would have turned any Jew into a lawbreaker in the eyes of the lay Jew, let alone those ardent official protectors of the law. Josephus, himself a loyal Jew, would have no doubt considered James a heretic. This contradiction disappears if we remove the identification of James as "the brother of Jesus, who was called Christ".

There is another interesting observation to note. The James passage talks about how he was tried and executed by the Sanhedrin, which is what is supposed to have happened to his brother Jesus. According to the Gospels, Pilate was an unwilling participant in the execution of Jesus. Yet although Josephus mentions Jesus to identify James, implying that Jesus was more famous than his brother, he inexplicably passes over the inviting opportunity to highlight the similarity between the fates of the two brothers. If James' trial and execution were worth mentioning, then surely the trial and execution of his much better known and far more important brother, presumably because of whom James was killed, would have been even more interesting to mention. Josephus either did not know that Jesus was executed or did not mention him at all.

3) The "tribe" description: The narrow and unglorified description of Christians as a "tribe" is written from a Jewish, rather than Christian, perspective. Some scholars have counterargued that this description is not

---

[12] Fatoohi, *The Mystery of the Historical Jesus*, 156-163.

necessarily demeaning or pejorative.[13] Even if it is, it would be a remnant from the original Josephan passage which would have been negative about Jesus.

4) Manuscriptal consistency: The Testimonium is present in all Greek manuscripts of book 18 of *Antiquities of the Jews*. It is found in all of the numerous manuscripts of the Latin translation, which was made in the sixth century. It also exists in an Arabic historical book from the tenth century, and in a Syriac historical book from the twelfth century. This argument is not as strong as it may seem:

> These facts must be balanced, however, by the sobering realization that we have only three Greek manuscripts of book 18 of *The Antiquities*, the earliest of which dates from the eleventh century.[14]

A few Greek manuscripts dating back a whole millennium, or even numerous Latin manuscripts that go back half a millennium after Josephus, do not make "manuscriptal consistency" a particularly strong argument.

In conclusion, the four arguments, individually and collectively, do not make a strong case for the partial authenticity of the Testimonium.

Let's now turn our attention to the far more likely possibility that Josephus has nothing whatsoever to do with the Testimonium.

10.2 Arguments That the Testimonium Is a Total Forgery

The view that the Testimonium was completely written by Christian hands does not exclude the possibility that Josephus wrote something demeaning and derogatory about Jesus that Christian copyists replaced with the surviving passage. This is what one scholar concludes:

> The simplest and most probable explanation for the text having been edited is not that it was neutral—let alone favourable—but rather that the Christian interpolator(s) did not like what (t)he(y) found, because (t)he(y) found it disturbing or offensive. The passage must have contained something, some negative description or a disparaging tone, that could not

---

[13] Meier, "Jesus in Josephus", 95.
[14] Ibid., 88-89.

be accepted, to the extent that some scribe felt compelled to alter it.[15]

Whether this is indeed the case or the Testimonium was authored from scratch by Christians, the conclusion is one and the same: the passage is not Josephan.

Let's examine why the Testimonium is almost certain to have been completely written by a Christian hand. There are six main arguments.

1) Christian-friendliness: The passage is effectively a set of affirmations that clearly either promote Christian beliefs about Jesus or generously praise him:

  i.   He was a "wise man".
  ii.   He was more than a man, i.e. at least partly divine: "If it be lawful to call him a man".
  iii.   He was a miracle worker: "He was a doer of wonderful works".
  iv.   He was a teacher of the truth and his followers were truth-seekers: "A teacher of such men as receive the truth with pleasure".
  v.   He was very influential and successful in his mission: "He drew over to him both many of the Jews and many of the Gentiles".
  vi.   He was the Jewish Messiah: "He was [the] Christ".
  vii.   He was raised three days after his death and appeared to his disciples: "For he appeared to them alive again the third day".
  viii. Prophets predicted numerous miraculous things about him: "The divine prophets had foretold these and ten thousand other wonderful things concerning him".

Scholars who advocate the partial authenticity view usually only consider the four statements that represent Christian confessions of faith (ii, vi, vii, viii) as Christian interpolations:

> ...if it be lawful to call him a man; ... He was [the] Christ. ...for he appeared to them alive again the third day; as the divine prophets had foretold these and ten thousand other wonderful things concerning him.

The obvious Christian tone of these statements has invited the apologetic suggestion that Josephus wrote them sarcastically or was

---

[15] Bermejo-Rubio, "Hypothetical Vorlage", 362.

implying that they reflect Christian beliefs.[16] This is not a plausible explanation. A competent writer like Josephus could not have done such a bad job of mocking Christian beliefs, allowing Christians to argue that he vouched for the veracity of their faith!

Scholars usually exclude the other four claims (i, iii, iv, v) about Jesus from the list of Christian forgeries. Let's study these claims and evaluate their respective authenticity arguments.

A) He was a "wise man": It is often argued that a Christian would not have described Jesus as a "wise man", as this falls short of how a Christian forger would have described him. Meier argues that "a Christian scribe would not deny that Jesus was a wise man, but would feel that label insufficient for one who was believed to be God as well as man".[17] He contends that describing Jesus as a man is Josephan and the following clause that elevates him above human, "if it be lawful to call him a man", is Christian.

The two successive clauses are tightly connected, so attributing them to two completely different sources is unconvincing. But, for the sake of argument, let's presume that describing Jesus as a "wise man" is indeed not a Christian practice. It could still be argued that to immediately qualify this description with "if it be lawful to call him a man" is a more subtle way to pass off a Christian view of Jesus as Josephan than adding a purely Christian statement.

B) He performed miracles: In trying to show this statement was also Josephan rather than Christian, it has been argued that the Greek word "paradoxa" that is translated here as "wonderful works" is "ambiguous; it can also be translated 'startling/controversial deeds' and the whole sentence can be read to simply mean that Jesus had a reputation as a wonder-worker".[18] Again, the suggestion is that the description can be neutral or of little significance. Yet not only does Josephus confirm that Jesus was a miracle worker without qualification or hesitation, but the whole point of reporting this is because it is significantly laudatory! Josephus uses the same description for the highly regarded prophet Elisha: "He also performed wonderful and surprising works by prophecy, and

---

[16] Bruce, *New Testament Documents*, 112.

[17] Meier, "Jesus in Josephus", 85.

[18] Van Voorst, *Jesus Outside the New Testament*, 89.

such as were gloriously preserved in memory by the Hebrews".[19] It is counterintuitive to claim that calling Jesus, in particular, a miracle worker amounted to anything less than acknowledging his elevated status.

C) He taught the truth and his followers were truth-seekers who received it with pleasure: It has been claimed that "Christian writers generally avoid a positive use of the word 'pleasure', with its connotation of 'hedonism', and it is difficult to imagine a Christian scribe using it here about Jesus' followers".[20] The point, surely, is not what other contexts the term "pleasure" could have been used in but its current context, which is obviously positive. Furthermore, the statement is unambiguous in presenting Jesus as a truth-teacher and his followers as truth-seekers. That any such activity is described as having been done with pleasure can only have positive connotations.

D) He successfully converted many Jews and pagans: Scholars have also pointed out that this claim could not have been made by a Christian because according to the Gospels, it is untrue.[21] In the Gospels, Jesus is shown coming into contact with only a few Gentiles, but these were not sought out by him; rather, they came to see him. Furthermore, in Matthew, he is said to have instructed the disciples not to preach to non-Jews:

> Go nowhere among the Gentiles, and enter no town of the Samaritans, but go rather to the lost sheep of the house of Israel. (Matt. 10:5-6)

Those who say that a Christian could not make this claim about the Gentiles miss the point of this fabrication. The forger is trying to make yet another commendatory remark about Jesus by portraying him as a *very successful preacher*. The claim that Jesus converted many Gentiles reflects the fact that when this statement was written, probably some three centuries after Jesus' time, Christianity had spread mainly among Gentiles. Also, Josephus could not have claimed that Jesus was a popular preacher because that was not the case (§5.2).

Two general arguments have been used to attribute these four, and indeed some of the other, statements to Josephus. First, he has used similar

---

[19] Josephus, *Antiquities*, 9.8.6.

[20] Van Voorst, *Jesus Outside the New Testament*, 90.

[21] Meier, "Jesus in Josephus", 93-94.

wording in his writings. This, of course, only means that Josephus *could have* written such phrases. But the problem is the context and meaning of the writing, not the wording. Josephus' description of the prophet Elisha as a miracle worker is not unexpected or suspicious but applying the same description to Jesus is.

Second, Christian authors could not have used such wording because it is not found in the New Testament or it can have negative connotations. Starting with the latter suggestion, again, the fact that the wording may carry negative meanings in other contexts is irrelevant. We are discussing a specific case in which the wording is used positively without any shadow of a doubt. As for the former suggestion, a Christian interpolator would not have *necessarily* used New Testament terminology when forging those passages. We cannot be sure who the interpolator was to presume that he would have used New Testament language anyway. Furthermore, we have already seen that the forger made the false claim that Jesus converted many Gentiles, not only Jews, even though this blatantly contradicted the New Testament. The writer does not show interest in complying with the New Testament's unambiguous statement that Jesus preached only to Jews and avoided Gentiles, so there is no justification to presume that he was more concerned with using New Testament terminology.

While some of the above four Testimonium statements do not promote *specifically* Christian beliefs, they are *not neutral*. Rather, they are highly laudatory and apply to the head figure of Christianity, no less. One of them even extends praise to his followers. In other words, they can only confirm the veracity of this faith. These statements could not have been written by a non-Christian, let alone a faithful Jew. They are *impossible* to reconcile with Josephus' Jewish beliefs. Not only the statements that promote specific Christian beliefs but even the other commendations could not have been said about a false teacher, as Jews who rejected Jesus' teaching saw him. This basic fact is often overlooked by scholars who argue that such statements are aligned with Josephus' style of writing.[22] They ignore the contradiction of these descriptions with Josephus' faith. For instance, Josephus describes Solomon, one of the

---

[22] E.g. Ibid., 90.

most revered men in Judaism, as being a man of wisdom,[23] so calling Jesus "wise" is not insignificant.

Early Christian writers knew that Josephus did not hold Christian beliefs. The early ascetic and theologian Origen of Alexandria (c.185-c.254 CE) twice stated that Josephus did not believe that Jesus was the Christ, while at the same time quoting freely from *Antiquities of the Jews* to argue in support of Christianity.[24] He showed no knowledge of the Christianity-promoting Testimonium.

When the Latin Catholic priest and historian Jerome quoted the Testimonium in 392 CE, he changed the clause "He was [the] Christ" to "he was believed to be the Anointed (Christ)".[25] This suggests that he believed that the passage was tampered with by Christians.

Also, a different version of the Testimonium was cited by the tenth-century Arab Melkite bishop of Hierapolis Agapius in his work *Kitāb al-'Unwān (Book of the Title)*. Significantly, some of the Christian claims have been removed, and what is left has been toned down, making Josephus only report what Christians claimed:

> Similarly Josephus, the Hebrew. For he says in the treatises that he has written on the governance of the Jews: 'At this time there was a wise man who was called Jesus. His conduct was good, and he was known to be virtuous. And many people from among the Jews and the other nations became his disciples. Pilate condemned him to be crucified and to die. But those who had become his disciples did not abandon his discipleship. They reported that he had appeared to them three days after his crucifixion, and that he was alive; accordingly he was perhaps the Messiah, concerning whom the prophets have recounted wonders'.[26]

These changes are an acknowledgement that the original text was written from a Christian perspective.

Removing some of the Christian statements, making Josephus only *report* the remaining Christian beliefs about Jesus, and keeping other laudatory descriptions does not produce a passage that is attributable to him. The passage is still far from being neutral about Jesus.

---

[23] Josephus, *Wars*, 8.2.5.

[24] Origen, *Against Celsus*, 1.47; Origen, *The Gospel of Matthew*, 10.17.

[25] Jerome, *On Illustrious Men*, 13.5.

[26] Pines, *An Arabic Version of the Testimonium*, 8-10.

An eighteenth-century translator of Josephus' complete works put forward the outlandish argument that Josephus was one of the Ebionites, an early Jewish Christian movement that believed that Jesus was the Messiah but did not believe in his divinity.[27] This apologetic hypothesis, which acknowledges the Christian character of the Testimonium, has no support in the writings of Josephus, Christians, and non-Christians.

2) **Passage unity**: The three statements that Jesus was not a mere man, he was the Christ, and he rose from the dead, which are accepted by all as Christian confessions, "exhibit a relationship of cause and effect with some other part of the passage. Either the entire passage has a single author, or the interpolator wove his additions into the text very skilfully".[28] Another scholar has noted that the phrases that are treated as Christian forgeries add up to twenty-nine words, which is as much as a third of the eighty-nine words of the Testimonium.[29] Removing those statements would fundamentally damage the textual integrity of the passage.

But given that all four superlative and laudatory statements about Jesus should be treated as Christian forgeries, as I argue, stripping these off would make the passage more or less disappear. This would only leave the reference to Jesus' crucifixion and the mention of the non-disappearance of his followers. The Testimonium's main focus is highlighting Jesus' supernatural and/or righteous attributes, which is why its attribution to Josephus has to be rejected. Removing these would leave a very short paragraph that does not make much sense or serve any purpose. It is possible, as we have already mentioned, that the forged text replaced one that is derogatory of Jesus.

3) **Late appearance**: The earliest citation of the passage goes back to the early fourth century by Eusebius.[30] Two centuries is plenty of time in ancient times to tamper with a text, but the fact that the passage is not cited until the fourth century argues against its partial authenticity.

Louis Feldman, the world's authority on Josephus, makes very significant observations leading to the conclusion that it was Eusebius

---

[27] Whiston, "Commentary", 8-9.

[28] Olson, "Eusebius and the "Testimonium Flavianum"", 308.

[29] Bermejo-Rubio, "Hypothetical Vorlage", 344.

[30] Eusebius, *The Proof of the Gospel*, I, 3.5, 143.

who authored the Testimonium and attributed it to Josephus. None of the apologetic fathers of the church of the second and third centuries mentions the Testimonium even though they quote Josephus on the interpretation of the Old Testament. Feldman names eight of these pre-Eusebian Christian authors. He acknowledges that this is evidence from silence but, rightly, points out the following:

> When the number of writers is so great and when these are writers who are very much involved with theological questions, especially questions regarding the nature of Jesus, the omission is striking.[31]

Feldman highlights the special case of Origen, who died in the middle of the third century. Origen cites *Antiquities of the Jews* seven times, including as many as five passages from book 18, which contains the Testimonium, without making any mention of this particular passage. Interestingly, Origen cited Josephus' alleged, less important reference to Jesus in the James passage. Furthermore, he even *falsely* attributed to Josephus saying that the fall of Jerusalem and the destruction of the temple was a punishment for the Jews for their responsibility for the death of James the Just, the brother of Jesus.[32] All this suggests that the version of the *Antiquities* that Origen had access to did not have the Testimonium.

A whole century after Eusebius, another eight church fathers referred to Josephus' works but none of them mentioned the Testimonium. The next mention of the controversial passage comes from Jerome at the end of the fourth century. The fifth century witnessed another four Christian writers who knew Josephus' writings but did not mention the Testimonium.[33]

Had any of those authors known of the existence of the Testimonium, they would have certainly used it in their polemics against the Jews. Even if it existed in a shorter form, as the partial authenticity theory states, they could have at least used it, for instance, to support the New Testament's claim that Jesus was an impressive miracle worker.

If Josephus had truly written something about Jesus and Christianity, it would have been negative. It would have served no purpose for

---

[31] Feldman, "Authenticity of the Testimonium", 15.

[32] Origen, *The Gospel of Matthew*, 2.10.17.

[33] Feldman, "Authenticity of the Testimonium", 16-17.

Christian authors to quote it.

4) Roman-unfriendliness: Leaving Josephus' beliefs aside, the fact that this Jewish historian was working for the Romans, whom the Testimonium presents as Jesus' supposed executioners, makes some of those Christian claims particularly problematic. This includes the claim that Jesus was the Messiah. Indeed, Josephus condemned all would-be Messiahs and popular leaders that the Romans opposed or killed. It is unreasonable to suggest that, for some unknown reason, he exempted Jesus from his typical pouring of scorn on such figures.[34] Yet in this passage, Josephus even goes out of his way to praise this particular rebel that the Romans condemned to death! He is also generous in praising Jesus' followers.

Even the Testimonium's claim that Pilate killed a "wise man" at the request of Jewish leaders is problematic. It portrays the Roman governor as a bit of an idiot. Writing for the Romans and under their patronage, Josephus could not have said that.

5) Out of context: The passage breaks the continuity of a narrative text that details a series of riots. It has nothing to do with the paragraphs that precede and follow it. There are two answers to this argument. While Josephus, like other ancient authors, wrote annalistically, he did at times interrupt the recounting of a certain chain of events to mention a different incident that took place at the same time. Additionally, footnotes and similar techniques that are used today for inserting intractable material that would otherwise break the main discussion were not known to ancient authors. This forced them at times to resort to digression.[35]

6) Lone mention: The Testimonium is preceded by the account of two incidents that caused tumult in Judea during the governorship of Pilate. Yet when the same two incidents are recounted in the *Wars of the Jews*,[36] there is no mention of Jesus. One unconvincing answer to this argument is that the Christians might have become more important by the time *Antiquities of the Jews* was written, about fifteen years later. This is not the case, though, as the number of Christians was still small at the

[34] Doherty, *Neither God Nor Man*, 562.

[35] Smallwood, "Introduction", 20-21.

[36] Josephus, *Wars*, 2.9.2.

time (§5.2).

These six arguments support the view that the Testimonium has nothing to do with Josephus. In my view, they heavily outweigh the arguments for partial authenticity. If Josephus wrote anything about Jesus, it would have been critical and derogatory, so completely different from the Testimonium. It would have been a passing reference without many details, as it was replaced by a short passage. A brief mention of Jesus would have confirmed that he was a minor figure and Christianity was still a small religion at the time. What we can be certain of, though, is that Josephus' surviving writings do not tell us anything about the historical Jesus, let alone confirm his crucifixion.

11

Classical Sources

Having examined Josephus in the previous chapter, we will now evaluate the other classical sources from the first two centuries. We first discuss the three sources that unambiguously mention Jesus' execution. Next, we examine another two that are claimed to refer to Jesus' death. Finally, we quickly review two sources that mention Jesus but not his death.

11.1 Cornelius Tacitus (117 CE)

Cornelius Tacitus (c.56-c.120 CE) occupied several important administrative positions in the Roman empire, including the Proconsul of Asia in 112-113. Generally considered to be one of the greatest Roman historians, Tacitus' major works are *Histories* and the unfinished *Annals*. The latter covers the period from the birth of the Roman empire in 14 CE to the death of Emperor Nero in 68 CE. It is considered to be the best source on the history of that period.

In this work, which was written around 117 CE, Tacitus describes in detail the great fire that engulfed Rome in 64 CE. It is in relation to this disaster that this pagan historian mentions the Christians and, more relevant to our subject, Jesus' death. To put down the rumour that the fire was ordered by him, Emperor Nero accused the Christians of arson and inflicted on them the worst of punishment:

> But neither human help, nor imperial munificence, nor all the modes of placating Heaven, could stifle scandal or dispel the belief that the fire had taken place by order. Therefore, to scotch the rumour, Nero substituted as culprits, and punished with the utmost refinements of cruelty, a class of men, loathed for their vices, whom the crowd styled Christians. *Christus, the founder of the name, had undergone the death penalty in the reign of Tiberius, by sentence of the procurator Pontius Pilatus*, and the pernicious superstition was checked for a moment, only to break out once more, not merely in Judea, the home of the disease, but in the capital itself, where all things horrible or shameful in the world collect and find a vogue.
>
> First, then, the confessed members of the sect were arrested; next, on their

disclosures, vast numbers were convicted, not so much on the count of arson as for hatred of the human race. And derision accompanied their end: they were covered with wild beasts' skins and torn to death by dogs; or they were fastened on crosses, and when daylight failed were burned to serve as lamps by night.

Nero had offered his Gardens for the spectacle, and gave an exhibition in his Circus, mixing with the crowd in the habit of a charioteer, or mounted on his car. Hence, in spite of a guilt which had earned the most exemplary punishment, there arose a sentiment of pity, due to the impression that they were being sacrificed not for the welfare of the state but to the ferocity of a single man.[1]

The authenticity of this passage has been questioned by a small minority of scholars on the basis that it is not mentioned by any of the early fathers of the church. Much of this passage is attested in a book by the Christian writer Sulpicius Severus in the early fifth century, but not earlier. The attribution of this text to Tacitus is generally accepted.

If Tacitus' passage relied on official Roman documents, it must be considered independent of Christian sources. Tacitus rarely names his sources, but it looks unlikely that he used official records.

First, there were two kinds of high-level records in Rome, the first of which is the court journal of the emperors. Tacitus himself reports that the royal archive was secret and closed, so he could not have used it. The second type of official records is the senate's archive. Because Judea was not senatorial but an imperial province, its governors would not have reported to the senate.

Second, at the time of his supposed crucifixion, Jesus was a minor Palestinian teacher with a small following (§5.2). His execution would not have been recorded in official records in Rome.

Third, Tacitus mistakenly called Pilate a "procurator", when in fact he was a "prefect". Judea was ruled by prefects from the removal of Herod Archelaus in 6 CE. In 41 CE, Emperor Claudius gave provincial governors the title "procurator of the empire". There is also a Roman inscription that describes Pilate as the "prefect of Judea". Among the differences between these two titles is that "prefect" was a military position, whereas "procurator" was a civilian financial administrator.

---

[1] Tacitus, *The Annals*, 15.44.

Tacitus used the title "procurator" anachronistically, as this title was more common in his own time than the historically correct title of "prefect". The significance of this error is that it "may indicate that he is not using an official imperial or senatorial document, which would not likely have made such a mistake".[2] It also throws some doubt on the *accuracy* of the account.

Fourth, official Roman documents could not have referred to Jesus with his Christian title, "Christus" or "Christ".

The fact that Tacitus did not rely on official Roman documents does not necessarily mean that his information is of Christian origin. Some scholars have, nevertheless, pointed out the possibility that Tacitus' reference to Jesus' death was based on what he learned from Christians.[3]

Attention has been drawn to a specific period in which Tacitus could have learned about Christians.[4] In 88 CE, he became a member of a priestly organisation whose responsibilities included supervising the practice of officially tolerated cults in Rome. Although Christianity was never officially tolerated, it is possible that in the course of working for the priestly college he gained knowledge about Christianity. Tacitus' passage shows that there was a Christian community in Rome as early as the middle of the seventh decade, just over thirty years after the crucifixion.

One critic has questioned the reliability of Tacitus' account, arguing that Christians had not become a distinct group by Nero's time, so he could not have targeted them specifically. She has also claimed that they were not called "Christians" until towards the end of the first century.[5] Paul's letters and the Gospels do not use "Christian" or any other specific term for Jesus' followers. This term occurs only three times in the New Testament, twice in Acts (11:25-26, 26:28) and once in the First Epistle of Peter (4:16). The first use reported by Acts is dated to around 45 CE, i.e. two decades before the Great Fire. But Ignatius, the second-century bishop of Antioch, was the first Christian writer to use this term with

---

[2] Van Voorst, *Jesus Outside the New Testament*, 50.

[3] France, *Evidence*, 23; Sanders, *Historical Figure*, 50; Wells, *Historical Evidence*, 17.

[4] Van Voorst, *Jesus Outside the New Testament*, 52.

[5] Moss, *The Myth of Persecution*, 133-134, 139.

some frequency.[6] If the name "Christian" was indeed not used until the end of the first century, then Tacitus' use of the term is anachronistic. This would further undermine its reliability and confirm that it describes events in terms of how they came to be understood later.

In conclusion, Tacitus' passage is highly likely based on the Christian tradition. The likelihood that it is not independent of Christian sources is further supported by the fact that Tacitus wrote almost nine decades after Jesus' supposed death.

11.2 Lucian of Samosata (165 CE)

Lucian (120-after 180 CE) was born in Samosata, today's Samsat in the south of Turkey, and died in Athens, Greece. He has over eighty books attributed to him. We have only this satirist's writings as a source of information on him.

One of his books is about the death of the Greek Cynic philosopher Peregrinus Proteus (c.100-165 CE), whom Lucian considers an imposter. Having been forced to flee his hometown in Anatolia after being accused of killing his father, Peregrinus went to Palestine. He converted to Christianity and became influential with Christians, which led to his imprisonment. His fellow believers continued to support him while he was in jail, supplying him with food and books. He was then released from prison by the governor of Syria who wanted to prevent him from dying a martyr. He went back to his hometown, but when he realised that the murder charge was still outstanding, he left again. He continued to live supported by Christians until they cut ties with him when they found him eating *prohibited food*. He later ended up in Greece, where he engaged in cynicism and political activities. He ultimately took his own life by burning himself near the Olympic Games of 165 CE.

The relevant part from Lucian's book, which was written shortly after 165 CE, starts by explaining how Peregrinus took advantage of the gullibility of Christians and became their new leader and prophet. It then states that he became second only to the Christians' first lawgiver, that is, Jesus, whom the book does not name but mentions his crucifixion:

> It was then that he learned the wondrous lore of the Christians, by associating with their priests and scribes in Palestine. And—how else could it

---

[6] Horrell, "The Label χριστιανός", 361.

be?—in a trice he made them all look like children, for he was prophet, cult-leader, head of the synagogue, and everything, all by himself. He interpreted and explained some of their books and even composed many, and they revered him as a god, made use of him as a lawgiver, and set him down as a protector, *next after that other, to be sure, whom they still worship, the man who was crucified in Palestine because he introduced this new cult into the world.*

Interestingly, Lucian thinks that Jesus was killed because he invented a new religion, not because he was deemed to be politically dangerous.

Lucian then goes on to talk about Peregrinus' imprisonment and the continued and unreserved support he received from Christians:

Then at length Proteus was apprehended for this and thrown into prison, which itself gave him no little reputation as an asset for his future career and the charlatanism and notoriety-seeking that he was enamoured of. Well, when he had been imprisoned, the Christians, regarding the incident as a calamity, left nothing undone in the effort to rescue him. Then, as this was impossible, every other form of attention was shown him, not in any casual way but with assiduity, and from the very break of day aged widows and orphan children could be seen waiting near the prison, while their officials even slept inside with him after bribing the guards. Then elaborate meals were brought in, and sacred books of theirs were read aloud, and excellent Peregrinus—for he still went by that name—was called by them 'the new Socrates'.

He then makes a second reference to Jesus and his crucifixion, again without naming him:

Furthermore, *their first lawgiver persuaded them that they are all brothers of one another after they have transgressed once, for all by denying the Greek gods and by worshipping that crucified sophist himself and living under his laws.* Therefore they despise all things indiscriminately and consider them common property, receiving such doctrines traditionally without any definite evidence. So if any charlatan and trickster, able to profit by occasions, comes among them, he quickly acquires sudden wealth by imposing upon simple folk.[7]

Lucian does not name Jesus but the clear references to the Christians leave no doubt that he is talking about Jesus when referring to the founder of their religion. Instead of naming Jesus, in line with the tone

---

[7] Lucian, *Peregrinus,* V, 11-13.

and purpose of his book, he uses the derogatory phrase "that one".[8]

Lucian wrote his book almost a century and a half after Jesus' time. He could only have acquired his information from Christian sources. Van Voorst[9] points out that it is unlikely that he took his information about Christianity from its sacred books, but he agrees with Meier[10] that "no doubt Lucian is reflecting the common knowledge 'in the air' at that time, not an independent source of historical data". Lucian's references to the crucifixion of Jesus do not constitute independent evidence of its historicity.

11.3 Celsus (175 CE)

A Greek philosopher and fierce critic of Christianity wrote around 175 CE a critical work on Christianity, *On the Ture Doctrine*. While this work did not survive, a large percentage of it was quoted by the third-century theologian Origen in his defence of Christianity. As we do not have Celsus' exact words, we need to be careful not to put too much emphasis on the exact words that Origen quotes.

Celsus mentions Jesus' crucifixion in two separate passages in the course of refuting Christian beliefs:

> More and more the myths put about by these Christians are better known than the doctrines of the philosophers. *Who has not heard the fable of Jesus' birth from a virgin or the stories of his crucifixion and resurrection?* And for these fables the Christians are ready to die—indeed do die.[11]
>
> The religion of the Christians is not directed at an idea but at *the crucified Jesus*, and this is surely no better than dog or goat worship.[12]

Celsus had read Matthew, Luke, and other Christian books. He also drew his information about Christianity from personal contact with Christians. He was familiar with Jewish sources, which he used to reject the virginal conception of Jesus and accuse Mary of adultery. Celsus was not an independent historical source on the crucifixion or any aspect of the history of Jesus.

---

[8] Van Voorst, *Jesus Outside the New Testament*, 61.

[9] Ibid., 64.

[10] Meier, "Jesus in Josephus", 92.

[11] Celsus, *True Doctrine*, 54.

[12] Ibid., 71.

11.4 Mara Bar Serapion (after 73 CE)

This unknown man wrote to his son an eloquent letter in Syriac from a Roman prison. The letter is preserved in one manuscript, now in the British Museum, and is dated to the seventh century. It suggests that the writer's city had been destroyed by the Romans who took him and others as prisoners. It also indicates that the writer was a follower of Stoicism, which is a philosophy of personal ethics. Stoics believe, among other things, that the person has to accept with content whatever life throws their way. The passage of interest and other parts of the letter show that the writer was not Christian.

Writing to his son about how even wise men may suffer persecution, Mara Bar (son of) Serapion goes on to say:

> What else can we say, when the wise are forcibly dragged off by tyrants, their wisdom is captured by insults, and their minds are oppressed and without defense? What advantage did the Athenians gain by murdering Socrates, for which they were repaid with famine and pestilence? Or the people of Samos by the burning of Pythagoras, because their country was completely covered in sand in just one hour? Or *the Jews [by killing]*[13] *their wise king, because their kingdom was taken away at that very time?*
>
> God justly repaid the wisdom of these three men: the Athenians died of famine; the Samians were completely overwhelmed by the sea; and *the Jews, desolate and driven from their own kingdom, are scattered through every nation.* Socrates is not dead, because of Plato; neither is Pythagoras, because of the statue of Juno; *nor is the wise king, because of the new laws he laid down.*[14]

Most scholars date the letter to shortly after the Roman conquest of the Armenian kingdom of Commagene in 73 CE, which the letter seems to refer to, but some have suggested that it could be from the second century.[15] The uncertainty in dating the letter is such that some scholars have extended the range of possible dates into the third or even fourth century.

The "wise king" is said to be a reference to Jesus. If so, then the letter could be one of the earliest references to Jesus' execution. Let's examine whether this is indeed the case.

---

[13] Van Voorst explains that the clause in the Syriac original lacks a verb but he concludes that the context indicates that killing is meant.

[14] Van Voorst, *Jesus Outside the New Testament*, 54.

[15] France, *Evidence*, 24.

Two main arguments support identifying the wise king as Jesus. First, Jesus is described as "king" in the Gospels, and particularly in his trial. But Jesus did not claim to be the king of the Jews (§5.4). Second, linking the destruction of the Jewish kingdom to the death of Jesus is a known Christian tradition (e.g., Matt. 23:37-39).[16]

But why did Mara not name Jesus then, especially since he named Socrates and Pythagoras? It is unreasonable to think that he did not know Jesus' name or his title as Christ yet supposedly knew who he was and how he was killed. There have been several attempts to explain this, including the suggestion that he concealed the name because it was the Romans who drove the Jews out of their land, so he would have wanted to avoid upsetting his captors.[17] This, like the other explanations, is unconvincing. The desolation of the Jews is taken by most scholars to refer to the first or second Jewish revolt against the Romans in 66-70 and 132-135 CE, respectively. The fact that it was the Romans who destroyed the Jewish state and, particularly after the second revolt, scattered the Jews is no secret to anyone for Mara to try and hide. This well-known information is the very reason that scholars have dated the letter to after the second revolt. Also, the writer explicitly accuses the Jews of killing their king, so he implicitly exonerates the Romans. More generally, to say that Mara gave enough information to identify the executed king as being Jesus but avoided naming him is a contradiction in terms.

Was he talking about someone whose name he was not sure of or did not know? This can be a possibility only if he meant someone who lived a long time earlier, so it could not be Jesus. Pythagoras and Socrates lived in the sixth and fifth centuries BCE, respectively, so the wise king of the Jews could refer to someone who lived at any time in several centuries. But, of course, we cannot be sure.

Significantly, if Mara's letter is talking about Jesus, then his statements about him contain historical inaccuracies. Accusing the Jews of unjustly "killing their wise king" implies that Jesus claimed to be the king of the Jews and/or they accepted that he was, both of which are untrue. For Jesus, the title "Messiah" was spiritual, not earthly. According to the New Testament, he presented himself as a spiritual saviour, and he carefully

---

[16] Ibid.

[17] Van Voorst, *Jesus Outside the New Testament*, 55.

and purposefully avoided and rejected any attempt to link him to any earthly kingship or political position or movement in general. The Jews never thought of Jesus as their king even though they believed that the Messiah is a king because they rejected his claim to messiahship (§5.4). If Mara indeed meant Jesus by the "wise king", then his description of Jesus as king of the Jews is historically wrong. It has also been pointed out that "wise king" is not a common Christological title.[18]

Furthermore, according to the Gospels, Pilate crucified Jesus in response to pressure from the Jews. From the Gospels' perspective, identifying the Jews exclusively as his murderers is inaccurate. Either Mara was not talking about Jesus or he was completely wrong in what he said about him.

There are two other inaccuracies in Mara's statement if it referred to Jesus. The kingdom of the Jews was not destroyed at the time of Jesus' death. No national Jewish disaster happened until forty years after the crucifixion. Also, Jesus did not bring new laws. Even if the unnamed Jewish king in Mara's letter was Jesus, his account is evidently highly unreliable.

Finally, what would have been Mara's likely sources on Jesus? We know that the earliest dating of Mara's letter is some four decades after Jesus, but it is likely to be later by as much as another century at least. Also, Mara was not someone who could have had access to Roman records on Jesus' execution, if such records existed at all. He may have got his information on Jesus from Jewish sources, which confirm the claim that they killed Jesus. But he is more likely to have got the information from Christians, given his positive view of Jesus and, particularly, his adoption of the Christian view that the Jews were punished for executing Jesus. This is what one scholar concludes:

> Mara's letter is not an independent witness to Jesus, for two main reasons. First, it obviously links the life of "the wise king" with his movement and its teachings, making it possible that Mara learned about the wise king from Christians. Second, its assertion that the Jews killed Jesus is dubious at best.[19]

To sum up, Mara's letter might well be completely irrelevant to Jesus' life, talking about someone else. But even if it meant Jesus, it fails the tests

---

[18] Ibid., 54.
[19] Ibid., 57.

of independence of Christian sources and accuracy.

11.5 Thallus (first century CE?)

The *potentially* earliest mention of Jesus' death by a non-Christian is quoted by the Christian chronographer Sextus Julius Africanus (c.180-c.250 CE). This travelling historian is thought to have lived in Alexandria, Jerusalem, and Rome, among other places. He is known for his five-volume history of the world, *Chronographiai*, which covers the period from the creation of the world to the year 221 CE.

Julius Africanus quotes a historian called Thallus about the darkness that, according to the Synoptic Gospels (Mark 15:33; Matt. 27:45; Luke 23:44), befell the earth from noon for three hours during Jesus' crucifixion. This is what Julius Africanus says:

> Concerning each of his deeds and his cures, both of bodies and souls, and the secrets of his knowledge, and his Resurrection from the dead, this has been explained with complete adequacy by his disciples and the apostles before us. A most terrible darkness fell over all the world, the rocks were torn apart by an earthquake, and many places both in Judaea and the rest of the world were thrown down.
>
> *In the third book of his Histories, Thallos dismisses this darkness as a solar eclipse.* In my opinion, this is nonsense. For the Hebrews celebrate the Passover on Luna, and what happened to the Saviour occurred one day before the Passover. But an eclipse of the sun takes place when the moon passes under the sun. The only time when this can happen is in the interval between the first day of the new moon and the last day of the old moon, when they are in conjunction. How then could one believe an eclipse took place when the moon was almost in opposition to the sun? So be it. Let what had happened beguile the masses, and let this wonderful sign to the world be considered a solar eclipse through an optical (illusion).[20]

There is too much ambiguity surrounding this quotation to make it of any value as a historical source on Jesus' crucifixion.

First, we do not have direct access to the text about the eclipse that Julius Africanus quotes, as Thallus' three-volume history of the world has been lost. Julius Africanus' work also has not survived. The above quote is preserved in the *Chronicle* of the Byzantine historian and ecclesiastic George Synkellos (Syncellus), who wrote five and a half centuries after

---

[20] Synkellos, *Chronography*, 391.

Julius Africanus. So, the surviving quote is a several-centuries-late, thirdhand citation of what Thallus is supposed to have written.

Second, Julius Africanus has rightly pointed out that an eclipse of the Sun occurs at the time of a new, not full, moon, which is when the Passover is celebrated and when the crucifixion supposedly took place. It is highly unlikely that a learned historian like Thallus would not have known this. Furthermore, Thallus must have also known that a solar eclipse does not last more than several minutes. The phenomenon he described, therefore, could not have been anything like the three-hour-long darkness in the middle of the month that the Gospels allege took place.

Third, Julius Africanus' refutation of Thallus' identification of the celestial phenomenon as a solar eclipse implies that *he* thought Thallus was referring to the darkness of the crucifixion. Yet there is no evidence in what he says that Thallus made a direct reference to Jesus, let alone his crucifixion. It is plausible, if not likely, that it was Julius Africanus who associated Thallus' eclipse with the darkness that took place during Jesus' crucifixion because of its date. He then went on to rebut Thallus' claim that this was a solar eclipse. Had Thallus mentioned the crucifixion, or even Jesus, Julius Africanus would have made sure we were made aware of it. This raises serious questions about the relevance of Thallus' eclipse record to Jesus' death.

This conclusion is further confirmed when we examine the continuation of Julius Africanus' passage in which he quotes the second-century Greek writer Phlegon on a solar eclipse:

> Phlegon records that during the reign of Tiberius Caesar there was a complete solar eclipse at full moon from the sixth to the ninth hour; it is clear that this is the one. But what have eclipses to do with an earthquake, rocks breaking apart, resurrection of the dead, and a universal disturbance of this nature?
>
> Certainly an event of such magnitude has not been recalled for a long time. But it was a darkness created by God, because it happened that the Lord experienced his passion at that time. And reason proves that the seventy weeks of years mentioned in Daniel were completed in this time.

Phlegon did not link the eclipse to Jesus' crucifixion, a crucifixion, or any other event. Luckily, Synkellos has also preserved Eusebius' quotation of Phlegon:

Phlegon, who composed a record of the Olympiads, also writes about these same events in his 13th book, with the following words: "In the fourth year of the 202nd Olympiad, there was an eclipse of the sun, greater than any that had been previously known. And night fell at the sixth hour of the day, so that the stars appeared in the sky. A great earthquake occurring throughout Bithynia overturned many sites in Nikaia". This is the witness of the man just mentioned.[21]

While Eusebius confirms that Phlegon said that the eclipse took place at the sixth hour, he did not attribute to him the claim that it lasted "to the ninth hour" or that it happened "at full moon". These additions are from Julius Africanus to make Phlegon confirm the Gospel's description of the darkness. Eusebius' account also does not mention that Phlegon linked the eclipse to Jesus in any way.[22] This makes it more likely that in the case of Thallus too, it was Julius Africanus, not Thallus, who linked the latter's report of an eclipse to Jesus' crucifixion.[23]

Fourth, Eusebius states that Thallus' history covers the period from the fall of Troy in 1184 BCE to the 167th Olympiad of 109 BCE. The end date of this chronology means that Thallus could not have said anything about the alleged eclipse that happened almost a century and a half later. However, other fragments of Thallus' history that are preserved in several sources indicate that he wrote about events at least until the time of the death of Jesus. This has prompted some modern scholars to claim that the figure 167 in Greek should be read as 207 instead and that this Olympiad took place in 49-52 CE, that is, after Jesus' time. What is certain, however, is that the dating of Thallus and his work is highly uncertain.

Fifth, Thallus remains a mystery character. Some have identified him as a Samaritan resident of Rome mentioned by Josephus, but this identification is based on conjecture.[24] Even if the attribution of the text is correct, the fact that its author cannot be positively identified makes it impossible to know how reliable any information he provides is.

Sixth, even if Thallus was indeed refuting a Christian argument when

---

[21] Ibid., 394.

[22] Carrier, "Thallus", 190.

[23] Adler and Tuffin, "Commentary", 466.

[24] Van Voorst, *Jesus Outside the New Testament*, 22.

stressing that the darkness was caused by a solar eclipse, "he likely knew about this darkness at the death of Jesus from Christians, either directly or indirectly, not from an independent source".[25]

In summary, it is extremely unlikely that Thallus' quote mentioned Jesus, let alone his crucifixion. But even if Thallus did and Julius Africanus, for some inexplicable reason, did not tell us, the fact that virtually nothing is known about Thallus means that we cannot consider him an accurate source of information. Additionally, if at all relevant, his quote might well be dependent on Christian sources. Thallus' very vague quote has no historical value for studying the historicity of Jesus' crucifixion. He was likely dragged unawares into the world of Jesus by Julius Africanus.

11.6 Sources That Do Not Mention Jesus' Death
In addition to the five we have discussed, there are another two early classical sources that mention Jesus, but they do not refer to his crucifixion or death. While they are not relevant to the specific subject of our study, I will briefly quote them here for interesting information on how Jesus and Christianity were perceived.

Our first source comes from Pliny the Younger (c.61-c.113). Around 112 CE, as governor of Pontus-Bithynia in Asia Minor, Pliny wrote a letter to Emperor Trajan in which he enquired about how to conduct the trials of Christians. Having not witnessed such trials before becoming governor, he did not know how to deal with those accused of following Christianity. He asked Trajan how far the examination should go, whether repenting and revoking Christianity entitles a former Christian to a pardon, and so on.

This is the part of Pliny's letter to Trajan in which Christ is mentioned:

> But this crime spreading (as is usually the case) while it was actually under prosecution, several instances of the same nature occurred. An anonymous information was laid before me containing a charge against several persons, who upon examination denied they were Christians, or had ever been so. They repeated after me an invocation to the gods, and offered religious rites with wine and incense before your statue (which for that purpose I had ordered to be brought, together with those of the gods), and even reviled the

---

[25] Ibid.

name of Christ: whereas there is no forcing, it is said, those who are really Christians into any of these compliances: I thought it proper, therefore, to discharge them.

Some among those who were accused by a witness in person at first confessed themselves Christians, but immediately after denied it; the rest owned indeed that they had been of that number formerly, but had now (some above three, others more, and a few above twenty years ago) renounced that error. They all worshipped your statue and the images of the gods, uttering imprecations at the same time against the name of Christ. They affirmed the whole of their guilt, or their error, was, that they met on a stated day before it was light, and addressed a form of prayer to Christ, as to a divinity, binding themselves by a solemn oath, not for the purposes of any wicked design, but never to commit any fraud, theft, or adultery, never to falsify their word, nor deny a trust when they should be called upon to deliver it up; after which it was their custom to separate, and then reassemble, to eat in common a harmless meal.[26]

The letter offers some information about how Christians lived and worshipped but it does not offer any on Jesus.

The second source comes from a friend of Pliny, Gaius Suetonius Tranquillus (c.70–c.140). Among other works, this prolific historian wrote, probably in 117-122 CE, biographies of twelve emperors. The sole passage of interest to us comes in his biography of Claudius (41-54 CE). Suetonius says the following about how Claudius dealt with the Jews:

Since the Jews constantly made disturbances at the instigation of Chrestus, he expelled them from Rome.[27]

Most scholars believe that the term "Chrestus" is a misspelling of "Christus". Suetonius' passage also indicates that he mistakenly thought that Christ was in Rome around 49 CE. These mistakes have been attributed to his poor knowledge of Jesus and Christianity.[28]

---

[26] Pliny, *The Letters,* II, 10.97.

[27] Suetonius, *The Lives of the Caesars,* II, 5.25.4.

[28] Van Voorst, *Jesus Outside the New Testament,* 38-39.

12

Jewish Rabbinic Sources

The earliest rabbinic literature, the *Mishnah* (Hebrew: "repeated study"), which codified the Jewish oral laws, was compiled over two centuries by many scholars. It was put in its final form early in the third century CE. The following centuries witnessed the development of two commentaries on the Mishnah, one in Palestine and another in Babylon. Each commentary, known as "Gemara" (Aramaic: "completion"), was then combined with the Mishnah and some auxiliary materials, known as "Tosefta" (Aramaic: additions), that did not make it into the Mishnah. The compiled work is known as the Talmud, which means "learning" or "instruction". The Palestinian Talmud, which is also called the "Jerusalem Talmud", was finalised towards the end of the fourth century, whereas its larger Babylonian counterpart, also known as "Bavli", took another century and a half to be completed.

The Mishnah and the Tosefta make no mention of Jesus by name. The Gemara passages that mention Jesus, which are highly defamatory, appear only in the Babylonian Talmud. Palestine, and accordingly Judaism there, was under the continuous and direct influence of Christianity, which led to anti-Jewish bias in the region. By the time the Palestinian Talmud was finalized, Christianity was the official religion of the Roman empire. Babylon, on the other hand, was under the rule of the Sasanians, who followed Zoroastrianism. The Sasanians and the Romans were enemies. In Babylon, there were even waves of persecution of Christians. Jews in Babylon may have even found themselves encouraged to express anti-Christian sentiments.[1]

There is one reference in the Talmud that deals with the execution of Jesus:

> *On the eve of the Passover Yeshu was hanged.* For forty days before the execution took place, a herald went forth and cried, "He is going forth to be

---

[1] Schäfer, *Jesus in the Talmud*, 113-122.

stoned because he has practised sorcery and enticed Israel to apostasy. Any one who can say anything in his favour, let him come forward and plead on his behalf". But since nothing was brought forward in his favour he was *hanged on the eve of the Passover*!—'Ulla retorted: "Do you suppose that he was one for whom a defence could be made? Was he not a Mesith [enticer], concerning whom Scripture says, 'Neither shalt thou spare, neither shalt thou conceal him?' With Yeshu however it was different, for he was connected with the government [or royalty, i.e., influential]". (b. Sanh. 43a)

This text contradicts the Synoptic Gospels but agrees with John in placing the killing of Jesus on the eve of the Passover. The accusations that he practised magic and led Jews into apostasy go against the Gospels' accounts. The passage has several other differences with the New Testament. Jesus was held for forty days, rather than overnight, after being sentenced to death; he was executed according to Jewish law by stoning; and the Jews had the power to execute him. "Hanging" here means crucifixion. This passage is followed by another that talks about Jesus having five disciples. Apart from Matthai whose name may be linked to Matthew, none of the names of the other four can be linked to any of Jesus' disciples in the New Testament.

The Talmud may also contain coded references to Jesus. The main ones are "Ben Pandira/Pantera" (son of Pandira/Pantera) and "Ben Stada" (son of Stada), who was an illegitimate son. This might be intended to refute Jesus' virginal conception. The following passage continues a discussion of making alterations to the skin as a way of invoking magical power:

It was taught. R. Eliezer said to the Sages: But did not Ben Stada bring forth witchcraft from Egypt by means of scratches [in the form of charms] upon his flesh? He was a fool, answered they, and proof cannot be adduced from fools. Was he then the son of Stada: surely he was the son of Pandira? - Said R. Hisda: The husband was Stada, the paramour was Pandira. But the husband was Pappos b. Judah?—His mother was Stada. But his mother was Miriam the hairdresser?—It is as we say in Pumbeditha: This one has been unfaithful to (lit., 'turned away from'—satath da) her husband. (b. Shab. 104b)

The passage shows confusion, including as to whether Stada was Mary or her husband.

There is a third passage in the Talmud, which was censored from other manuscripts from the era of Christendom, that suggests that Yeshu,

Ben Stada, and Ben Pandira are the same person. Repeating almost word-for-word a part of b. Shabbat 104b and borrowing from b. Sanhedrin 43a the reference to the hanging on the eve of the Passover, this passage identifies Ben Stada as the victim:

> And this they did to Ben Stada in Lydda, and they hung him on the eve of Passover. Ben Stada was Ben Padira. R. Hisda said: "The husband was Stada, the paramour Pandira. But was not the husband Pappos b. Judah? - His mother's name was Stada. But his mother was Miriam, a dresser of woman's hair? As they say in Pumbaditha, This woman has turned away from her husband, (i.e. committed adultery)". (b. Sanh. 67a)

There are other passages that confirm the stoning of Ben Stada for deceiving people.[2]

Some scholars have accepted that Ben Pandira and Ben Stada are both pseudonyms for Jesus,[3] but others dismiss most claimed coded names, including Ben Stada, and accept only Ben Pandira.[4] The latter is said to be reasonably identifiable with Jesus because of external evidence.[5] The third-century Christian theologian Origen quotes Celsus, the Greek critic of Christianity, writing around 180 CE, who cited Jewish stories accusing Jesus' mother of adultery involving a Roman soldier:

> When she was pregnant she was turned out of doors by the carpenter to whom she had been betrothed, as having been guilty of adultery, and that she bore a child to a certain soldier named Panthera.[6]

Commenting on the only Talmudic passage that mentions the name Jesus and his execution, Van Voorst thinks that it is likely that "this short narrative seems to be an inner-Jewish explanation and justification of how one famous criminal, Jesus of Nazareth, was put to death, and implicitly a warning to stay away from his movement".[7] He goes on to conclude:

> The presentation of Jesus' trial and death in b. Sanhedrin 43a seems to

---

[2] Herford, *Christianity in Talmud and Midras*, 79.

[3] Ibid., 35-39; Dalman, *Jesus Christ in the Talmud*, 8-10. Schäfer, *Jesus in the Talmud*, 7-8; Wróbel, "The Rabbinic Anti-Gospel", 55.

[4] Klausner, *Jesus of Nazareth*, 20-22; Van Voorst, *Jesus Outside the New Testament*, 114.

[5] Van Voorst, *Jesus Outside the New Testament*, 117.

[6] Origen, *Against Celsus*, 32.

[7] Van Voorst, *Jesus Outside the New Testament*, 119.

represent a Jewish rebuttal to Christian traditions about Jesus' death; it cannot be claimed to represent early, independent information about Jesus, even though according to the Synoptic accounts some leading Pharisees were present at the trial of Jesus.[8]

Van Voorst concludes that the Talmudic passages about Jesus are rather late, not earlier than the second century:

> While we cannot be sure, given the paucity and difficulty of the evidence, the third-century rabbis seem to have had no traditions about Jesus that originated in the first century. Beside the rabbis' typical disinterest in history and confused knowledge of the first century, what the rabbis say about Jesus appears to be the product of at least the second century.[9]

Some[10] have suggested that b. Sanhedrin 43a may have come from the early second century, whereas others have proposed that the most explicit Jesus passages are even later, dating them to the late third to the early fourth century.[11]

It is critical to note that the Talmud's accounts of Jesus were not concerned with history as such. They were intended to defame Jesus and present him in the worst possible way. In the course of doing so, the Talmudic writers did not spare Jesus and his mother an accusation. They wanted to provide an alternative history to the Christian tradition.

Another significant, but not unexpected, observation is that Jewish writers became interested in Jesus only as a result of Christianity's growing presence. Significantly, the Hellenistic Jewish philosopher Philo, who was contemporary to Jesus, makes no mention of him even when he criticises Pilate's brutality.[12] Justus of Tiberias, another first-century Jewish historian, is also silent on Jesus.

In conclusion, there are no historically reliable rabbinic accounts of Jesus, including his trial and execution. In addition to being late, those passages are polemical responses to Christian beliefs. These statements about Jesus have no historical value.

---

[8] Ibid., 121.

[9] Ibid., 120.

[10] Theissen and Merz, *The Historical Jesus*, 75.

[11] Schäfer, *Jesus in the Talmud*, 8.

[12] Philo, *The Embassy to Gaius*, X, 299-305.

13

The Historical Unreliability of Non-Christian Sources

Five facts stand out about the references to Jesus in non-Christian sources from the first two centuries CE.

First, there are only a handful of sources that mention him at all and even fewer that refer to his execution. If we discard Josephus' Testimonium as a Christian forgery, then we end up with only three sources that unambiguously mention Jesus' execution: Tacitus, Lucian, and Celsus. Of course, the larger the number of sources, the easier the assessment of the reliability of their reports. Having this very small number of sources limits considerably our ability to cross-examine and verify their accounts.

Second, the space that these sources have allocated to Jesus is tiny, no more than a couple of sentences. Works of the historians who were contemporary to Jesus have all been lost, but that does not explain why those later writings show little interest in him.

That there are only a handful of sources on Jesus' crucifixion and they mention him almost casually is contrary to what a reader of the Gospels would have expected about such a popular and influential teacher, spiritual revolutionary, and impressive miracle worker. This would be even more shocking to Christians given Jesus' known influence and status in history.

Yet, in his own time, Jesus was not known beyond his small circle of followers. During his life, he had little impact on the Jews and Palestine in general. Immediately after he was gone, Christianity was a small sect. His low profile is also attested to by the fact that he remained a minor figure for many decades afterwards. As has been strikingly put, "When he was executed, Jesus was no more important to the outside world than the two brigands or insurgents executed with him — whose names we do not know".[1] The Gospels' image of Jesus' grand impact in his lifetime is undoubtedly unhistorical (§5.2). This is reflected in the paucity of his mentions in surviving sources and the passing nature of those references.

Jesus' profile started to grow with the gradual spreading of Christianity and the increase of his followers. Ironically, it was Christians who made Jesus popular rather than it being him who made them and Christianity popular. As has been succinctly observed, "Christianity was of some interest, Christ himself was of small interest, and 'the historical Jesus' of very little interest"[2] to classical writers and historians. As also stated by the same author, "Roman writers seem to have considered Christianity an important topic only when it became a perceived threat to Rome".[3] This started to happen only many decades after the time of Jesus.

Third, our earliest non-Christian resources date to at least some ninety years after the crucifixion, so they do not provide eyewitness testimony. They must have been based on earlier oral and written tradition. This, in turn, means that it is almost certain that they were influenced by Christian tradition.

Tacitus wrote his account on Jesus almost half a century after Mark wrote his Gospel, itself at best a secondhand account. By then, Christian groups were found in various places and their beliefs had become relatively well known. It is beyond doubt that references to Jesus in Roman sources are all derived from Christian oral and written reports.[4] They cannot be used to corroborate the earlier Christian sources, namely the Gospels. This is how one New Testament scholar assesses the available sources:

> The first thing to be said about non-Christian historical evidence for Jesus is that there is not much of it, at least from a period close enough to the events to be of any value as an independent witness to Jesus as seen through non-Christian eyes.[5]

In addition to the fact that those early sources could have only taken

---

[1] Sanders, *Historical Figure*, 49.
[2] Van Voorst, *Jesus Outside the New Testament*, 69.
[3] Ibid., 70.
[4] Sanders, *Historical Figure*, 49.
[5] France, *Evidence*, 19.

their information from Christian sources, written and oral, directly and indirectly, their accounts are further compromised by the fact that they saw "Christ through Christianity. Christianity as a movement is their primary, perhaps their only, concern". [6] The developments that Christianity went through after Jesus were projected back on him.

Fourth, there is no official Roman record of Jesus' trial and death. This looks natural as Jesus was too insignificant for his execution to make it into the records of the empire.[7] Another possibility is that such a record has been lost as happened to various writings from that era. It may also be argued that the silence of the Roman records reflects the fact that the supposed killing of Jesus by the Romans never took place! What no one disputes, though, is that the alleged crucifixion is not attested in Roman official records.

This, again, means that none of the early non-Christian writers could have taken their information about the crucifixion from official Roman archives. This, in turn, makes it more likely that their sources on the crucifixion were Christian. This is how this has been excellently summarised:

> What classical writers know about Jesus comes almost completely from Christians. They seem to have little or no knowledge about him independent of Christianity. Given factors described above, we should not expect such information, or be surprised at its absence. The only possible exception is Tacitus, but even here it is more likely that he derived his information from Christians, either directly or by way of his friend Pliny the Younger. As a consequence, we obtain no reliable information about Jesus from the classical writers that we do not have in the Christian writings of this time.
>
> It seems that early traditions about Jesus did not pass independently of Christianity through the classical Roman world and surrounding areas. In all probability, Pilate did not send any report to Rome about Jesus, nor was there any early report about him to the emperors. To judge from how Pliny and Tacitus write, Christianity was not well known among Romans at the turn of the century. When those who write today on the topic of Christ in classical authors often sound the refrain, "We gain nothing new about Jesus from this writer", this is perhaps based on an unreasonable expectation that something

---

[6] Van Voorst, *Jesus Outside the New Testament*, 72.
[7] France, *Evidence*, 19-20.

new about Jesus should come from them.[8]

Fifth, the later a source is, the more inaccurate it is likely to be. Even if in the highly unlikely case that a non-Christian source did not use Christian tradition, directly or indirectly, the source having been written at least ninety years after the events means that the information reached the author through multiple layers of reporting. Every time a piece of information is reported, it is likely to suffer some deliberate or unwitting change. The more distant the date of a source from Jesus' time, the less reliable its information on him.

The inevitable conclusion from reviewing the surviving non-Christian sources on Jesus is that they can be of no help for the study of the historical Jesus. I do not see how they can be even of "supplementary" value, as some suggest:

> What survives of pagan and Jewish records of the trial and subsequent execution of Jesus is of too late a date, too secondary a character, too fragmentary a nature, and too tendentious to be of more than supplementary value in a systematic attempt to reconstruct the history of the case. The accounts from Christian sources—chiefly the Gospels—are both earlier in date and fuller in their description.[9]

We have already seen that while "earlier" and "fuller", the Gospels are themselves highly unreliable.

Of course, none of this means that the crucifixion of Jesus was not historical. But it does mean that there is no independent source on what exactly happened.

---

[8] Van Voorst, *Jesus Outside the New Testament*, 72-73.
[9] Winter, *The Trial of Jesus*, 1.

III

The Genesis of a Belief

14

Alternative Scenarios

The supernaturality of the resurrection has, understandably, prompted scholars to consider natural alternatives to the Gospel version of events. This endeavour is further justified by the historical unreliability of the Gospels. Like other episodes of Jesus' crucifixion in the Gospels, the empty tomb and post-resurrection appearances suffer from inconsistencies and irredeemable contradictions (§1.17-19). There are specific reasons to reject each episode. The reliance of the early Roman and Jewish sources on Christian tradition, as we saw in the second part of the book, makes them incapable of lending external support to the Gospel narratives. One widely held view is that the resurrection account is a late editorial addition to the story. As the concept of a *suffering Messiah* was completely alien to Judaism (§4), the related *resurrected Messiah* must also be unhistorical.

In their rejection of the traditional Christian reading of the New Testament, some scholars have rejected the historicity of the empty tomb and post-crucifixion appearances of Jesus. Many other scholars have taken a middle ground in proposing certain natural events they say were behind these reports, thus accepting that something happened but it had nothing to do with the rising of Jesus from death. Any alternative version of events is bound to reject some parts of the Gospel narratives and interpret others in a non-traditional way. A detailed study of all those theories is beyond the scope of this book, but we will briefly review the main alternative scenarios that have been proposed.[1]

14.1 The Crucifixion
One radical theory that could help to explain the empty tomb and Jesus' appearances in natural terms is that Jesus did not die when he was

---

[1] For more details, see Allison, "Explaining the Resurrection"; Vermes, *Nativity, Passion, Resurrection*, 435-441; Theissen and Merz, *The Historical Jesus*, 476-482.

crucified. Reference is at times made to Mark (15:43-44) where Pilate is said to be surprised that Jesus had died so quickly when Joseph of Arimathea went to him to seek permission to bury the corpse. The suggestion is that this may hint that Jesus was taken for burial before he was dead.

Advocates of the theory of non-fatal crucifixion often cite a report by Josephus about someone who survived crucifixion as proof that this extremely cruel method of execution did not always lead to death:

> And when I was sent by Titus Caesar with Cerealins, and a thousand horsemen, to a certain village called Thecoa, in order to know whether it were a place fit for a camp, as I came back, I saw many captives crucified, and remembered three of them as my former acquaintance. I was very sorry at this in my mind, and went with tears in my eyes to Titus, and told him of them; so he immediately commanded them to be taken down, and to have the greatest care taken of them, in order to their recovery; yet two of them died under the physician's hands, while the third recovered.[2]

The earliest form of the non-fatal crucifixion theory was proposed by the German theologians Karl Friedrich Bahrdt, late in the eighteenth century, and Heinrich Paulus, early in the nineteenth century. Versions of this theory include suggestions that Jesus fell into a deep swoon on the cross, pretended to have died, or put himself in a state of self-hypnosis. It is claimed that he was treated in the tomb, or that he managed to gather whatever energy he had left after his ordeal to escape the tomb. Surviving the crucifixion is then used to explain the emptiness of Jesus' tomb and his appearances to his disciples.

These theories have been roundly rejected on medical grounds and due to their failure to explain Jesus' post-crucifixion history. While surviving a crucifixion is not impossible, it is highly unlikely.[3] Unsurprisingly, even when rushed off the cross while still alive and given good medical treatment, two of Josephus' three acquaintances died. The one who lived was almost certainly left with serious disabilities and severe health problems. Jesus' crucifixion is not reported to have been cut short or followed by top emergency medical help.

In addition to the fact that the crucifixion would have left Jesus

---

[2] Josephus, *Life*, 25.
[3] Edwards, Gabel, and Hosmer, "Death of Jesus Christ".

incapacitated and hardly able to move a limb, this scenario presumes that someone must have helped him out of the tomb. The alternative scenario that Jesus' dead body was moved from the tomb by someone, which we will study soon, is a far more realistic, though still unlikely, explanation of the empty tomb.

Surviving the crucifixion is hardly an explanation for the appearances either. The image of a half-dead crucifixion survival, perhaps with broken limbs and certainly in a general state of health that requires intensive medical treatment, is a far cry from the glorious figure that Jesus' followers are reported to have seen. These theories were rejected as early as 1835 by the German liberal Protestant theologian David Friedrich Strauss.[4] This is what one modern critic had to say:

> This explanation stretches the limits of the imagination and has been rightly rejected by almost all critical scholars. The Romans were experts at crucifixion, and it is inconceivable that they would have botched the job. The incidental references to the soldiers leaving Jesus' legs unbroken and blood and water coming from the spear wound in his side provide additional evidence of his death (John 19:32-37). Even if Jesus were still alive when laid in the tomb, the chances are practically nil that he could recover from the severe trauma of flagellation, crucifixion, bleeding, and exposure.[5]

The theory that Jesus was not dead when he was taken down from the cross introduces more problems than those it tries to solve.

14.2 The Empty Tomb

The Gospels disagree on who visited Jesus' tomb on Sunday, at what time, who was already there, and what exactly happened (§1.17). As noted by one liberal Episcopal Bishop, "Almost every detail of the resurrection of Jesus appearing in one Gospel is contradicted in another Gospel".[6] But the Evangelists agree that the tomb was found to be empty by the visitors; Jesus' body was not there. Paul, on the other hand, makes no mention of the empty tomb.

Notably, while the empty tomb is presented as evidence that Jesus was physically raised, none of the Gospels claims that his resurrection was

---

[4] Strauss, *The Life of Jesus*, 736-738.
[5] Strauss, *Four Portraits*, 512-513.
[6] Spong, *Why Christianity Must Change or Die*, 15.

witnessed by any of the visiting women! They are introduced as eyewitnesses of the *emptiness* of the tomb, not of its *becoming empty* by the resurrection of the dead body. Not even the one or two men that the Synoptic Gospels claim were already there when the women arrived are said to have witnessed the alleged resurrection. The Synoptists also agree that no one who knew Jesus came physically close enough to confirm that it was indeed Jesus on the cross (§1.13), so Jesus' crucifixion and resurrection are both without eyewitnesses. Jesus' appearances after the crucifixion are no evidence that he was crucified and resurrected.

While Mark (16:4), Luke (24:2), and John (20:1) claim that the stone on the tomb had already been rolled back by the time the women visited, Matthew (28:2) claims that an angel descended from heaven and rolled the stone back while the women were there. This seems to suggest that Jesus rose without needing to remove the stone, which itself seems to suggest the resurrection was not corporeal. This could mean that the Gospel authors did not have an eyewitness of the resurrection because it was spiritual, not corporeal, hence inaccessible to the human eye. Either way, as no one witnessed Jesus leave the tomb, it was natural for alternative scenarios to the Christian interpretation of the empty tomb to emerge, and there has not been a shortage of alternatives.

Probably the earliest alternative scenario was put forward in the first half of the nineteenth century by the German scholar Hermann Samuel Reimarus who considered Jesus an unsuccessful political claimant. He argued that Jesus died and did not rise but the tomb was found empty because his disciples stole his body from the tomb. This version of the story, which is not considered seriously today, makes use of a reference in Matthew to such a claim being prevalent among the Jews, although it is presented as a Jewish, rather than Christian, act of fraud:

> Some of the guard went into the city and told the chief priests everything that had happened. After the priests had assembled with the elders, they devised a plan to give a large sum of money to the soldiers, telling them, "You must say, 'His disciples came by night and stole him away while we were asleep.' If this comes to the governor's ears, we will satisfy him and keep you out of trouble." So they took the money and did as they were directed. And this story is still told among the Jews to this day. (Matt. 28:11-15)

But how credible is Matthew's suggestion that the Jews *bribed* the guards to make up the story about the disciples stealing Jesus' body? The Jews did not believe that Jesus was the Messiah and even devised and carried out the plan to have him crucified. When told by the guards that Jesus' body had disappeared from the tomb, the Jewish leaders could not have seen anything miraculous in this disappearance. Their natural reaction would have been to think that the guards themselves were involved in some foul play or ignored their duties. This is what the Roman governor would have naturally also thought, as confirmed by the Jews' promise to the guards to *satisfy the governor and keep them out of trouble*, should what happened come to his notice.

Yet the Jews, according to Matthew, did not consider the possibility that the guards were at fault or involved in the disappearance of the body. Instead, they inexplicably accepted that this disappearance implies something supernatural that threatens their view of Jesus, so their response was to bribe the guards! The Jews pre-empted how the story of the disappearance was going to be interpreted by Jesus' disciples even before the latter did that! Matthew's account is obviously written from a Christian perspective.

A second suggestion, which was first put forward anonymously in 1799, is that Joseph of Arimathea, who buried Jesus on Friday, later moved the body to another tomb for one reason or another. For instance, the first tomb may have been temporarily used because it was nearby so the body could be quickly buried before the start of the Passover. Indeed, John (19:41) states that a new tomb had been prepared but not used in a garden next to the crucifixion place, so Joseph of Arimathea used it to bury Jesus. The visitors were not aware that the body was later moved, so they went to the first tomb on Sunday and found it empty.

A third theory claims that as the women who came to visit Jesus' tomb were strangers to Jerusalem and it was still dawn with little light, they lost their way. They went to the wrong tomb, which happened to be empty.

A fourth claim, which is far more credible and utilises details of the Roman practice of crucifixion, is that the crucified Jesus was not buried. The Romans reserved punishment by crucifixion for the lower classes who had few rights, such as slaves and people outlawed from society who disturb the Roman order, for violent criminals, and for political rebels. As if crucifixion was not brutal enough, the Romans often combined it with other forms of torture, including at least flogging. This is noted in the Gospels as they claim that Jesus was scourged before being crucified (Matt. 27:26). Crucifixion was used as a deterrent, so to make it as effective as possible, it was carried out in public. To inflict maximum humiliation on the victim, a prominent place was chosen for the public display of the naked victim, such as a theatre or the place of the crime. This is how the first-century Roman rhetorician Quintilian proudly described this:

> Whenever we crucify the guilty, the most crowded roads are chosen, where the most people can see and be moved by this fear. For penalties relate not so much to retribution as to their exemplary effect.[7]

What is particularly relevant here is that the Romans frequently denied burial to victims of crucifixion. A study that compiled a long list of Roman crucifixions concluded the following:

> Crucifixion was aggravated further by the fact that quite often its victims were never buried. It was a stereotyped picture that the crucified person served as food for wild beasts and birds of prey. In this way his humiliation was made complete. What it meant for a man in antiquity to be refused burial, and the dishonour which went with it, can hardly be appreciated by modern man.[8]

One prominent scholar on the historical Jesus notes that "it was actually nonburial that made being crucified alive one of the three supreme penalties of Roman punishment (along with being devoured alive or burned alive)".[9]

It has been counterargued that, while available evidence shows that victims of Roman crucifixion were not allowed burial, this was confined to wartime. During peacetime, the Romans would have allowed the burial of those crucified outside the walls of Jerusalem.[10] There is no convincing evidence to support this view. On the other hand, there were exceptions to the practice of nonburial when a Roman holiday was approached or when a request was made by a friend of the Roman

---

[7] Hengel, *Crucifixion in the Ancient World*, 50.

[8] Ibid., 87–88.

[9] Crossan, *The Birth of Christianity*, 542.

[10] Evans, "Jewish Burial Traditions".

governor. But neither of these two applied in Jesus' case.

Furthermore, even if Jesus was buried, he would not have received the kind of honourable burial that the Gospels describe. The body would probably have been dumped in a common grave rather than a private tomb.[11]

Inexplicably, Jesus' followers did not try to spread the news about the unique and immensely impressive miracle of the empty tomb to convert others. The Gospels suggest that this information was kept secret, even though its proselytising impact would have been particularly powerful. Also, the longer this miracle was kept secret, the less verifiable and credible it would have become, as alternative dismissive explanations would have sounded more likely to outsiders.

There is one last point to raise. Any spreading news about the emptiness of Jesus' tomb would have reached the Roman prefect. Pilate would not have believed that Jesus had risen from death or had been taken to heaven. He would have done everything in his power to get to the bottom of this absurd Christian rumour and make sure that his decision to execute Jesus did not backfire, resulting in the executed man attaining further exaltation and making him look like a fool. He would have first had the tomb inspected. If it was found truly empty, he would have thought of two possibilities. First, Jesus' body was stolen and the stories about his rising from death were fabricated by his followers. Pilate would have sent his soldiers to investigate the matter, capture the body thieves, and expose the sham. The body in the tomb was supposed to have been guarded, so Pilate was indeed keen on the body not being taken away.

Second, Jesus did not die and was rescued from the tomb. In this case, Pilate would have had his soldiers look for the rescued half-dead Jesus, capture him, and have him killed for sure this time. There is no indication whatsoever in the Gospels that either of these scenarios happened. Pilate is portrayed as a moron who did not know about or bother to investigate the amazing miracle that involved someone that he had just publicly executed!

14.3 The Appearances
As is the case with their empty tomb accounts, the Gospel narratives of

---

[11] Goulder, "Jesus' Resurrection", 193.

the appearances of the risen Jesus are riddled with irreconcilable contradictions (§1.18). The traditional Christian position overlooks those discrepancies and accepts at face value the Gospel accounts that Jesus appeared to his followers in the flesh. At the other end of the scale, some scholars consider the reports of Jesus' post-mortem appearances as fraudulent claims. An alternative to these extreme positions is to consider the appearances as "subjective" experiences.

This interpretation was put forward by David Friedrich Strauss in the first half of the nineteenth century. He notes that Jesus' appearance to Paul was visionary rather than in the flesh. The subjectivity of Paul's experience may be inferred from the fact that his companions on his journey to Damascus did not see Jesus. In this case, the claim that they heard the voice has to be false. But it is clear that Paul's description of his encounter with Jesus did not involve seeing a physical Jesus. Paul mentions his experience in the course of citing Jesus' other appearances (1 Cor. 15:8). This suggests that Paul believed that all of Jesus' other appearances were of the same nature as his, i.e. they were visionary.[12] Strauss argued that Jesus did not appear in reality to anyone after his death but that a state of mind made those followers believe that they had seen him. Their visual experiences of seeing their master were completely subjective.

It is logical for subjective visions to be attributed to the beliefs of the person having them. But this cannot explain Paul's vision of Jesus because he experienced it while persecuting Christians. This objection has itself been rejected by the counterargument that conversion-related visions are known phenomena in which people change the direction of their lives.[13] In other words, a vision is not necessarily the outcome of a person's beliefs.

"Visions" is one way of describing those subjective experiences. A more negative label for the subjectivity of the experiences is "hallucinations". This makes the experiences pure delusions, whereas the term "vision" allows for more nuances. A vision may imply someone's access to an experience that is not accessible to another.

Examining the various accounts shows that not all sightings of the

---

[12] Strauss, *The Life of Jesus*, 740.
[13] Goulder, "Jesus' Resurrection", 193-194.

risen Jesus are supposed to be bodily appearances. Descriptions of different appearances suggest that they were not of the same nature but represented dissimilar experiences and phenomena. Jesus' appearance to Paul was in the form of heavenly light. In one appearance to his disciples, Jesus suddenly appeared in the middle of a room whose door was locked, suggesting that he could not have appeared in corporeal form. Yet he goes on to show them the wound in his side which he sustained when crucified, indicating that he was there in the flesh (John 20:19-20). In a later appearance, he invites Thomas to touch the wound in his body to believe that he was present in the body (John 20:27). Another appearance to two disciples represents yet a more different experience, as Jesus seems to have looked so different that they did not recognise him! Other appearances were met with doubts by those who experienced them. For whatever reasons, it did not look credible to those followers that they had seen Jesus (§1.19). This is particularly baffling given the Gospels' claim that Jesus had foretold the disciples of his future execution and rise from death. Different accounts talk about different experiences, so there is no standard definition for what a Jesus appearance is supposed to have meant exactly. Talking about Jesus "appearances" as one phenomenon, usually to reinforce belief in the resurrection, is misleading.

It has also been claimed that these subjective visions of Jesus, which were interpreted to mean that he was alive, led to the creation of the myth of the empty tomb:

> The first resurrection appearances are more likely to be visionary experiences *interpreted* as a bodily raised figure, which meant that the early accounts of Paul and Mark could assume an empty tomb even if historically this was not the case.[14]

Another alternative scenario, which we have already mentioned, is that Jesus survived the crucifixion. While this makes his appearances to his followers corporeal, it is hardly a credible proposition.

---

[14] Crossley, "Against the Historical Plausibility", 171.

15

Unshakable Faith

Like the crucifixion, the resurrection of Jesus is a cornerstone of the Christian faith. Its central role in Christian theology is attested in the earliest writings, Paul's letters. As he cogently put it when addressing fellow Christians, "If Christ has not been raised, your faith is futile and you are still in your sins" (1 Cor. 15:17). Similar to the crucifixion, the resurrection is unattested by early sources that are independent of the Christian tradition. Yet there is still a fundamental difference between the two events. Execution by crucifixion is a *natural* event that happened to numerous people throughout history, so its historicity may be entertained without subscribing to any *supernatural* beliefs, whether Christian or not. Indeed, the overwhelming majority of historians, including those who would not describe themselves as Christians or believers in the miraculous, accept that Jesus was executed.

Conversely, the resurrection is a supernatural event whose historicity can be seriously considered only by people who believe in miracles and, more specifically, accept a Christian version of it. A person who does not believe in the supernatural cannot accept Jesus' rising from the dead because such an event is a natural impossibility. A non-Christian believer in the supernatural would consider Jesus' resurrection possible, but they would still likely see it as belonging to Christian theology rather than history proper. Only a Christian believer, who by definition believes in the supernatural, accepts that this particular miraculous event did happen.

Unsurprisingly, the historicity of the resurrection has been rejected by non-Christian scholars. It has also been dismissed by some scholars who confess Christian faith but do not read the Gospels literally, do not consider them inerrant, and/or are not inclined to accept such a supernatural occurrence.

Jesus' resurrection was not witnessed directly by anyone, according to the Gospels. It was concluded by Jesus' close followers from two distinct sets of events: visitors to his tomb found it empty and he appeared after his burial to various people. The empty tomb and the appearances, therefore, have been dismissed by those who do not accept that Jesus was raised from the dead, as we have already seen.

I should mention a composite argument by those who maintain that the crucifixion and resurrection are both historical. It is most associated with N. T. Wright, a prominent New Testament scholar and Anglican Bishop, who detailed it in his seminal book *The Resurrection of the Son of God*. In his defence of the traditional Christian position, Wright argues that the emergence of the early Christian belief in the resurrection of Jesus, which is a concept of resurrection that did not belong to the Jewish environment in which it rose, is best explained by accepting the Gospels' assertions of both the empty tomb and the post-crucifixion appearances:

> Neither the empty tomb by itself, however, nor the appearances by themselves, could have generated the early Christian belief. The empty tomb alone would be a puzzle and a tragedy. Sightings of an apparently alive Jesus, by themselves, would have been classified as visions or hallucinations, which were well enough known in the ancient world. However, an empty tomb and appearances of a living Jesus, taken together, would have presented a powerful reason for the emergence of the belief.[1]

Unsurprisingly, Wright's argument does not suffer from a paucity of critics. Most scholars do not accept this two-millennia-old traditional Christian belief. This is an example of a retort:

> Yes, historically something happened shortly after Jesus' death, but the evidence hardly demands anything as spectacularly dramatic as a bodily resurrection in the sense that it would be an unparalleled event in human history and would leave an empty tomb. The list of eyewitnesses in 1 Cor. 15:5-8 gives no evidence pointing in the direction of the bodily resurrection as an historical event, except in the sense of a visionary experience. The earliest empty tomb story we have (Mark 16:1-8) suspiciously makes it clear that the only witnesses to the empty tomb told no one (16:8). All the other Gospel narratives make good sense in the context of creative storytelling, including the grounding of present beliefs in the life, death and resurrection of Jesus. I would suggest that these conclusions are much more historically probable than there being a bodily resurrection and empty tomb in the sense

---

[1] Wright, *The Resurrection*, 686.

Wright claims.[2]

Even liberal Christian scholars disagree with Wright's historical Christian belief. For instance, theologian and Bishop John Shelby Spong gives supremacy to New Testament texts over Wright's claim that the Christian belief about the resurrection reflects what actually happened. More specifically, Spong argues that the apostle Paul was completely oblivious to the story of the resurrection as recounted in the Gospels. Paul, he maintains, did not believe that Jesus' resurrection was corporeal, which is why he makes no mention whatsoever of the empty tomb tradition (also Acts 13:28-31; §8):

> For I handed on to you as of first importance what I in turn had received: that Christ died for our sins in accordance with the scriptures, and that he was buried, and that he was raised on the third day in accordance with the scriptures. (1 Cor. 15:3-4).

Accordingly, Jesus' appearances also were not of a raised body:

> Our eyes have been shaped for so long by the Gospels that even when we are reading Paul's words, Gospel concepts dramatically distort our understanding of what Paul actually wrote. There is no sense at all in Paul of a physical resurrection of Jesus back into the life of this world. God did not, for this apostle, raise Jesus from the grave back to life on this earth. Rather, for Paul, God raised Jesus from death into God's presence; from the grave to God's right hand.[3]

In general, arguing that the emergence of a particular belief among a group of ancient people must indicate the historicity of a particular set of events suffers from an irredeemable weakness. Beliefs may arise and develop, and at times die, for reasons that have nothing to do with the historicity, veracity, or objectivity of the narratives and details underlying those beliefs. Fabrication, wishful thinking, incomplete information, misperception, misinterpretation, misrecollection, and any cognitive flaws of the human mind and subjective experience can individually or collectively be responsible for a belief. While it is methodologically sound to try to trace a route from established history to belief, the same cannot be said of the reverse process. Trying to recover history from belief can

---

[2] Crossley, "Against the Historical Plausibility", 186.

[3] Spong, *Resurrection*, 50.

be highly speculative and is particularly susceptible to confirmation bias, as we saw with the embarrassment and discontinuity criteria of authenticity (§8). Depending on the details of the case, this speculation can be extreme, as in the case of Wright's application of this method, concluding from the *belief* in Jesus' empty tomb and his appearances that the crucifixion *must* have happened, as opposed to concluding that some of Jesus' followers *believed* that it did.

In the previous chapter, we reviewed the main alternative scenarios to the traditional literal Christian interpretation of the three episodes of the resurrection narrative: the crucifixion, the empty tomb, and the post-crucifixion appearances. Scholars have proposed scenarios that occupy different spots on the credibility spectrum. However, there is one particular alternative version of events that we did not encounter: Jesus was not crucified! Contrary to the controversial nature of the resurrection, the crucifixion of Jesus is always treated as a certainty, so the possibility that Jesus could have escaped the attempt to crucify him is never entertained.

This is how James Dunn, a prominent professor of theology and a minister of the Church of Scotland, affirms this unshakable confidence in the historicity of the crucifixion of Jesus:

> Two facts in the life of Jesus command almost universal assent. They bracket the three years for which Jesus is most remembered, his life's work, his mission. One is Jesus' baptism by John. The other is his death by crucifixion. Because they rank so high on the "almost impossible to doubt or deny" scale of historical "facts", they are obvious starting points for an attempt to clarify the what and why of Jesus' mission.[4]

Any attempt to look into the possibility that Jesus was not crucified would automatically draw the accusation of lacking serious scholarship, at times explicitly, as in the words of the late Geoffrey Parrinder, professor of comparative religion, Methodist minister, and author of *Jesus in the Qur'an*:

> Secular historians also accept the crucifixion as a fact. No serious modern historian doubts that Jesus was a historical figure and that he was crucified,

---

[4] Dunn, *Jesus Remembered*, 339.

whatever he may think of the faith in the resurrection.[5]

It is not uncommon to misleadingly claim that the historical certainty of the crucifixion is supported by Jewish and Roman evidence. This is one such statement by an Evangelical New Testament scholar, which is not particularly discreet in pointing the finger of accusation at Muslim scholars:

> No serious historian of any religious or nonreligious stripe doubts that Jesus of Nazareth really lived in the first century and was executed under the authority of Pontius Pilate, the governor of Judea and Samaria....The death of Jesus is not only affirmed (or at least presupposed) in every writing of the New Testament and early Christianity, it is attested by early Jewish and Roman writers as well.[6]

It is certainly true that this conviction about the execution of Jesus is shared even by scholars who are not influenced by Christian faith. For example, the Jewish author Paul Winter wrote a book that discussed in detail numerous internal inconsistencies, contradictions, and historical problems in the Gospel accounts of Jesus' trial. Yet this did not stop him from making this bold statement:

> That Jesus died by crucifixion, and that his cross bore an inscription stating the cause for which he had been sentenced, is the one solid and stable fact that should be made the starting point of any historical investigation dealing with the Gospel accounts of his trial.[7]

This certainty looks even more baffling coming from an author who also confirms that while the Gospels are the best available sources on the resurrection, they lack any corroborating sources and are not written as historical accounts but to convey a religious message![8]

It is undeniable that the overwhelming majority of scholars accept that Jesus was crucified. Historians are supposed to assess past events on the scale of probability, and most would confidently say it is as certain as any ancient historical event can be that Jesus was crucified. Yet the Synoptists claim that the crucifixion had no direct eyewitness among Jesus'

---

[5] Parrinder, *Jesus in the Qur'an*, 116.

[6] Evans, "The Shout of Death", 3.

[7] Winter, *The Trial of Jesus*, 109.

[8] Ibid., 1-2.

followers (§1.13). Do the early sources really justify the level of conviction that borders on certainty that Parrinder, Dunn, and the overwhelming majority of Western scholars stress? What exactly is it based on?

16

The Crucifixion between Theology and Selective History

In this chapter, we will see that the certainty about the historicity of the crucifixion is the outcome of compounding two errors:

- Treating theological writings as historical sources
- Unjustifiably ignoring sources that deny that Jesus was crucified

16.1 Historicising a Theological Crucifixion

Excluding Josephus' Testimonium, which is a Christian forgery, there are only three non-Christian sources from the first two centuries that mention Jesus' death. There are another two that mention him but not his crucifixion. In addition to their relative lateness, all five rely on Christian sources, so they do not provide independent historical testimony on Jesus. This leaves us with Christian writings as the only sources on Jesus. But the Gospels themselves, as is the case with Paul's writings, are unreliable as historical documents.

The absence of independent sources on Jesus' life combined with an enormous interest in his history creates considerable pressure to accept the New Testament's version of history, even if this position can be sustained only through a cherry-picking approach. There is almost an element of desperation in the interest of scholars, not only of lay people, in what the New Testament says about Jesus. There is a strong need to know how he lived, what he said and did, and how he died, and the New Testament books are seen as the only sources to satisfy this need.

The unreliability of the Gospels has made some scholars, albeit a very small minority, go as far as advocating the fantastic theory that Jesus never existed! I am far from advocating the view that there is no history in the Gospels, but identifying accurate historical details cannot be done with any reasonable level of certainty. What we can confidently conclude is that the Evangelists, writing several decades after Jesus, *believed* that he was executed by Pilate under pressure from Jewish leaders. Despite the historical unreliability of the Gospels, we have to accept that this belief was already widespread a few decades after his time. To put it differently, *there is no evidence that Jesus was executed, but it is certain that decades after he was gone, Christians already believed that he was crucified by the Roman governor at the request of the Jewish authorities.* There is no evidence to confirm or reject Jesus' alleged execution, but there is evidence that a perception that he was killed had developed by the time the first Gospel was written some three or four decades after Jesus. This is the only certain conclusion that can be drawn from the early sources.

Parrinder has rightly argued that whether the crucifixion occurred or not "has a vital bearing on the understanding of the life of Jesus, and on the reliability of the Gospel and all the New Testament".[1] But this concern exposes a fundamental flaw in the way some scholars, in particular of the Christian faith, have dealt with the question of the historicity of the crucifixion: conflating history and theology to the point of treating theology as history. Rejecting the historicity of the crucifixion does not only affect the belief in how Jesus' life ended, but it also undermines the unique salvational message that is attached to his crucifixion. This message is the very foundation of Christian theology in Paul's writings and the Gospels. Dismissing this message leads to a completely different reading of Jesus' life that fundamentally changes the Christian faith.

Furthermore, it is generally accepted that theology was a major driver in the writing of the New Testament. One common approach to understating the significance of this fact for the historical value of the Gospels is to point out that the latest Gospel of John shows a far more advanced theology than the earliest of Mark. The implication is that we can treat Mark, followed by Matthew and Luke, more as historical documents than John. This may well be the case, but let me explain why I see overplaying this to be misleading.

The earliest New Testament books are Paul's letters. These are earlier even than Mark. Yet these are unambiguously theological rather than historical writings. Furthermore, they do not even attempt to claim otherwise. Theology was already guiding Christian writings when Mark

---

[1] Parrinder, *Jesus in the Qur'an*, 117.

set out to write his account of Jesus' life. Evidently, in this case, "early" does not mean "historical" and "earlier" does not equate to "more historical".

The fact that the crucifixion of Jesus is at the heart of this theology should make us wonder how much attention was given to history in Christian writings. Unlike theologians and historians of the Christian faith, secular historians have no faith-driven interest in affirming the historical foundations of New Testament theology. But considering the historicity of the crucifixion beyond doubt fails to account for the significant role of theology in the recorded narrative. Just about every detail of the crucifixion narrative has been doubted or rejected, yet the crucifixion itself is said to be a certainty! In general terms, this is the equivalent of accepting the historicity of an ancient incident even though every detail of it is at least questionable. This probably puts the crucifixion in the company of a tiny number of such ancient events!

16.2 Unjustified Selective Admission of Sources

Accepting the historicity of the crucifixion is, critically, albeit subtly, a process of choosing between two mutually exclusive Gospel accounts. Following their claim that Jesus was crucified, the Gospels go on to say that he was raised from the dead. Confirming that he was not found in his tomb, they then mention instances of him appearing after his resurrection to his disciples and some women. Paul extends the list of those who saw him to over five hundred of his male and female followers. Unsurprisingly, these sources differ on whom Jesus appeared to (§1.18). But what concerns us here is the very claim that he appeared to some people after his resurrection.

Scholars of the Christian faith have no problem in accepting the historicity of both the crucifixion and the appearances. After all, this is what their faith is built on. Historians who accept that Jesus was crucified but read the New Testament without influence by a commitment to its faith reject his post-resurrection corporeal appearances because they are supernatural. This may sound like a completely justifiable decision given that it is a choice between a supernatural claim and a natural alternative. But there is a serious flaw in this logic. Describing the appearances as supernatural is the result of accepting that Jesus was crucified and, inevitably, died! Had he not died, which all accept his crucifixion would have led to, his physical appearances would have been fully acceptable, because they would have been natural occurrences. If there was no crucifixion, there was no death and resurrection, so Jesus' controversial appearances were no less natural than any of his earlier appearances that are reported in the same sources. After all, everyone accepts that the Gospel writers injected supernaturality into various episodes of Jesus' life.

Let us turn this argument on its head. If a historian concluded that Jesus was indeed physically seen after his crucifixion, they would treat those sightings as natural appearances. Accordingly, they would reject the mutually exclusive claim that he was crucified!

It is not as if the crucifixion accounts are more reliable than those of the appearances. Like many Gospel narratives, the story of the appearances has its problems, but it is nowhere near as problematic as the crucifixion narrative. The latter is riddled with incoherence, inaccuracies, and outright historical fallacies from the arrest to the resurrection.

Why, then, is there this uncompromising reluctance to consider the possibility that the crucifixion never happened? This is how the author of *Jesus Outside the New Testament* explained the thinking of the scholarly establishment in excluding such sources:

> Some popular treatments of Jesus outside the New Testament have also dealt with Jesus in the Qur'an and later Islamic traditions, in legends about Jesus' putative travels to India and Tibet, his grave in Srinagar, Kashmir, and so forth. Scholarship has almost unanimously agreed that these references to Jesus are so late and tendentious as to contain virtually nothing of value for understanding the historical Jesus. Since they have formed no part of the scholarly debate on Jesus, we will not examine them here.[2]

Two reasons for the *scholarly* exclusion of these sources are pointed out: lateness and tendentiousness. Let's discuss the merits of both as a justification for excluding the Qur'an, which denies the crucifixion of Jesus.

The Qur'an dates back to the beginning of the seventh century, more specifically 610-632 CE. Its account of Jesus' life is, therefore, *six centuries* later than the events. This is immensely late, not least if we take into account the fact that the Gospels, which were written *decades* after Jesus, are themselves considered late. But there are Christian sources that denied

---

[2] Van Voorst, *Jesus Outside the New Testament*, 17.

Jesus' crucifixion centuries before the Qur'an.

The Second Treatise of the Great Seth and *The Coptic Apocalypse of Peter* from the third century, and less clearly *The First Apocalypse of James*, deny Jesus' crucifixion and claim that a substitute suffered it instead. We will discuss these sources in more detail later (§22.1). The discovery of these tractates in 1945 failed to allow the crucifixion of a substitute theory to be admitted into the never-ending, and almost unconstrained, scholarly debate to reconstruct and reinterpret Jesus' history. It may be argued that these tractates are still very late, but they advocate a claim that lived much earlier!

Scholars were already aware of this alternative theory of the crucifixion before these three sources came to light. Writing around 185 CE, Irenaeus, bishop of Lyon, attributed the claim that someone else was crucified instead of Jesus to the Egyptian Christian teacher Basilides who lived in the early second century. This takes the substitute interpretation of the crucifixion back to not much later than the Gospel of John and other New Testament books! The lateness argument cannot be sustained.

Furthermore, the substitute claims are also said to be based on docetism. This is the belief that Jesus was incorporeal, so Jesus could not have been the subject of the physical punishment of crucifixion. The earliest known accusation of the Qur'anic version of the crucifixion as being docetic goes back to the monk John of Damascus. Writing around a century after the Prophet Muhammad, this is how he accused him of composing the Qur'an:

> This man, after having chanced upon the Old and New Testaments and likewise, it seems, having conversed with an Arian monk, devised his own heresy. Then, having insinuated himself into the good graces of the people by a show of seeming piety, he gave out that a certain book had been sent down to him from heaven.

He then goes on to critically and inaccurately summarise the Qur'an's version of the crucifixion:

> And he says that the Jews wanted to crucify Him in violation of the law, and that they seized His shadow and crucified this. But the Christ Himself was not crucified, he says, nor did He die, for God out of His love for Him

took Him to Himself into heaven.[3]

The docetism label has certainly played a big role in the dismissal of those claims out of hand. This, however, is effectively a judgment about history informed by theological preference. What is particularly significant is the observation of some that New Testament books, including the Gospels, seem to contain rebuttals to docetism.[4] For instance, when Jesus makes his final appearance to his disciples, Luke (24:38-41) says that they thought he was a ghost, making Jesus admonish them and ask them to touch his hands and feet to satisfy themselves that he was present in the flesh. If docetism predates the Gospels, then it must go back to the early days of Christianity. That, surely, isn't late!

Let's further critique the lateness argument but in a rather novel manner by looking at the present. The scholarly study of the historical Jesus, which is permeated by endless polemics, has produced a wide range of views, even without considering mythicism. This is known to anyone who is even moderately familiar with this discipline. One prominent scholar has labelled this "stunning diversity" as "an academic embarrassment" before going on to say:

> It is impossible to avoid the suspicion that historical Jesus research is a very safe place to do theology and call it history, to do autobiography and call it biography.[5]

These wildly diverse opinions are, tellingly, interpretations of the same texts, mainly the Gospels, and to some extent Paul's letters. They range from accepting Jesus' divinity and all supernatural aspects of his life, death, and resurrection, at one extreme, to a complete rejection of any aspect of supernaturality in his story, at the other. They occupy a wide spectrum from a literal reading of the text to as free a reading as one can imagine. Just about every New Testament claim about Jesus has been accepted, rejected, and differently interpreted by numerous scholars—all reading the same text! The confidence and vigour with which every side defends their interpretation makes this situation all the more startling and often rather amusing. One would be forgiven for thinking that the

---

[3] John of Damascus, *Fountain of Knowledge*, 153-154.
[4] Price, *Shrinking Son of Man*, 326-331; Yamauchi, "Docetic Christology", 5-7.
[5] Crossan, *The Historical Jesus*, xxviii.

interpretations are the sources and the New Testament texts are their interpretations!

Indeed, one New Testament scholar, who is also an ordained elder of the Presbyterian Church in the USA, has this to say about the role of a scholar's precommitment in steering their interpretation of the text, citing two scholars at opposing ends of the spectrum of opinions:

> People's arguments regarding the origins of Christianity are unavoidably driven by large assumptions about the nature of the world, assumptions that cannot often if ever be the upshot of historical investigation. Goulder's preference for a naturalistic explanation of Jesus' resurrection did not grow out of his study of the ancient Christian materials but was rather brought to them. Similarly, Wright's passionate belief in the traditional Christian confession was not the result of his historical researches but rather an article of faith that has informed his scholarly work from its inception.[6]

This situation is a perfect example of what psychologist Jonathan Haidt once famously described, though in a completely different context, as the emotional tail wagging the rational dog.

How does this almost unlimited diversity of interpretation of the same text inform our criticism of the argument of *lateness* against the non-crucifixion claim? It tells us that when this many opposing *new* interpretations are allowed into the debate, no interpretation or claim should be excluded because of its *age*, certainly not when it is fourteen centuries older than the modern debate and its many competing biographies of Jesus!

The second reason for rejecting the Qur'an and those early Christian sources is their supposed tendentiousness. I do not think we need to spend many words showing the hollowness of this argument unless it is claimed that Paul's letters, the Gospels, or any New Testament book are not tendentious! No reasonable person would make such a claim.

We have to accept that almost all of what is claimed to be known about Jesus, regardless of how much history is appealed to for support, comes at least partly from faith. This applies to Jesus' alleged execution. Even when a particular detail of Jesus' life in whatever source is considered compatible with known history, this should only mean that the veracity of this detail cannot be ruled out, not that its historicity is

---

[6] Allison, "Explaining the Resurrection", 133.

beyond doubt. It is *partly* an act of faith to declare a claim about Jesus to be *more likely*, but it is *completely* an expression of faith to be *absolutely certain* of it.

Christian scholars have successfully popularised the view that the New Testament is more historical than the Qur'an. Unsuspecting people who have not studied closely the sources are often misled into thinking that there is an independent version of Jesus' history and that the New Testament's is, if not completely then at least largely, in agreement with that history. Sources that disagree with the New Testament, such as the Qur'an, are then positioned as *unhistorical* and *inaccurate*. The reality is that there is cyclical logic in operation here: the history of Jesus' life that the New Testament has *created* is often cited as independent historical evidence in support of the Gospel accounts! Sources that disagree with the New Testament are, expectedly, discredited as historically unreliable. This is a real crucifixion of truth that is attested by history.

I hope to have shown why the exclusion of the Qur'an's *unique* account of Jesus' life from the scholarly discussion of the historical Jesus is unscientific. In the fourth part of this book, we will focus on the Qur'an's explanation of the crucifixion, which has been claimed to be a version of docetism. We will see how wrong this claim is and why the Qur'an's version of history is, on the contrary, *unique*.

IV

The Crucifixion in the Qur'an

17

The Qur'an Interprets Itself

In the fourth and last part of this book, we will focus on what the Qur'an says about the crucifixion of Jesus. Before we embark on this task, I should briefly introduce the methods of interpreting the Qur'an and my specific approach.

Scholars have established several methods to interpret the Qur'an. These may be classified into three main groups, depending on the main sources of interpretation: tradition (*naql*), personal opinion (*ra'i*), and the Qur'an itself.

The tradition-based approach relies on interpretations attributed to the Prophet Muhammad and early authorities from his Companions, i.e. believers who met him, and the Successors, i.e. believers who met Companions. One obvious risk with this method is the false attribution of interpretations to the Prophet Muhammad, which is common in Ḥadīth literature. Also, interpretations by people other than the Prophet could mainly reflect the reasoning of their respective interpreters, which may or may not be more accurate than the reasoning of later exegetes. In effect, for an interpretation by a Companion or Successor to be given special authority, it has to be at least influenced by the Prophet. Yet this is often impossible to prove. Not unexpectedly, reported interpretations of the same text can be contradictory.

Interpretation by opinion effectively covers every interpretative attempt in which neither the Qur'an nor tradition is the central source of interpretation. The main role is taken by the scholar's reasoning. Using their judgment, the exegete may use any information available to them from any source and integrate it into a complete interpretation. An interpretation by opinion is influenced by the person's linguistic skills, relevant knowledge, and analytical skills, even though it may call on tradition for support.

Interpretation by the Qur'an treats the book itself as its main source of interpretation. Personal reasoning remains the main tool of analysis. This method does not exclude the use of extra-Qur'anic information, such as Ḥadīth and historical and linguistic sources, which may even be necessary. This approach is, rather, characterised by two principles. First, it gives the Qur'anic text unchallenged interpretive authority. It is both the source and the interpretation. Second, it considers using the Qur'an a requirement, without which any interpretive attempt is likely to fail to capture the text's meaning accurately and/or fully.

In theory, a Qur'anic text may be linguistically analysed and interpreted as a standalone passage with no reference to any other verses if it is found to be complete in meaning. This *may* provide an accurate understanding of the passage in question, but this interpretation cannot be *confirmed* without studying its context. The immediate context of the passage is found in its surrounding verses. But even this may not be sufficient for a full and wholly accurate interpretation. The interpretation requires consulting the passage's broadest and fullest context, which would be all relevant passages and terms in the Qur'an.

Unsurprisingly, using the fundamental hermeneutical principle of "the Qur'an interprets itself" does not eliminate the differences between exegetes. It still leaves considerable room for personal reasoning and preference. It does, however, reduce, limit, and clarify such disagreements.

We find references to this well-known, long-established, and most reliable interpretative principle in the works of the earliest Muslims. Imam 'Alī Ibn Abī Ṭālib, the Prophet Muhammad's confidant and the first to embrace his message, is reported to have described the Qur'an as follows:

> Its parts speak through each other and its parts bear witness to each other.[1]

In his interpretation of the verse "Allah has sent down the best of speech—a consistent Book" (39.23), Ṭabarī (310/922) attributes to the Successor Saʿīd Ibn Jubayr (95/714) the following saying about the Qur'an's description of itself as "a consistent Book" (*kitāban mutashābihan*):

> Its parts are consistent with each other, its parts confirm each other, and its parts point to each other.

---

[1] 'Alī Ibn Abī Ṭālib, *Nahj Al-Balāgha*, 337.

The earliest exegetical work that mentions this interpretive rule seems to be Zamakhsharī's (538/1143). In its commentary on verse 30.23, it states, "The most correct meaning is the one that the Qur'an points to". According to Ibn Taymiyya (728/1328):

> The best method is to interpret the Qur'an using the Qur'an. What is mentioned in general in one place is specified in other, and what is abbreviated in one place is detailed in another.[2]

The twentieth-century scholar Ṭabāṭabāʾī has insightfully pointed out that the principle that the Qur'an is self-explanatory comes from the Qur'an itself. In the introduction to his voluminous exegesis, he observes the following:

> The Almighty said, "We have sent down to you the Book as clarification for all things" (16.89). God forbid, the Qur'an cannot be a "clarification for all things" but not a clarification of itself! The Almighty said, "a guidance for the people and clear proofs of guidance and distinction" (2.185), and the Almighty said, "We have sent down to you a clear light" (4.174). How can the Qur'an be "guidance", "proof", "distinction", and "clear light" for people in all their needs but not suffice them in their need for it, which is the biggest need? The Almighty said, "Those who strive for Us, We will surely guide them to Our ways" (29.69). What strife is greater than striving to understand His Book? Which way guides to Him more than the Qur'an?[3]

Treating the Qur'an as one unit of text necessitates that it is consulted on its interpretation.

Applying the principle of *the Qur'an interprets itself* in the current study means that we will not only study verse 4.157, which is the only verse that explicitly mentions Jesus' crucifixion, denying that it happened. We will also study its surrounding verses for its immediate context. But references to Jesus' story are scattered in several chapters in the Qur'an. To fully and accurately understand what the Qur'an says about Jesus' crucifixion, we must study all relevant verses. Furthermore, we will need to consult other parts of the Qur'an that do not deal with Jesus' story to correctly and fully understand certain terms that also occur in verses about him.

In the coming chapters, we shall see that many, if not most, studies of

---

[2] Ibn Taymiyya, *Muqaddima*, 93.

[3] Ṭabāṭabāʾī, *Al-Mīzān*, I, 11.

the crucifixion, and Jesus in general, in the Qur'an fail to fully use the Qur'an for interpretation. This is the case even when a study claims, explicitly or implicitly, to follow this approach. This shows in various interpretations that seem to account for some verses but fail to explain or even contradict others. The failure to consider *all* relevant verses is a fundamental flaw in the application of the method of *the Qur'an is its own interpreter*.

18

Why Did the Jews Try to Kill Jesus?

In chapter 5, we concluded that the Gospels state or imply that the Jewish leaders wanted to eliminate Jesus because he was very critical of them, made offensive statements about the temple, caused a disturbance there, and moved to preach in Jerusalem. In this chapter, we will study the reasons for the Jewish move to eliminate Jesus according to the Qur'an.

There are three basic facts about Jesus' story in the Qur'an that I should first state:

- He escaped the attempt on his life.
- The Jews are named as being responsible for the unsuccessful attempt to kill Jesus. No third party is mentioned.
- There is no *direct* explanation of why they wanted to kill him.

We will deal with the first two points in detail in the coming chapters, focusing here on the third.

To understand why the Jews wanted Jesus dead, we need to look at his sayings, actions, and image for things that the Jewish leadership could have found so offensive and/or threatening as to decide to kill him. But we should not necessarily look for something *unique* about him because killing a prophet was not unique in Jewish history. The Qur'an reiterates several times, albeit without giving details, that the Jews killed unnamed prophets. The Old Testament also mentions this fact (1 Kings 18:4), as does Jesus in the Gospels (Matt. 23:31). We will discuss this point in more detail in the next chapter.

In the following sections, we will review how Jesus presented himself and was seen, before concluding the chapter with a discussion of what could have led to the extreme hostility that he was subjected to.

18.1 Prophet and Messenger

Jesus is called a "prophet" (*nabī*) (3.84; 4.136, 163; 19.30; 33.7). The Qur'anic concept of "prophet" differs from its Biblical counterpart. A prophet in the Qur'an is someone whom God has given revelations to and has commissioned to call people to His way. Adam, Noah, Abraham, Jacob, and Moses, to name a few, were all prophets. Prophethood is the highest spiritual status in the Qur'an. A prophet in the Old Testament is someone who receives prophecies from God and speaks for Him.

Jesus is called a prophet in the Gospels as well. He called himself a prophet (Matt. 10:41), the disciples called him so (Luke 24:19), and the public did the same (Mark 8:28).

Jesus is also described in the Qur'an as a "messenger" (rasūl) (2.253; 3.49, 53; 4.157, 171; 5.111; 61.6). Applied to anyone that God commissions to deliver a message, a "messenger" is a broader title than "prophet". Every prophet is a messenger, but the reverse is untrue. For instance, angels who deliver communications to certain humans are called messengers (e.g. 11.69), but they are not prophets.

Jesus is described as a messenger in the Gospels as well. For instance, he said, "I was sent only to the lost sheep of the house of Israel" (Matt. 15:24).

18.2 The Messiah

The Qur'an calls Jesus "the Messiah" (al-Masīḥ) eleven times in nine different verses. It occurs three times alone (4.172; 5.72; 9.30), three times in the phrase "the Messiah, Jesus son of Mary" (3.45; 4.157, 171), and five times in "the Messiah son of Mary" (5.17 twice, 72, 75; 9.31). The implication is clear: Jesus presented himself as the Messiah.

Like his image in the Gospels, Jesus of the Qur'an was a spiritual teacher who had no overt or covert political agenda. Unlike the Gospels, the Qur'an does not link Jesus to King David or associate him with royalty. He must have disappointed the Jewish public with his claim that the Messiah they had been long expecting to liberate them from the Romans and re-establish the historical state of Israel was a product of their imagination and wishful thinking. This would have limited his appeal to the Jews, except for the minority who were open to his corrective teachings.

The Gospels call Jesus "Christ" fifty-four times. While many scholars argue that Jesus never called himself the Messiah, several statements by him leave no doubt that he claimed to be the Messiah, even if these were in response to a question or remark from someone else.[1]

18.3 Receiver of New Scripture

The Qur'an affirms several times that Jesus was sent by God to confirm the Torah of Moses. It also states that God revealed to him a new book called "Injīl":

> We sent, following in their (the prophets') footsteps, Jesus, the son of Mary, confirming that which came before him in the Torah; and We gave him the Injīl, in which there is guidance and light, and as a confirmation of that which preceded it of the Torah, and as guidance and admonition for the god-fearing. (5.46)

The Injīl, which is mentioned twelve times in the Qur'an, was revealed to complement the Torah, not to replace it. This being the case, it was probably much smaller in size than the Torah. The word "Injīl" is an Arabisation of the Greek εὐαγγέλιου (euangelion). This term, which means "good news", was translated into Anglo-Saxon as god-spell, which later became "Gospel".[2]

The repeated reference to Jesus' mission as a "confirmation" of the Torah indicates that the Qur'an portrays him as a revivalist and reformist of Judaism, rather than a radical teacher who tried to replace it with a completely new faith. I should point out that this fourteen-century-old Qur'anic image of Jesus is also what historical Jesus research in the last few decades has led Western scholarship to conclude. In the past, Jesus used to be presented in opposition to Judaism rather than being placed within it as a reformist.[3]

To be sure, Jesus' new revealed book may have consisted of mere spiritual advice or may also have included new legislation about the believer's way of life. Either way, the Injīl did not replace the Torah but supplemented it. Non-Christian scholarship on Jesus sees him very much as a Jewish teacher preaching within the framework of Judaism, although Christian theologians are more likely to read the Gospels and Paul's writings to mean that Jesus, at least, relegated the law to the background and replaced it with grace as the means of salvation (§5.3).

---

[1] Fatoohi, *The Messiah in Islam, Christianity, and Judaism.*

[2] Fatoohi, *The Mystery of the Historical Jesus*, 501-512.

[3] Wassen, "The Jewishness of Jesus".

The Qur'an challenges the "People of the Book", that is, the Jews and the Christians, in the city of Medina to apply the Torah and Injīl (5.66-68). This means that both books were, partly or completely, available at the time. An obvious question is whether these two are to be equated with the Old Testament and the Gospels or New Testament, respectively. The Qur'an expressly accuses the Jews of tampering with "the book" (e.g. 5.41)—that is, the book that was revealed to Moses—and disagrees with some historical information in the Old Testament. It also unambiguously rejects episodes of the history of Jesus in Gospels, such as his alleged crucifixion, as well as New Testament theology. So, the answer to this question must be negative. It is likely, though, that the Old Testament, in particular, and the New Testament contain material from the Torah and the Injīl, respectively.

Many scholars reject the Qur'an's claim that Jesus had received a divine book while others suggest that the Qur'anic Injīl is an inaccurate and confused reference to the Gospels. They argue that there is no evidence that Jesus had written revelation. This claim, in fact, is one example of the application of double standards to the Qur'an and New Testament. Scholars have embraced the twentieth-century concept of the *hypothetical* document "Q", which is supposed to have been one source of the Gospels of Matthew and Luke. Indeed, two other presumed documents, "M" and "L", are also said to have been used by Matthew and Luke, respectively (§7.1). These hypothetical documents have become standard concepts in New Testament scholarship. The historicity of these documents is treated as a foregone conclusion by most scholars. If the historicity of any hypothetical pre-Gospels source is seriously considered, which is the case with Q, M, and L, then the Qur'anic Injīl should be considered at least as likely to have existed.

The concept of "gospel" is inconsistently used in the New Testament. It appears to mean the news about Jesus' message, the message itself, and the act of proclaiming that news or message. The Qur'an leads us to conclude that the inconsistent concept of "gospel" in the New Testament is a corruption of the "Injīl", the name of Jesus' book. Interestingly, the earliest evidence of the use of "gospel" for a written document is from the second century. If "gospel" was never connected to writings, why did it develop to mean a written document? Using the term for a biography of Jesus is certainly a late development of the term, as is the use of "gospel" in the plural.

We know that the Christian community at the time of Jesus was so small that it was possible for his teachings to be changed and for his history to be reported in contradictory accounts. It should not be seen as far-fetched to expect Jesus' book to have become fused with other writings, particularly if his oral teachings and Injīl passages were confused with each other. I have discussed the Injīl in more detail elsewhere.[4]

18.4 Law Reformer

The following verse confirms that Jesus, instructed by God, relaxed some aspects of the law by legalising things that until then were prohibited:

> And [I have come] confirming what was before me of the Torah and to *make lawful for you some of what was forbidden to you.* I have come to you with a sign from your Lord, so fear Allah and obey me. (3.50)

The wording is clear that this is not a reference to new *interpretations* of the law but the *abrogation* of previous prohibitions. Mentioning the new allowances after stating, again, that Jesus confirmed the Torah indicates the limited scope of these unexplained allowances. This image is closer to the position of nonconfessional scholarship, that the Gospels indicate that Jesus had his own interpretations of legal matters, than the view of many Christian theologians that Jesus intentionally and repeatedly broke the law and even abolished it altogether (§5.3). Nevertheless, the Qur'an's portrayal of Jesus' relationship to the Mosaic law is distinct from other views.

Being changes to the Mosaic law in the Torah, the new relaxations were probably revealed in the Injīl rather than as verbal instructions by Jesus.

18.5 Forerunner of Another Prophet

In addition to reiterating that Jesus confirmed the Torah, the following verse reveals another objective of his mission:

> When Jesus, the son of Mary, said, "O children of Israel, I am a messenger of Allah to you confirming what came before me of the Torah and bringing good tidings of a messenger to come after me, whose name is Aḥmad". But when he came to them with clear proofs, they said, "This is clear magic".

---

[4] Fatoohi, *The Mystery of the Historical Jesus*, 357-388.

(61.6)

The Gospels portray John the Baptist as the forerunner of Jesus. The Qur'an's short account of John (19.12-15) occurs immediately before one of the longest passages on Jesus, but it does not link the missions of the two prophets. The Qur'an states, however, that Jesus was himself a forerunner of the Prophet Muhammad. The names "Muhammad" and "Ahmad" are both superlatives from the same Arabic root *ḥmd* (praise). This is aligned with the Qur'an's portrayal of Jesus as a non-eschatological figure whose coming had nothing to do with the end of the world, let alone signalled its imminence. It is also congruent with the Qur'anic message that the different prophets proclaimed the same core message, even if their specific legal and social teachings reflected the eras and milieus in which they appeared.

18.6 Miracle Worker

The Qur'an describes Jesus as an exceptional miracle worker. It attributes to him eight different kinds of miraculous feat:

- Speaking in infancy
- Supernatural precociousness
- Creating figures of birds from clay and then giving them life
- Healing blindness
- Healing albinism or serious skin diseases
- Raising the dead
- Knowing what people ate and stored in the privacy of their homes
- Bringing down from heaven a table of food

Jesus in the Gospels also has an impressive catalogue of wonders, including healings, prophecies, clairvoyance, and nature-control miracles, such as walking on water. The most reported type of miracle in the Gospels is healing. Healing miracles may, in turn, be subdivided into healing diseases, exorcisms of devils, and resurrections of dead people.[5] The miracle in the Qur'an of Jesus speaking as an infant is found in apocryphal writings, such as *The Arabic Gospel of the Infancy*. Making birds out of clay and giving them life is another miracle that does not

---

[5] Ibid., 437-500.

appear in the Gospels but is found in apocryphal sources, such as *The Infancy Gospel of Thomas.*[6]

As explained earlier (§5.2), in Judaism, supernatural feats did not necessarily make the performer be seen as good or evil. Rather, his perceived religious status would have led to his wonders being understood as godly or magic. The Qur'an gives the same picture of how Jesus' miracles were perceived:

> When Allah said, "O Jesus, son of Mary! Remember My favour on you and your mother when I supported you with the Spirit of Holiness, making you speak to people in the cradle and when middle-aged; [remember] when I taught you the Book, Wisdom, the Torah, and the Injīl; [remember] when you created out of clay the figures of birds by My permission, then you breathed into them and they became birds by My permission, and you healed the blind and the leper with My permission; [remember] when you raised the dead by My permission; and [remember] when I restrained the Children of Israel from you when you came to them with clear proofs. But those who disbelieved among them said, '*This is nothing but clear magic*'". (5.110)
>
> But when he came to them with clear proofs, they said, "*This is clear magic*". (61.6)

Those who dismissed Jesus' claim to prophethood and messiahship saw his wonders as acts of magic, whereas the believers accepted them as miracles facilitated by God.

18.7 What Provoked the Jews against Jesus?

Let's now assess Jesus' various descriptions in the Qur'an to see which could have provoked his opponents among the Jewish authorities to the point of seeking his death.

Jesus' correction of the concept of the Messiah would not have appealed to many people, but it is unlikely to have made him a serious religious enemy that deserved nothing less than death. A claim to messiahship was not blasphemous or a religious crime in Judaism (§3.8). Furthermore, a peaceful Messiah would have been particularly harmless and unthreatening to the authorities.

It is also difficult to see why Jesus' revelation that another prophet would come in the future would have led to persecution. While these

---

[6] Ehrman, *Lost Scriptures*, 58.

two claims may not have resulted in his persecution, Jesus' other claims made him the target of serious animosity.

Declaring oneself to be a prophet and messenger from God could have prompted an accusation of making a false claim about God and misleading the Jewish public. Deuteronomy (18:20-22) stipulates that even if a genuine prophet attributes to God something that He had not said, then he must be killed. In the case of Jesus, his very claim of having a revelation from God was rejected, so it is not implausible that this was used as a pretext to seek his death.

Claiming to receive written revelation from God would only have magnified his guilt in the eyes of his opponents. His claim that the Injīl only supplemented, not abrogated, the Torah would not have been enough to dismiss the perception that the new book was a fake and illegal rival to the Torah. The legalisation of prohibitions, even if minor dietary things, could only have further heightened all accusations and accentuated Jesus' guilt as far as the religious authorities were concerned.

Accusing Jesus of being a false prophet would have meant considering his miracles as magic facilitated by the devil. This is a serious accusation.

There is a critical point to note. It is sensible to look for what the Jewish leaders considered to be legal and theological indiscretions by Jesus that led them to want to kill him. But whatever Jesus was accused of may not necessarily be true, as the law could have been dishonestly used to justify his prosecution. After all, the Qur'an, the Old Testament, and the New Testament all confirm that prophets were unjustly killed by Jews. For instance, dismissing Jesus' claim to prophethood was not necessarily a true objective judgment but a defensive emotional response. Seeing Jesus as a serious threat to their authority and being more interested in keeping their privileges than being students of the truth and servants of God, religious leaders would have laid any accusations against Jesus to eliminate him.

If not the *main* motives behind the persecution of Jesus, rivalry, envy, and ill feeling might have at least played a *major* role. Both Mark (15:10) and Matthew (27:18) claim that Pilate realised that the Jewish authorities handed Jesus over to Pilate "out of jealousy". Jesus' impressive miracles, in particular, might have been a major cause of jealousy. We saw in the previous section that his wonders were described as "magic" by his enemies because they did not believe in his mission. It is equally possible that this negative labelling of his miracles was the product of pure jealousy. Other Jewish teachers did not have anything like Jesus' miracles to testify to their righteousness, so they could have seen his wonders as indirectly undermining their standing and authority. This, in turn, would have triggered ill feeling towards Jesus. This seems to be supported by God's words to Jesus:

> And [remember] *when I restrained the Children of Israel from you* when you came to them with clear proofs. But those who disbelieved among them said, '*This is nothing but clear magic*'. (5.110)

The "clear proofs" are the miracles, so the verse links them to the hostility towards Jesus that required divine intervention to protect him.

As I observed earlier (§5.3), because we do not have reliable and detailed information about Jesus' career as a spiritual teacher, we cannot speculate about what exactly happened to him. We do not know which factors drove what events that culminated in the attempt to kill him.

19

The Qur'an's Denial of Jesus' Crucifixion

The Qur'an holds Jesus in very high esteem. He is not only a prophet, which is already the most revered status in the Qur'an, but he belongs to an elite group of prophets. While historical details in the Qur'an are limited, Jesus' story is found in seven chapters (3, 4, 5, 19, 43, 57, 61). The amount of details of his story, including his mother's, is second only to the prophet Moses'. We will encounter many of those verses in the rest of the book.

The Qur'an presents a completely different and much briefer picture of the final stage of Jesus' life than that found in the Gospels. Its disagreements start with rejecting the claim that Jesus was killed or crucified by the Jews, which is the focus of this chapter. We will study the main verse on this issue and the consensus of Muslim scholarship since its inception that this verse denies the crucifixion. All other related verses and how the Qur'an cannot be read as doing anything other than denying the crucifixion will be gradually brought into the discussion in other chapters.

19.1 The Non-Crucifixion Verse

The striking denial of Jesus' crucifixion is made as clear as can be in verse 4.157. To properly and fully understand it, we need to also study other related verses. In this section, we will focus on 4.157 and the verses leading to it, which provide immediate contextual information that is critical for interpreting this verse:

> The People of the Book ask you [O Muhammad!] to bring down to them a book from heaven. They had asked of Moses greater than that and said, "Show us Allah plainly". So, the thunderbolt struck them for their wrongdoing. Then they took the calf [for worship] after clear proofs had come to them. We pardoned that. We gave Moses a clear authority. (153)
>
> We raised over them the mount for their covenant and We said to them,

"Enter the gate while prostrate". We said to them, "Do not transgress on the Sabbath", and We took from them a solemn covenant. (154)

[We cursed them] for breaking their covenant, rejecting the signs of Allah, killing prophets unjustly, and saying, "Our hearts are covered". Rather, Allah has sealed them because of their disbelief, so they do not believe except for few. (155)

And for their disbelief and their saying against Mary a grave slander, (156)

And saying, "We have killed the Messiah, Jesus, the son of Mary, the messenger of Allah". They did not kill him, nor did they crucify him, but it was made to appear so to them. Those who differ over it are in doubt about it. They have no knowledge of it except the following of conjecture. They did not kill him with certainty. (157)

Rather, Allah raised him to Himself. Allah is invincible, wise. (4.158)

Verse 4.153 first criticises the Jews at the time of the Prophet Muhammad for demanding that he show them a book descended from heaven. They asked for this as proof of his claim that the Qur'an was revealed to him by God. God responds by pointing out that their fellow Jews at the time of Moses made an even greater demand, asking him to make it possible for them to see God to believe him. This transgression is referenced in another verse in the Qur'an that addresses the Jews directly:

[Recall] when you said, "O Moses, we will never believe you until we see Allah plainly". So the thunderbolt overtook you as you looked on. (2.55)

The closest reference to this event in the Old Testament seems to be the following:

Then the Lord said to Moses, "Go down and warn the people not to break through to the Lord to look; otherwise many of them will perish." (Exod. 19:21)

Having gone up to Mount Sinai as instructed by God, Moses was ordered to go down to warn his followers against bypassing some physical boundaries to see God. The Qur'an, on the other hand, talks about a demand that Moses' followers made of him. The ending of 2.55 suggests that they carried out whatever they meant to do in anticipation of seeing God, but they were instead struck by a thunderbolt.

Verse 4.153 goes on to make another criticism of Moses' followers, which is taking a calf for a god. This grave sin is mentioned several times in the Qur'an (2.51-54, 92-93; 4.153; 7.148-150). The episode of the golden calf is also found in the Old Testament (Exod. 32:1-33).

Verse 4.154 references other events that reflect the failure of Moses' followers to honour their covenant with God, including keeping the Sabbath (also 2.65; 4.47). The sanctity of the Sabbath and the command to cease work on it is mentioned in many places in the Old Testament, the first of which is in Exodus (16:23). It also reports several violations by the whole community and by individuals (e.g. Exod. 16:27; Num. 15.32-36).

The Qur'an goes on in 4.155 to confirm God's condemnation of the Jews for breaking their solemn covenant, rejecting His signs, killing prophets without justification, and claiming that their hearts are "covered". The seriousness of the killing of prophets is underlined by its mention in several verses (2.61, 87, 91; 3.21, 112, 181, 183; 5.70), without naming the victims. This charge needs to be discussed in detail because of its particular relevance to the Qur'an's account of the crucifixion.

The Old Testament describes the killing of the priest Zechariah son of Jehoiada (2 Chron. 24:17-22), who is called a "prophet" in rabbinic writings (b. Git. 57b), and the prophet Uriah son of Shemaiah (Jer. 26:20-24). They are dated to the ninth century and the end of the seventh century BCE, respectively. The prophet Jeremiah, who was contemporary to Uriah, also came close to facing death (Jer. 26:11). We also find passing references to the killing of *multiple prophets*. Jezebel, the wife of Ahab, King of Israel, is said to have been involved in "killing the Lord's prophets" (1 Kings 18:4). This multiple murder is also mentioned by the prophet Elijah who, after running for his life, complained to God:

> The Israelites have forsaken your covenant, thrown down your altars, and *killed your prophets* with the sword. I alone am left, and they are seeking my life, to take it away. (1 Kings 19:9)

There is also a fifth-century BCE reference to the mass murder of prophets, which may be the same as the one mentioned by Elijah, in which several inhabitants of Judah are reported to have complained to God about their Israelite ancestors:

> They were disobedient and rebelled against you and cast your law behind their backs and *killed your prophets*, who had warned them in order to turn them back to you, and they committed great blasphemies. (Neh. 9:26)

The Jews' killing of many prophets is also reported in the New Testament. Paul (1 Thess. 2:15) accuses the Jews of killing "both the Lord Jesus and the prophets". Significantly, this accusation is repeatedly mentioned in a scathing attack by Jesus in a speech to the public (also Luke 11:49, 13:34; Acts 7:52):

> Woe to you, scribes and Pharisees, hypocrites! For you build the tombs of the prophets and decorate the graves of the righteous, and you say, "If we had lived in the days of our ancestors, we would not have taken part with them in *shedding the blood of the prophets.*" Thus you testify against yourselves that you are descendants of those who *murdered the prophets.* Fill up, then, the measure of your ancestors. You snakes, you brood of vipers! How can you escape being sentenced to hell? Therefore I send you prophets, sages, and scribes, *some of whom you will kill and crucify,* and some you will flog in your synagogues and pursue from town to town, so that upon you may come all the righteous blood shed on earth, from the blood of righteous Abel to the blood of Zechariah son of Barachiah, whom you murdered between the sanctuary and the altar. Truly I tell you, all this will come upon this generation. "Jerusalem, Jerusalem, the city that *kills the prophets* and stones those who are sent to it!" (Matt. 23:29-37)

Zechariah son of Barachiah is not Zechariah son of Jehoiada mentioned earlier. He is the one to whom the Old Testament's Book of Zechariah is attributed. This seems to be a misidentification by Matthew, while Luke (11:51) does not name Zechariah's father.[1] The charge against the Jews of killing many prophets is also found in Jewish and Christian writings.[2]

The Qur'an's attribution to Jews at the time of the Prophet Muhammad of something that was committed by other Jews in the past does not mean the inheritability and transferability of guilt. It only accuses the new generation of thinking like their predecessors, highlighting their intention and willingness to follow in the footsteps of their ancestors. This is a device used by the Qur'an repeatedly whose use is not confined to the Jews. This is one example that talks about the disbelievers in general:

> Those who do not know say, "Why does Allah not speak to us or there

---

[1] Kalimi, "Prophet Zechariah".
[2] Reynolds, "Killers of the Prophets".

come to us a sign?" So spoke those before them like their words. Their hearts resemble each other. We have made clear the signs to people who are certain. (2.118)

In another verse, the Qur'an rhetorically asks whether different generations rejected God's messengers because the earlier peoples advised the later ones:

> Similarly, no messenger came to the peoples before them but they said, "A magician or a madman". (52) Have they advised each other about this? Rather, they are a transgressing people. (51.52-53)

After answering its rhetorical question in the negative, the verse goes on to explain that adopting the same attitude and way of thinking led different generations to the same transgression.

The Qur'an also states that the disbelievers tried to kill the Prophet Muhammad:

> As those who disbelieve plan to restrain you, kill you, or evict you. They plan, and Allah plans, and Allah is the best of planners. (8.30)

This verse does not identify the disbelievers as the Jews, but it is certain to include them as the early Muslims were at war with several Jewish tribes in Medina. Early biographies of the Prophet and other Muslim sources state that some Jews tried to assassinate him. One attempt was made by the Banū al-Naḍīr in breach of their peace treaty with the Muslims. This failed attempt made the Muslims attack this Jewish tribe and remove it from its land.[3] This battle and eviction are referred to in the Qur'an (59.2-3). The Banū al-Naḍīr then retaliated by provoking Arab tribes to attack the Muslims. The attackers were joined by the Jewish tribe of Banū Qurayḍa, besieging the Muslims in Medina. This siege, which ultimately failed,[4] and the following fighting, known as "the Battle of the Trench", are mentioned in some detail in a Qur'anic chapter that is accordingly named "the Alliances".

The other accusation against the Jews in verse 4.155 is that they claim that their hearts were "covered". This has been interpreted in two different ways. First, the Jews claimed that their hearts were already full of knowledge, so they did not need the teaching of prophets. Second,

---

[3] Al-Wāqidī, *Al-Maghāzī*, I, 363-383.
[4] Ibid., II, 440-480.

they claimed that their hearts were closed to the prophets' teaching. This interpretation seems to mirror a criticism of the Jews by the Christian Stephen of being "uncircumcised in heart" (Acts 7:51). The concept of the circumcision of the heart is also found in the Old Testament (Jer. 9:26) and Paul's writings (Rom. 2:29). I agree with the first interpretation for two reasons. The Qur'an uses different terminology for the state of the heart described in the second interpretation, calling it "sealed" (*khatama*) (e.g. 2.7, 45.23). Also, it does not sound reasonable to say that the Jews would have confessed to an irrational rejection as their defence!

Verse 4.156 moves us from the Jews' transgression against unnamed prophets to their specific rejection of and hostility towards Jesus, as well as his mother. Given that they rejected his claim that he was sent by God, let alone that he was the awaited Messiah, it is no surprise that they did not believe in Mary's virginal conception. This major miracle is confirmed by the Qur'an in more than one place (3.42-47; 19.16-22). The Jews accused Mary of becoming pregnant with Jesus illegitimately. We have already discussed such accusations in rabbinic writings and their refutations by early Christian writers (§12).

We now come to the main verse of interest, 4.157. It starts by adding the Jews' boast that they killed Jesus to the sinful acts listed in the previous verses. The description "the messenger of Allah" has been attributed by some exegetes to God and by others to the Jews. In the former case, it would be a confirmation of Jesus' status by God. If, instead, it is a part of the Jews' claim, which is how I read it, it is a sarcastic ridiculing of Jesus' claim to having been sent by God. I am inclined to this reading because it is aligned with the fact that the title "Messiah" is used by the Jews derisorily in their claim. The Jews' use of the title "Messiah" sarcastically contrasts their perception that they killed Jesus with their longstanding belief that the awaited Messiah was going to be an invincible and victorious military leader, thus deriding Jesus' claim to messiahship. Also, it seems a more natural reading of the text to consider God's response to the Jewish claim to be starting with His refutative retort that "they did not kill him, nor did they crucify him".

Condemning the Jews for "saying" (*qawlihim*) that they killed Jesus is preceded by two other claims they made that are described using this very term. The first claim is that their hearts are covered and the second is of their slander against Mary, both of which the Qur'an clearly rejects as false. There is no justification, then, to suggest that the third condemned "saying", which is killing Jesus, is anything other than a false claim too.

Also, in verse 155, the Qur'an condemns the Jews for "killing" prophets, yet in the case of Jesus, the Jews are denounced for "saying" that they killed him. Had they truly killed him, the condemnation would also have been of the "killing", not of bragging of the killing. This can only indicate the falsehood of their claim.

It is difficult to see how the verse could have been clearer in rejecting that the Jews killed Jesus, in particular when it goes on to equally emphatically deny that they crucified him. By following its denial of the killing with *specifically* rejecting that he was crucified, the Qur'an dismisses any claim that Jesus suffered a nonfatal crucifixion. This is one scenario that has been suggested by some as an alternative to the Gospels' narrative (§14.1). Verse 4.157 is unambiguous that Jesus was not killed or even nonfatally crucified.

When boasting that they killed Jesus, the Jews did not lie but *mistakenly thought* that they killed him. This is clarified when their claim is contrasted, using the word "but" (*lākin*), with the corrective statement "it was made to appear so to them". This indicates that there was some grounds for the Jews' misguided belief that they crucified Jesus. As we will discuss later, they did indeed try to kill him, but they ended up killing someone else by mistake.

The *appearance* statement, in particular, has caused most of the disagreement among Muslim exegetes on 4.157, even though they all agree that the verse rejects the historicity of the crucifixion. It is also at the centre of the disagreement between Muslims and other scholars who share their consensus, on the one hand, and scholars who suggest that the Qur'an does not deny the crucifixion, on the other. Some Western scholars have used an incorrect interpretation of this statement to reject what the earlier part of the verse emphatically says, that Jesus was not killed, even though the meaning of the first part is completely independent of how its explanation, "it was made to appear so to them", may be interpreted. We will revisit this subject later (§22.2).

The verse goes on to say, "Those who differ over it are in doubt about it". The subject of this difference is the clarification just mentioned in the verse, i.e. that Jesus was not killed or crucified but that the claimants wrongly thought so. The verse concludes by emphasising that the Jews' claim is not based on real knowledge and certainty. Denying they were certain about Jesus' death indicates that they did not do all that could be done to ascertain that they did indeed kill him. They tried to kill him but they failed; their claim to the contrary was not based on sufficient evidence.

As 4.157 is the only verse that directly addresses the claim that Jesus was crucified, let's further study its natural reading. Breaking it up into its constituent statements shows that it explicitly and unambiguously denies the historicity of this event:

i.   The Jews' claim is stated: "We have killed the Messiah, Jesus, the son of Mary, the messenger of Allah".

ii.   The claim is unambiguously denied: "They did not kill him, nor did they crucify him".

iii. The Jews' confusion is explained: "But it was made to appear so to them".

iv.   Those who say otherwise are not certain about their claim: "Those who differ over it are in doubt about it".

v.   Their claim is not based on evidence but guessing and speculation: "They have no knowledge of it except the following of conjecture".

vi.   The verse concludes with another firm confirmation that the claim is false and is not based on certainty: "They did not kill him with certainty". (4.157)

Statements i, ii, and iii have this general structure, respectively: *they claim they did X; they did neither X nor Y; but it appeared to them that they did*. This simple breakdown of the structure of the first half of the verse shows that it could not have been any clearer in denying the substance of the Jewish claim. If these three *negations* of the claim that the Jews killed or crucified Jesus are somehow read as *confirmation* of his crucifixion, as some Western scholars do (§20), then there is hardly any verse in the Qur'an that cannot be claimed to mean the exact opposite of what it appears to say! Such disregard for the basics of language would make the Qur'an unintelligible. I cannot recall any other Qur'anic verse that has been subjected to such astonishing misreading.

Finally, I would like to add a note about the Arabic word root *ṣlb*, which I have translated as "crucify". This word appears in the Qur'an in a verbal form six times (4.157; 5.33; 7.124; 12.41; 20.71; 26.49) and in a noun form twice (4.23; 86.7). In one instance, Pharaoh makes this threat to the magicians who accepted Moses' claim to being God's messenger:

> I will surely cut off your hands and your feet on opposite sides, and I will crucify you (*uṣallibannakum*) on the trunks of palm trees. (20.71)

This use may indicate that *ṣlb* means some kind of execution by suspension. As I have already pointed out (§5.5), there is some debate about how Jesus was allegedly crucified, whether he was nailed to a cross—and what shape it had—or was suspended until he died. By the time of the Qur'an, the classical interpretation of the crucifixion of Jesus using a T-shaped cross or a variation of it was already long established. The Qur'an rejects the historicity of the crucifixion anyway, so a discussion of the exact form that this unhistorical *ṣlb* took is meaningless.

Having stressed that Jesus was not killed or crucified, the Qur'an goes on in verse 4.158 to explain what happened to him: "Allah raised him to Himself". Using the word "rather" (*bal*) to describe God's raising of Jesus as a corrective fact to the Jews' misconception that they killed him is another confirmation of the failure of their attempt on Jesus' life. The word "but" is used in 4.157 to contrast the fact that the Jews did not kill Jesus with their contrary claim, and "rather" is used in 4.158 to contrast God's raising of Jesus with the Jews' uncertain claim to killing him. The verse's use of "invincible" to describe God is another confirmation that His will to rescue Jesus prevailed over the scheming of those who wanted to crucify him. We will discuss verse 4.158 in more detail later in the book.

19.2 The Consensus of Muslim Exegetes

Like scholars of other scriptures, Muslim exegetes are not particularly renowned for easily agreeing when interpreting their sacred text. Some of this disagreement is because a Qur'anic text can genuinely accommodate different interpretations, which may be intended anyway. But even when the text looks to be unambiguous and naturally and spontaneously suggestive of one specific reading, it is not uncommon to find multiple interpretations on offer. This phenomenon can be easily witnessed in any meta exegetical work that compiles the opinions of various scholars, such as Ṭabarī's (310/922), which is the earliest such work. Ṭabarī's tome is particularly significant because it is the closest historically to the first generations of Muslim exegetes.

I need to stress that I do not advocate that the popularity of an interpretation means that it is correct, accurate, or even more plausible than alternatives. But in the absence of an alternative explanation, a rare consensus of exegetes must be considered indicative of the *absolute clarity* of the text and, accordingly, the accuracy of the agreed interpretation. This is more so when surrounding and related verses do not show the same unanimity in interpretation. This is the case with the Qur'anic statement on the crucifixion. More specifically, the consensus on the interpretation of 4.157 immediately breaks down in the following and related verse, 4.158.

The earliest exegetes of the Qur'an disagreed on why the Jews wrongly thought that they killed Jesus, how he escaped the crucifixion, and what exactly happened to him afterwards. Yet virtually all early exegetes agreed that the Qur'an denies that Jesus was crucified.[5] This is confirmed by Ṭabarī, who cites several authorities from the first century and a half after the revelation of the Qur'an. These include the Companion 'Abd Allāh Ibn 'Abbās (68/687); the Successors Mujāhid Ibn Jabr al-Makkī (104/722), al-Qāsim Ibn Abī Bazza (114/732), Wahb Ibn Munabbih (114/732), Qatāda Ibn Di'āma (117/735), and Ismā'īl al-Suddī (127/744); and 'Abd al-Malik Ibn Jurayj (149/767) and Ibn Isḥāq (151/768).

Over the centuries, exegetes from various schools of thought continued to uphold the view that the Qur'an categorically denies that Jesus was crucified. They include Sunnis, such as Ṭabarī, Māwardī (450/1058), Qurṭubī (671/1273), Bayḍāwī (685/1292), and Sayyid Quṭb (1386/1966); Shias, such as Ṭūsī (460/1068), Ṭabresī (548/1154), and Ṭabāṭabā'ī (1402/1981); Mu'tazilīs, such as 'Abd al-Jabbār Ibn Aḥmad (415/1024) and Zamakhsharī (538/1143); and Sufis, such as Qushayrī (465/1072) and Najm al-Dīn Kubrā (736/1335). Muslim exegetes have almost unanimously understood the Qur'an as rejecting the historicity of the crucifixion of Jesus.

Even the small minority of scholars who argue that Jesus died on the earth rather than in heaven after being raised, such as Ibn Ḥazm al-

---

[5] Robinson, *Christ in Islam and Christianity*, 140.

Andalusī (456/1064),[6] confirm that he was not crucified. Prominent twentieth-century scholars who share this view include Muḥammad ʿAbduh (1905), his student Muḥammad Rashīd Riḍa (1935), Muṣṭafā al-Marāghī (1945), Muḥammad Shaltūt (1963), Muḥammad Ibn ʿĀshūr (1973), Muḥammad Abū Zahra (1974), and Muḥammad al-Ghazālī (1996).[7]

It is significant that this unanimity appeared and continued among exegetes who were perfectly familiar with the contradictory Christian view. They were well aware that written and oral Christian tradition uncompromisingly confirmed the crucifixion of Jesus. It is not, either, that Muslim scholars were not in the habit of incorporating Christian, and for that matter Jewish, tradition into their exegeses; they did that. Yet they never borrowed its most fundamental claim that Jesus was put to death on the cross. Furthermore, accepting that Jesus was killed would not necessarily have entailed accepting the theology of the cross, which the Qur'an rejects. After all, Muslims knew that the death or killing of prophets never produced any suffering and redemption theology. Again, we have to conclude that they must have seen the Qur'an as so unequivocal that not a single one of them entertained the alternative scenario as a possible interpretation of the text.

An exception to this unanimity seems to have first appeared as late as the fourth century of Islam and was promoted by Ismāʿīlī scholars. Ismāʿīlism is a Shia branch that considers Imam Jaʿfar al-Ṣādiq's (148/765) second son, Ismāʿīl, his father's successor. As Ismāʿīl died before his father, some Ismāʿīlīs consider his son, Muḥammad, as the seventh and last Imam instead. The number seven is an essential cornerstone of their typology, which is why they are also known as the "Seveners". In contrast, the largest branch of Shiism considers Mūsā al-Kāẓim, another son of Ṣādiq, as his successor and the seventh Imam. They also accept five other Imams after him, the last of whom is Muḥammad son of Imam Ḥasan al-ʿAskarī, hence their name the "Twelvers". The Twelvers and Ismāʿīlīs both believe that their last Imam went into occultation and will come back at the end times.

Ismāʿīlī scholars have practised esoteric forms of "taʾwīl"

[6] Ibn Ḥazm al-Andalusī *Al-Muḥallā*, I, 43.
[7] Shalabī, *Al-Masīḥiyya*, 64-67.

(interpretation) of the Qur'an and Islamic tradition and developed a mystical understanding of history. Their hermeneutical methods include attributing spiritual properties to letters and the use of numerology, which they borrowed from other cultures. Early Ismā'īlīs saw history as consisting of seven phases in which they incorporated Judaism, Christianity, and other pre-Islamic religions, such as Zoroastrianism. The last phase is ushered by the return of the eschatological figure of the hidden Imam. The "Mahdī", as this figure is known to most Muslims, or "Qā'im",[8] as Ismā'īlīs prefer to call him, plays a central role in Shia theology. Given that Islamic tradition, albeit extra-Qur'anic, claims that Jesus will return at the end times when the Qā'im emerges, Jesus is given a special role in the unfolding events. This special role seems to be the door through which his crucifixion was admitted into Ismā'īlī thought.[9]

The earliest of the rare Muslim scholars who claimed that the Qur'an confirms the crucifixion of Jesus seems to be Abū Ḥātim al-Rāzī (322/933). This Ismā'īlī scholar wrote a polemical book that contains his refutations of various atheistic claims by the famous philosopher and physician Abū Bakr Ibn Zakariyyā al-Rāzī. The two met and debated many times. One broad argument by Abū Bakr against the veracity of religion is the many differences between the various religions. Abū Ḥātim dedicated a whole chapter to disproving forms of this argument that use various facts, such as the Qur'an's rejection of the claim of the Jews and Christians that Jesus was crucified. He refers to the claim of unnamed scholars that Jesus died in the body but was alive in the spirit, offering a reconciliatory explanation.[10]

It is important to note that Abū Ḥātim's work is not exegetical and does not engage with the Qur'anic text in any depth. His objective is not to analyse what the Qur'an says independently of any external influences. His interpretation is openly motivated by his focus on winning the argument against his rival, which, in this case, meant claiming that the Qur'an can be read to accommodate the crucifixion of Jesus. He wanted

---

[8] "Mahdī" means "guided one", implying being guided to the truth, and "Qā'im" means "establisher", indicating the one who establishes God's will. These titles have been given other meanings.

[9] Daftari, Al-Ismā'īliyyūn.

[10] Al-Rāzī, A'lām Al-Nubuwwa, 168-170.

to show that there was no contradiction between the Qur'an and the New Testament.

Significantly, in another work, *Kitāb al-Iṣlāḥ*, Abū Ḥātim adopts the unanimous interpretation that the Qur'an rejects the historicity of the crucifixion of Jesus.[11] This work is an interpretation of Qur'anic verses, which further confirms that upholding the crucifixion in his other work was polemical. It is a position that he didn't need and, more relevant to the point here, couldn't take when interpreting the Qur'an. Even the esoteric nature of his commentary did not make Abū Ḥātim claim that Jesus was crucified.

Abū Yaʿqūb al-Sijistānī (331/942), a contemporary of Abū Ḥātim, also upheld the historicity of Jesus' crucifixion. He talked about it in a book that elaborates on his esoteric philosophy. Sijistānī's only concern is to interpret the crucifixion of Jesus and the symbol of the cross in terms of his understanding of the roles of the Imams and the Qāʾim. Neither the Qur'an nor any other Islamic tradition is quoted, let alone discussed, when Sijistānī presents his theory.[12]

Half a century after Abū Ḥātim and Sijistānī, another Ismāʿīlī author called Jaʿfar Ibn Mansūr al-Yaman (380/990) advocated the Gospels' claim that Jesus was crucified. In this work, which is biographies of prophets, Jesus' life is mainly based on the Gospel accounts. This book does not concern itself with what the Qur'an says on the crucifixion, so no verse is quoted or discussed.[13] Jaʿfar Ibn Mansūr's view is indisputably based on the Gospels and possibly other Christian traditions.

Another relatively early instance of this view comes from the Brethren of Purity (Ikhwān al-Ṣafāʾ). This group, which was formed in the fourth century AH (tenth century CE), combined Greek philosophy with Islamic thought and is believed to have had close links to Ismāʿīlism. The Brethren of Purity considered all religions authentic. One of their fifty-two epistles talks about Jesus and reveals their view that his human body was crucified. They consider this a confirmation of the immortality of the soul. Like the Ismāʿīlī works we have reviewed, the writings of the Brethren of Purity are not interpretations of the Qur'an. They simply

---

[11] Al-Rāzī, *Al-Iṣlāḥ*, 243-246.

[12] Al-Sijistānī, *Al-Yanābīʿ*, 146-149.

[13] Ibn Mansūr al-Yaman, *Asrār Al-Nuṭaqāʾ*, 223-225.

give an account of Jesus' life with no reference to any Islamic tradition, Qur'anic or otherwise.[14]

Understandably and unsurprisingly, these few esoteric Ismāʿīlī works have not had any impact on the exegetes of the Qur'an. Their acceptance of the historicity of the crucifixion of Jesus is driven by the need of their Qāʾim-based doctrine and they reflect clear influence by esoteric philosophies. Most importantly, these works are not exegetical. To be sure, they do not pretend that their belief in the historicity of Jesus' crucifixion is an interpretation of what the Qur'an says. They do not relate it to Prophetic ḥadīths either. As acknowledged by Todd Lawson in his book *The Crucifixion and the Qur'an*, these Ismāʿīlī authors used the alleged crucifixion as "a way of propagating their own typologically iterative view of salvation and eschatology". Having reviewed classical and well-known exegeses from different eras and confirmed their uniformity in rejecting the historicity of Jesus' crucifixion, Lawson goes on to express his surprise and disappointment that the Ismāʿīlī view has not had any influence on Islamic exegetes, including those of the Shia persuasion, as he accepts the historicity of the crucifixion.[15] Contrary to Lawson's sentiments, it would have been completely inexplicable if such a blatantly doctrinal and plainly un-Qur'anic view was seriously considered by any exegete worth his title. Unfortunately, Lawson's book, which claims to study the development of the interpretation of the crucifixion in Islamic scholarship, fails to inform its reader of the significance of the consensus of Muslim scholars over the centuries while it overstates the weight of the few dissident voices. The overall picture that Lawson's book paints is misleading but it has been accepted by some scholars.[16]

In the second half of the nineteenth century, the Indian Muslim scholar Sayyid Ahmad Khan suggested that Jesus was indeed crucified but did not die on the cross. He treated the Qur'an's denial that Jesus was crucified to mean that it did not lead to his death. This is far more of an attempt to read a prior idea into the text than read an interpretation from

---

[14] Ikhwān al-Ṣafāʾ, *Rasāʾil*, IV, 28-32.

[15] Lawson, *The Crucifixion and the Qur'an*, 94-95.

[16] Mevorach, "Qur'an, Crucifixion, and Talmud"; Reynolds, "The Muslim Jesus"; Reynolds, "Introduction", 10.

it.

Sayyid Ahmad Khan was probably familiar with the non-fatal crucifixion theory, which first appeared in Europe late in the eighteenth century. This is what he had to say:

> Crucifixion itself does not cause the death of a man, because only the palms of his hands, or the palms of his hands and feet are pierced. The real cause of death is that when someone is hanged on the cross for four or five days, he dies because of the pains of the pierced hands and feet, combined with the endured hunger, thirst and exertion... When we bring the whole event into historical connection, it is clear that Christ did not die on the cross, but something happened there which caused people to believe that he died... After three or four hours Christ was taken down from the cross, and it is certain that at that moment he was still alive. Then the disciples concealed him in a very secret place, out of fear of the enmity of the Jews... and they spread the rumour that Christ ascended to heaven.[17]

Sayyid Ahmad Khan adopted a strict *rationalistic* approach to reading scriptures. He also interpreted the virginal conception and Jesus' miracles as natural events that did not involve any supernatural elements. He followed this approach in his exegesis of the Qur'an, *Tafsīr al-Qur'an*. In an earlier work, which is an Islamic reading of the Old and New Testaments that does not accuse them of textual corruption, he had accepted the virginal conception.[18] Sayyid Ahmad Khan accused Muslim exegetes of being influenced by Christian beliefs. His uncompromising naturalistic interpretation of scriptures that vividly describe miracles and the world of the unseen was never going to convince many.

One person that seems to have been influenced by Sayyid Ahmad Khan is his contemporary Mirza Ghulam Ahmad, the founder of the Ahmadiyya movement, which is also known as "Qādyāniyya", after the town of "Qādyān", Punjab, in which Ahmad was born. He first held the standard Muslim belief about Jesus but he changed his view in 1891 claiming that God informed him that Jesus had died.[19] Ahmad, who also claimed to be the Messiah and the Mahdī, further developed Sayyid Ahmad Khan's theory. He argues that an earthquake kept the Jews busy

---

[17] Baljon, *The Reforms*, 107–108.

[18] Rahman, "Interpretation", 27.

[19] Dard, *Life of Ahmad*, 50.

with their safety so they presumed that Jesus died on the cross without having the opportunity to confirm it.[20] Jesus survived this ordeal, received medical treatment, and went on to live in Kashmir, India, where he died and was buried. Ahmad quotes the Qur'an but his focus is on developing his peculiar story of Jesus' crucifixion and travel to India. This form of hagiography cannot be treated as exegesis. Ahmad's interpretation does not have support beyond his followers. It is worth noting that most Muslims consider Ahmadiyya to have contravened Islamic beliefs too fundamental for this movement to still represent Islam.

In summary, the consensus of Muslim exegetes over the centuries that the Qur'an denies the crucifixion of Jesus confirms the unequivocalness of its statement. Creedal differences, pluralism of interpretation, ingenuity, critical thinking, and breaking with tradition did not lead scholars to understand the Qur'an as doing anything other than denying that Jesus was killed or crucified. This unanimous understanding is not an interpretation that relies on historical, theological, or any other specific extra-Qur'anic information. It is simply a reading that calls on the ability of the exegete to understand plain Arabic. The relatively new phenomenon of a minority of Muslim scholars joining others in reading Jesus' crucifixion into the Qur'an can only be the result of an a priori belief in the historicity of the alleged event. This is what we will discuss next.

---

[20] Ahmad, *Jesus in India*, 57-58.

Reading the Crucifixion into the Qur'an

Like their Muslim counterparts, most non-Muslim scholars agree that the Qur'an is clear in rejecting the historicity of the crucifixion of Jesus. But an increasing number of scholars have been challenging this consensus, arguing that it is an incorrect interpretation of the text. The denial of the crucifixion, they claim, is a product of the process of interpretation, not something that is intrinsic to the text.[1] They have also been joined by some Muslim thinkers, but their number remains tiny, contrary to the suggestion of some.[2] Some argue that the Qur'an is agnostic on the historicity of Jesus' crucifixion while others go as far as suggesting that it confirms the crucifixion.

In this chapter, we will explore what drives this alternative reading of the Qur'anic text and its hermeneutical methods.

20.1 The Need to Deny the Denial

Two different goals can be seen driving the claim that the Qur'an does not deny Jesus' crucifixion. The first is specific to Muslims while the second is shared by Muslims and non-Muslims. Both objectives are present, albeit the second more indirectly than the first, in the below quote from Mahmoud Ayoub, a Lebanese-American professor of religious studies. Ayoub is often cited as proof of the emerging trend among Muslim scholars to not read the Qur'an as denying the crucifixion (italics are mine):

> Why then, it must be asked, does the Qur'an deny the crucifixion of Christ in the face of apparently overwhelming evidence? *Muslim commentators have not been able convincingly to disprove the crucifixion.* Rather, they have compounded the problem by adding the conclusion of their

---

[1] Lawson, *The Crucifixion and the Qur'an*, 19.
[2] Mevorach, "Qur'an, Crucifixion, and Talmud", 9.

substitutionist theories. The problem has been, we believe, one of understanding. Commentators have generally taken the verse to be a historical statement. This statement, like *all the other statements concerning Jesus in the Qur'an, belongs not to history but to theology in the broadest sense.*[3]

The **first** goal is to defend the inerrability of the Qur'an. Some Muslim attempts are driven by the belief that the crucifixion of Jesus and his consequent death are historical facts. The view that the Qur'an denies the crucifixion would mean that it makes a historically false claim. This reading of the Qur'an would not "answer convincingly the charge of history".[4] This, in turn, would mean that it cannot be the Word of God, the Omniscient. The suggestion that the Qur'an confirms, or at least does not deny, the historicity of Jesus' death on the cross aims to protect its credibility and status as divine revelation.

Ayoub does not only accuse all Muslim scholars over the centuries of misinterpreting the wording of verse 4.157. He argues that their understanding is misguided at an even more fundamental level because, contrary to what exegetes have always thought, the Qur'an does not talk history but theology. This is the standard view of non-Muslim scholars who deny the Qur'an's denial of the crucifixion.[5] Ayoub further generalises this unsubstantiated claim to cover all that the Qur'an says about Jesus. There is no justification, either, for restricting this generalisation to Jesus' story. It must be equally applicable to all Qur'anic stories of past prophets, such as Moses, Abraham, and Joseph. This inescapable conclusion is, in my view, manifestly absurd.

The "overwhelming evidence" and Muslims' failure to "disprove the crucifixion" that Ayoub is referring to can only mean his acceptance that Jesus' crucifixion is a historical fact. So, he accepts that the Gospels talk history, at least on this matter. Yet he denies the Qur'an the same treatment, presumably to protect it. Ayoub implies that the Gospels' crucifixion-based theology, which he presumably does not endorse, is based on history, but he leaves the Qur'an's theology as self-referential and with no basis in history. This is no protection of the credibility of the Qur'an.

---

[3] Ayoub, *A Muslim View of Christianity*, 176.
[4] Ibid., 156.
[5] Fry, "The Quranic Christ", 216.

This conflation of history and theology and switching between them conveniently is all too common in studies that claim that the Qur'an does not deny Jesus' crucifixion, as we shall see more in the next section. It can easily lead to contradictory or nonsensical conclusions. For instance, Ayoub's acceptance of the historicity of Jesus' crucifixion and treatment of the Qur'anic statement as theological is guided by his acknowledgement and appreciation of the centrality of the crucifixion in Christianity. Yet if Ayoub is to be consistent in consulting history about this claim, it would tell him that the concept of a suffering Messiah does not exist in the Old Testament, was never part of the Jewish faith, is contrary to the centuries-old Jewish concept of the Messiah, and appeared only with Christianity! What should be done now about this irreconcilable conflict between history and the suffering Messiah of the New Testament? If protecting the theology of the cross is the main goal, the suffering Messiah should somehow be read into history. Alternatively, if history is the main concern, which is presumably behind Ayoub's reading of verse 4.157, then the theology of the suffering Messiah has to go, which is the Qur'an's position.

This takes me to the **second** goal of rejecting the Qur'an's denial of the crucifixion, which is to seek better reconciliation between Islam and Christianity. Ayoub says that the aim of his study that asserts the death of Jesus on the cross is to "promote constructive and meaningful dialogue among the men and women of faith in the two communities".[6] Here is a clearer description of this objective by a Christian theologian:

> Q 4:157-58 has become an important exegetical site for repairing the broken relationship between Christianity and Islam. Typically, authors with this goal have hoped to shift attention away from the Qur'an's supposed denial of the crucifixion in Q 4:157 and instead attempt to find common ground in its affirmation in Q 4:158 that God raised Jesus to Godself. Christian scholars, hoping to present the Qur'an in a more positive light to Christian readers, have labored to prove that these verses need not be interpreted as a denial of the crucifixion.[7]

In their enthusiastic pursuit of this commendable objective, scholars have jumped at anything that may look like it leads to this goal or has the

---

[6] Ayoub, *A Muslim View of Christianity*, 157.
[7] Mevorach, "Qur'an, Crucifixion, and Talmud", 2.

potential to do so. One telling example is their immense interest in a critically acclaimed 1954 Arabic novel, *Qarya Ẓālima*, whose theme is the crucifixion of Jesus. Its author, a Muslim thinker called Muhammad Kamel Hussein, is at most agnostic as to the identity of the crucified,[8] and the novel is philosophical rather than historical or exegetical, yet it is often hailed as an example of a change in the way Muslims read what the Qur'an says about the crucifixion. Ayoub, astonishingly, called Hussein "perhaps the first Muslim attempt to see the cross in its true meaning",[9] the Methodist minister and academic Geoffrey Parrinder described the author as "one of the most outstanding modern writers",[10] and the Anglican bishop and prolific writer Kenneth Cragg translated it into English.[11] Another Christian theologian described the novel as "notable among works of modern Muslim scholarship in transcending the polemics between Muslims and Christians over the historicity of the crucifixion".[12] This quote, like Ayoub's, shows once again the fundamental problem of conflating theology and history, as its praise of the novel's transcendence of history occurs in a paper that presumes the historicity of crucifixion!

The main obvious problem with conflating history and theology is that history is universal and objective whereas theology is confined and subjective. At best, theology is an interpretation of history; in the extreme, it is self-referential. By definition, an interpretation does not inherit the objective authority of its source. By conveniently switching between history and theology, arguments become fundamentally flawed and communication, understanding, and accommodation become all but impossible.

Whether Jesus was crucified is not an inconsequential question of history. To deny the crucifixion is to challenge the legitimacy of Christian theology, which is based on and held together by the suffering Messiah.[13] Yet the Qur'an is explicit in rejecting the Christian theology

---

[8] Majlī, *Muhammad Kamel Hussein*, 227.
[9] Ayoub, *A Muslim View of Christianity*, 175.
[10] Parrinder, *Jesus in the Qur'an*, 112.
[11] Hussein, *City of Wrong*.
[12] Mevorach, "Qur'an, Crucifixion, and Talmud", 12.
[13] E.g. Fonner, "Jesus' Death", 447-448.

of redemption and, more generally, the idea of one person bearing or inheriting the sin of another. This makes denying the Qur'an's denial of the crucifixion futile unless denying the Qur'an's rejection of redemption theology is its next target.

Yet we know that the Messiah's crucifixion was never accepted by the Jews as well, even though rabbinic sources state that they killed Jesus as they rejected his messiahship. A couple of decades after Jesus' death, Paul (1 Cor. 1:23) wrote that the *crucified Christ* is a "stumbling block to Jews" and "foolishness to Gentiles". Was this 2000-year-old issue ever resolved? Despite its significant theological differences with Christianity, Islam always viewed Jesus far more favourably than Judaism did, as the former confirms his messiahship while the latter considers him a false claimant and teacher.

Positing the crucifixion as the core issue in Christian-Muslim rapprochement is a highly suspect view. Which outlook causes the most difficulty for the believers of these two great religions: Islam's portrayal of Jesus as a noble nondivine prophet whom God spared humiliating death by crucifixion or the dominant image among Christians of Muḥammad as a career fraudster? Giving the crucifixion priority over and more significance than more serious issues is false rapprochement and interfaith dialogue but genuine service to Christian theology. This is how Rabbi Walter Homolka, professor of Jewish theology, has succinctly described the fundamental problem in this approach by Christian scholars towards both Judaism and Islam:

> One of the great achievements of the Enlightenment was creating a basis on which religions could live side by side. Sadly, it was for the most part only Jewish academics who consistently championed this new paradigm in nineteenth-century Germany. The problems faced by Jewish academics and intellectuals in the nineteenth century are, *mutatis mutandis*, comparable to the problems many Muslims are currently experiencing in the West—and this despite the West's insistence on its Christian-but-secular, pluralist, and tolerant traditions. The problems that Muslims and Islam are now facing show how little the Christian mainstream has actually learned from its century-old struggle with Judaism. All too often, secular politicians and systems also follow this Christian attitude. Christianity, therefore, needs to relativize its absolutist claims if there is to be true Christian-Jewish or Christian-Muslim dialogue and a West that is de facto, and not simply de

jure, pluralist.[14]

Finally, while efforts to bring different faiths closer are commendable, these studies greatly overplay the impact of the Qur'an's denial of the crucifixion on the Christian-Muslim relationship. This exaggeration shows, in my view, a gap between professional theologians and historians working in their institutional settings and the average Muslim and Christian in the wider world. We must not forget that the Qur'an not only reveres Jesus but also portrays him as a very special prophet. It is in the mundane politics of the everyday world, not in spiritual concerns and theological differences, that interfaith relations are broken and opportunities to mend them are found. Even when religious piety is openly claimed as the motive for conflict, it is almost always a cover for ulterior motives. I wish that faith drove people's behaviour to the extent that reconciling theological differences would result in mending relationships in this non-spiritual world, but that is not the case. Let's not credit religion with a bigger role than it actually has. This exaggerated influence is the bedrock of the anti-religion propaganda of many atheist activists.

20.2 The Denial Interpreted as Confirmation

We will now see how denying the Qur'an's denial of Jesus' crucifixion is not the result of exegetical efforts that brought new insights to the reading and interpretation of the text. It is, rather, essentially a theological exercise. We will also see that every form of this interpretation is fundamentally flawed.

The Qur'an is clear that Jesus was mortal. Jesus' death, which we will discuss in detail later (§23), has been claimed to refer to the crucifixion. There are serious objections to this claim. **First**, putting aside highly creative and convoluted interpretations, which we will discuss in this section, the Qur'anic text can only mean that Jesus did not die by crucifixion. **Second**, there is no link whatsoever in the Qur'an between Jesus' death and the crucifixion.

Third, the Qur'an mentions that God raised Jesus to Himself (4.158) as a counterclaim to the Jews' claim that they killed him, which means that he did not die on the earth. Indeed, the overwhelming majority of

---

[14] Homolka, *Jewish Jesus Research*, 113.

Muslim scholars think that Jesus continues to live somewhere in heaven and will die after he descends to the earth again at the end times and finishes his work. This exegetical delay to Jesus' death is the result of the eschatological role he will allegedly play. In his commentary on 3.55, Ṭabarī attributes to Wahb Ibn Munabbih the claim that God made Jesus die for three hours and then raised him. Even this death is not linked to the crucifixion. He also attributes to Ibn Isḥāq the claim that Christians believe that he died for seven hours and was then brought back to life.

Some modern Muslim scholars think that Jesus died on the earth after a life of normal length. They still do not link his death to the crucifixion. We will review the different opinions on the death and raising of Jesus later (§23-25).

Western scholars often claim that verse 4.157 is not a statement about the *historicity* of the crucifixion of Jesus.[15] This is a misunderstanding of the Qur'an, it is suggested, that Muslims have failed to correct for fourteen centuries.[16] Noting that verse 4.156 criticises the Jews for making a false calumnious accusation against Mary, scholars have proposed that 4.157 does not deny that Jesus *was killed* but rejects the *Jews' claim to the responsibility* for his death. This interpretation discards what the Qur'an *explicitly* states in favour of the claim that it *implicitly* says the opposite!

We have already discussed the unambiguity of 4.157 in rejecting the crucifixion of Jesus and we have supported it with several observations. I would like to briefly mention one of them here. Two verses before 4.157, the Qur'an condemns the Jews for the *actual* "killing of the prophets unjustly". It makes no sense to suggest that the case of Jesus, if the Jews had indeed killed him, was for an unknown reason an exception, so the Qur'an's denouncement is targeted at the falsehood of the Jews' claim for responsibility! The subject of condemnation is the *attempt to kill Jesus*, even though God foiled it. Nevertheless, let's examine the various forms of the alternative interpretation that the Qur'an does not deny the crucifixion.

The Qur'an's rejection of the Jews' claims about Mary and Jesus has been claimed to be a response to the Bavli. We have already reviewed

---

[15] Lawson, *The Crucifixion and the Qur'an*, 27.
[16] Mourad, "The Death of Jesus in Islam", 380.

Talmudic derogatory texts about the two most sacred figures of Christianity (§12). The ultimate goal of this approach, which is not short of adopters,[17] is to show that 4.157 is a counterargument to the Jewish claim of responsibility, not to the belief that Jesus was crucified.[18] It has even been suggested that "the sequence of events in Jesus' execution in the Talmud, first stoning and then hanging, can be read as corresponding to the Qur'an's double-denial that the Jews 'did not kill him, nor did they crucify him'".[19] In his enthusiasm to link 4.157 to b. Sanhedrin 43a, this scholar ignores the fact that "stoning" is mentioned several times in the Qur'an (e.g. 11.91), yet in the case of Jesus it talks about killing, not stoning. Why would the Qur'an not use the Talmud's exact descriptions, if that is what it meant to say? Furthermore, the Qur'an does not refer to any of the other details in that Talmudic passage. The only alleged link between the Qur'an and the Talmud's passage is not a link at all. Finally, it is more natural to read the Qur'anic text as a *general* confirmation that Jesus was not killed followed by the *specific* denial of his crucifixion.

Treating Qur'anic verses on Judaism and Christianity as largely borrowed and adapted from Jewish and Christian sources by the Prophet Muhammad has dominated Western studies of the Qur'an.[20] The Prophet Muhammad is said to have been very familiar with Jewish and Christian writings and beliefs, yet he is also criticised for his inexplicable ignorance and misunderstanding of basic information. To use the above example, both Christian and rabbinic writings insist that the Jews were responsible for the crucifixion of Jesus. Yet the Prophet Muhammad is said to have inexplicably decided to exonerate the Jews! Why he would have this verse almost immediately after another accusing the Jews of the killing of prophets is also left unaddressed. Even when the Qur'anic text fundamentally disagrees with Jewish and Christian sources, the foundational assumption that Qur'anic verses are effectively derivative texts, or at least influenced by them, is still as eagerly applied, albeit this time to dismiss the originality of the Qur'an.

Having denied that 4.157 denies the historicity of Jesus' crucifixion,

---

[17] Leirvik, *Images of Jesus Christ in Islam*, 36.

[18] Leirvik, "Jesus in Modern Muslim Thought", 141.

[19] Mevorach, "Qur'an, Crucifixion, and Talmud", 12.

[20] Pregill, "The Hebrew Bible and the Quran".

scholars move on to find theological meanings for its supposed rejection of the Jews' claim to being Jesus' executioners. One popular view is that 4.157 denies the ability of man, represented by the Jews, to defeat the will of God, represented by his agent Jesus, even though the latter is said to have been killed.[21] Another flavour of this view is that the verse confirms that it is God who gives life and death, so had He not permitted the killing of Jesus, it would not have happened.[22] These are further examples of reading a simple historical statement through the spectacles of theology.

Confirmation of this misreading is also made by likening verse 4.157 to the following verse:[23]

> You [O you who have believed] did not kill them, but it was Allah who killed them. You [O Muhammad] did not throw when you threw, but it was Allah who threw that He might test the believers with a good test. Indeed, Allah is hearing and knowing. (8.17)

This verse is thought to explain a particular incident in Badr, the first major battle of the Muslims. The verse reminds the believers, including the Prophet, that it was God's power that truly defeated their enemies. This reminder is particularly relevant given that the Muslims were outnumbered three to one.

The flawed attempt to use 8.17 to interpret 4.157 shows the extent to which scholars are willing to go to deny the latter its obvious meaning. First, verse 8.17 makes its point by allegorically replacing the believers with God as the true actor. Likening 4.157 to 8.17 falsely *implies* that the former verse has a similar metaphor. Second, the Qur'an presents the human actions in 8.17 as essentially good because they are taken by believers to defend themselves against a violent enemy. But the attempt to crucify Jesus is described as evil, so attributing it to God is theologically untenable. Third, the Qur'an had just condemned the Jews for killing prophets, as it does in other verses, and no one can suggest that it meant that God killed them; so what justification is there for treating Jesus'

---

[21] Ayoub, *A Muslim View of Christianity*, 176; Mourad, "Jesus's Crucifixion and Death", 356; Parrinder, *Jesus in the Qur'an*, 119; Lawson, *The Crucifixion and the Qur'an*, 41.

[22] Kaltner and Mirza, *The Bible and the Qur'an*, 80; Reynolds, *The Qur'ān and the Bible*, 181.

[23] Parrinder, *Jesus in the Qur'an*, 120; Fonner, "Jesus' Death", 445; Anderson, *The Qur'an in Context*, 245.

situation differently? Finally, the Qur'an follows its denial of the crucifixion by revealing a second action that He *explicitly attributes to Himself*, which is raising Jesus.

Another creative interpretation gets around the verse's clear statement that Jesus was not killed by likening him to martyrs whom the Qur'an describes as alive with God:[24]

> Do not say about those who are *killed* in the way of Allah, "They are dead". Rather, they are alive, but you do not perceive it. (2.154)
> Do not think of those who have been *killed* in the cause of Allah as dead. Rather, they are alive with their Lord, receiving provision. (3.169)

This attempt ignores the fundamental fact that both verses explicitly talk about believers who were "killed", whereas Jesus is described as having been saved.[25] The confirmation of verses 2.154 and 3.169 that martyrs are alive with God did not stop them from unambiguously stating that they were indeed killed. Like 2.154 and 3.169, 4.157 and many other verses are informational (*khabariyya*), so they state what the Qur'an considers to be facts. Informational verses must not be confused with rhetoric, allegories, euphemisms, and other such linguistic devices. If informational verses were treated as anything less than manifest and direct statements of facts, the Qur'an would become unintelligible.

In another example of the history-cum-theology and theology-cum-history that has blighted studies of 4.157, the verse is understood as a historical, rather than theological or historical-theological, statement. Its denial of the Jews' responsibility for Jesus' crucifixion, it is argued, reflects the fact that it was the Romans, not the Jews, who executed him.[26] This claim has been rightly rejected because if the verse intended "to indicate that it was God or the Romans and not the Jews who crucified Jesus this would surely have been stated explicitly".[27]

Contrary to what Western scholars suggest, in accusing specifically the Jews of the attempt to kill Jesus, the Qur'an is completely aligned with the Gospels' narrative. I have already discussed this in detail (§5.3-5), so I will only make a passing mention of the main facts here. Pilate

---

[24] Parrinder, *Jesus in the Qur'an*, 113; Mourad, "The Death of Jesus in Islam", 371.

[25] Robinson, *Christ in Islam and Christianity*, 109.

[26] Lawson, *The Crucifixion and the Qur'an*, 8.

[27] Robinson, *Christ in Islam and Christianity*, 115.

got involved in the perceived crucifixion of Jesus only at the request of Jewish leaders. The Roman authorities would not have even heard of Jesus had it not been for the Jewish leaders, let alone would they have taken an interest in him, and even less would they have thought of killing him (§5.4). Jesus was a little-known spiritual teacher who, significantly, never advocated violence and rejected any attempt to politicise his mission. He was brought to the attention of the Roman governor by the Jewish authorities. They, on the other hand, had strong reasons to have Jesus eliminated. He was perceived to be a growing threat to the religious establishment (§5.3, §18.7).

I should also point out that the crime that the Qur'an accuses the Jews of is far less serious than its counterpart in the Gospels because the Qur'anic Jesus escaped the crucifixion. The Qur'an accuses the Jews of the *intention* and *preparation* to kill Jesus, whereas the Gospels charge them with his *actual* crucifixion.

The full theological potential of the *creative* readings of 4.157 to make it say that Jesus died on the cross is realised when it is combined with a *literal* understanding of the reference of 4.158 to God's raising of Jesus to heaven. This is how the Qur'an is made to confirm the Gospels' narrative that Jesus died on the cross and God raised him to heaven:[28]

> If the Qur'an's statement (in Q 4:157) that "the Jews" did not really kill Jesus is a metaphysical affirmation rather than a literal or historical denial, then its statement (in Q 4:158) that "God raised him up to Himself" can be read as an affirmation of the story of Jesus' resurrection and ascension as told in the New Testament.[29]

> Explanations abound; however, most Muslim commentators couple their understanding of Q 4:157-58 with Q 3:55 in order to assert that someone other than Jesus died and that God rescued Jesus from the plot of the Jews and raised him up to heaven. But scholars have noted that when these verses are viewed within this sūra's broader rhetorical context—centered on rebuking the Jews for their perfidy and demonstrating God's control over life and death—it is clear that these verses affirm the death and resurrection of Christ.[30]

---

[28] Reynolds, "The Muslim Jesus", 240; Mourad, "Jesus's Crucifixion and Death", 354.

[29] Mevorach, "Qur'an, Crucifixion, and Talmud", 14.

[30] Bridger, *Christian Exegesis of the Qur'ān*, 98.

I have to agree with Neal Robinson's conclusion that "the attempt of some Christian apologists to circumvent the Qur'anic denial of the crucifixion is disingenuous in the extreme".[31]

The full picture of the flaws in denying the Qur'an's denial of the crucifixion of Jesus will become even clearer in the coming chapters as we analyse more relevant Qur'anic passages.

---

[31] Robinson, *Christ in Islam and Christianity*, 115.

21

Divine Protection and Rescue

Verse 4.157 is the only one that mentions the attempt to crucify and kill Jesus. Verses 3.54 and 5.110 mention God's general protection of Jesus, which must include foiling any attempts on his life, even though they make no express mention of the crucifixion.

The first verse that alludes to the Jews' attempt to kill Jesus and his miraculous escape, 3.54, is quoted here with its surrounding verses:

> But when Jesus perceived disbelief from them (the Children of Israel), he said, "Who are my supporters for the cause of Allah?" The companions said, "We are Allah's supporters. We believe in Allah, and do you bear witness that we are Muslims. (52) Our Lord! We have believed in that which You have sent down and we have followed the messenger, so write us down among those who bear witness [to the truth]". (53) They (the Children of Israel) planned, and *Allah planned; Allah is the best of planners.* (54) When Allah said, "O Jesus! I am taking you (*mutawaffika*), raising you to Me, and cleansing you of those who disbelieve, and setting those who follow you above those who disbelieve until the Day of Resurrection. Then to Me you shall all return, and I shall judge between you concerning what you differed on". (3.52-55)

These verses follow a rather lengthy account of Mary's birth and virginal conception (3.35-47) and Jesus' miracles (3.48-49). Verse 3.49 describes Jesus as a "messenger to the Children of Israel" (3.49), so the disbelieving people in the above verses are the Jews, as clarified in the translation.

The "disbelief" in 3.52 is not simply people's refusal to believe in Jesus. That was something he faced from day one and it was visible for all to see. The verb "perceived" (*ahassa*) denotes something new and subtle. The verse highlights a specific point in Jesus' mission when the negative reaction to his public teaching developed into something far more sinister than mere rejection.

Naturally, Jesus' followers had already been countering defamatory propaganda and false accusations that discredited him and his teachings. But having sensed the escalated danger, he wanted to confirm that his closest followers would offer him any form of protection that he may end up needing. They confirmed their total loyalty to him and their commitment to protecting him (3.52-53). At this point, Jesus probably did not know that God had a plan to rescue him by raising him.

Verse 3.54 shows that the hostility towards Jesus escalated into a plot to kill him. God responded to the Jews' conspiracy with a counterplan of His own to foil theirs, stressing that He is "the best of planners". This strongly implies a miraculous intervention in Jesus' escaping of the crucifixion. Verse 3.55 then explains that the divine plan to rescue Jesus culminated in *raising* him. This miraculous raising is more grandiose in supernaturality than the earlier divine intervention that helped Jesus avoid the arrest and crucifixion.

Verse 3.54 has particularly significant symmetry with the second half of verse 8.30:

> As those who disbelieve plan to restrain you, kill you, or evict you. They plan, and Allah plans, and Allah is the best of planners. (8.30)
>
> They (the Children of Israel) planned, and Allah planned; Allah is the best of planners. (3.54)

The difference in the tense of the verbs is because 8.30 describes the then ongoing situation of the Prophet Muhammad, whereas 3.54 reports past events from Jesus' life. We know from history that verse 8.30 means that God was going to foil all plans against the Prophet Muhammad. It is logical to conclude that its symmetry with 3.54 indicates that the latter similarly means that God thwarted the conspiracies to harm and kill Jesus.

In verse 3.55, God promised Jesus that He was going to raise him and cleanse him of the disbelievers. This *promised rescue* cannot be reconciled with the image of Jesus' *crucified corpse* being in the hands of his enemies and then carelessly disposed of or buried after that *most painful and humiliating ordeal*! What sense would it make for God to promise Jesus to *rescue* him when He actually meant to *recover his ravaged and desecrated body*? Why would God raise the *corpse* and call this an act of raising *Jesus*? Would cleansing not entail protecting Jesus from the defilement that his body would suffer if it was allowed to be crucified rather than recovering it after being completely dishonoured? Why would God allow the death by crucifixion to happen just to then intervene to *miraculously* raise the body? None of this would make any sense to Jesus, his followers, his enemies, or anyone for that matter. It makes sense for the body to be raised only if it is to continue to live wherever it is taken to. Also, if God raised only Jesus' soul or his status, as some Muslim scholars have started to argue the verses imply, then describing this as a cleansing of Jesus of the disbelievers would hardly make sense either. The act of cleansing means separating the impurities and the target of purification from each other. We will discuss raising Jesus and the various interpretations in detail later (§25).

As we will see later, the root verb of *mutawaffika* can mean "take" or "cause to die". The latter is often quoted by scholars to support their denial of the Qur'an's denial of the crucifixion. Reading 3.55 in context shows that it could not be talking about God causing Jesus to die. The latter misunderstanding would mean that God carried out the plot against Jesus on behalf of the Jews, not that He foiled it as 3.54 tells us! This is why I have translated *mutawaffika* as "taking you". We will analyse this verb in more detail later (§24).

In the second verse about God's protection of Jesus, He first reminds Jesus of some of the miracles He enabled him to perform before mentioning His intervention to fend off his adversaries:

> When Allah said, "O Jesus, son of Mary! Remember My favour on you and your mother when I supported you with the Spirit of Holiness, making you speak to people in the cradle and when middle-aged; [remember] when I taught you the Book, Wisdom, the Torah, and the Injīl; [remember] when you created out of clay the figures of birds by My permission, then you breathed into them and they became birds by My permission, and you healed the blind and the leper with My permission; [remember] when you raised the dead by My permission; and [remember] *when I restrained the Children of Israel from you* when you came to them with clear proofs. But those who disbelieved among them said, 'This is nothing but *clear magic*'". (5.110)

Jesus' preaching and miracles happened over several years. God's restraint of the Jews protected Jesus from repeated attempts to harm him. This harm would have included hostilities of varying seriousness, from verbal abuse and physical attacks to the attempt to kill him. Perhaps there was more than one failed attempt on Jesus' life, the last of which was the crucifixion that ended with the wrong person being put on the cross. It is not possible to tell.

The mention of repeated efforts to cause Jesus harm indicates that God's speech in 5.110 took place late in Jesus' life, probably after he was raised. One counterargument that it may have happened before the crucifixion instead is that it is followed by an account of the miracle of Jesus bringing a feast from heaven for his disciples, which is likely to have happened shortly before the crucifixion:

> When I inspired the companions, "Believe in Me and My messenger". They said, "We believe. Bear witness that we are Muslims". (111) When the companions said, "O Jesus son of Mary! Can your Lord send down for us a table of food from heaven?" He said, "Fear Allah, if you are true believers". (112) They said, "We wish to eat of it, have our hearts be at ease, know that you have spoken the truth to us, and be witnesses to it (the table)". (113) Jesus son of Mary said, "O Allah our Lord! Send down for us from heaven a table of food, that it may be a feast for the first and the last of us, and a sign from You. Give us sustenance; You are the best of Sustainers". (114) Allah said, "I shall send it down for you, so whoever of you disbelieves afterwards I will punish him with a torment that I do not inflict on anyone among all the nations". (5.111-115)

That 5.110 precedes 5.111-115 should not *necessarily* mean that it reports a chronologically earlier event. Indeed, the yet earlier verse of 5.109 talks about the Day of Resurrection, the most distant future event. The fact that 5.110 and 5.111 both start with "when" (*ith*) indicates a change of timeline and context. We will revisit this point and verses 5.109-119 later in the book (§26.2).

On the other hand, there are stronger indications that God's speech in 5.110 took place after He raised Jesus. The mention of God frustrating the plans against Jesus in 3.54 is followed in 3.55 by the explanatory promise that He would take and raise him. Conversely, verse 5.110 reports God's protection of Jesus from the Israelites as something that had already happened. Also, there is no explanation or promise of divine actions to follow, suggesting that God was talking about past events, ones which Jesus had experienced. Verse 5.110 sounds very much like a *recap* of God's favours to Jesus.

Besides, Jesus' speaking in his middle age appears as a promise by God to Mary in verse 3.46 (§23.1), but in 5.110 the verse reports it as something that has already happened. If so, this speech must have been many years after Jesus was raised.

Verse 5.110 has an interesting symmetry with 3.54. God's planning to protect Jesus in 3.54 is mentioned after recounting his miracles in earlier verses. The same sequence is found in 5.110. We have already noted that verses 3.54-55 indicate that there was a divine intervention in rescuing Jesus from the crucifixion. The same can be concluded from 5.110 if the speech happened after the crucifixion. Even if that speech was before the crucifixion, God's repeated intervention to protect Jesus means it remains highly likely that rescuing him from crucifixion did involve divine help.

An important observation I made about 3.54-55 also applies to 5.110. If Jesus had been crucified, God's reminder in 5.110 of His protection of Jesus would make no sense. This argument stands even if the speech in 5.110 happened before the crucifixion. God would not remind Jesus of repeatedly protecting him from the hostility of the Jews if He was going to later abandon him to the fatal ordeal of the crucifixion! Had Jesus been crucified, such a reminder would be even more difficult to make sense of given that it was revealed in the Qur'an some six centuries after the event.

In the next chapter, I will argue that Jesus escaped the crucifixion and another person was wrongly put to death in his stead. This *natural* scenario must have been facilitated, as 3.45 and 5.110 suggest, by *supernatural* intervention at some points. The latter rescued Jesus from the crucifixion and was followed by a greater miracle that saved him from his enemies for good by raising him to heaven.

Without divine intervention of the type that made Jesus' miracles possible, he could not have escaped the persistent hostility of his enemies. In his commentary on 4.157, the great twentieth-century scholar Muḥammad Mitwallī al-Shaʿrāwī makes this insightful observation:

> The combination of the two controversies of Jesus' birth and taking in his message indicates to us that reason must be consistent in its interpretation. When reason addresses the birth of Jesus the son of Mary, the person must conclude that it did not happen according to an existing norm. When God informs us that the Children of Israel planned to kill Jesus the son of Mary and that Allah raised him to Himself, the matter is also discordant [with what is normal]. We have to believe what Allah told us. Reason must remember that the birth was discordant, so why wouldn't the end also be discordant?
>
> In the same way we have believed that Jesus the son of Mary came into

being without a father, we must believe that, in the end, God raised and took him. The birth would have been beyond the boundaries of reason, had God not informed us of it. Similarly, the taking has to be accepted within what God told us. Both Jesus' birth and end were miraculous. If we recognise the first miracle of the birth, we must consider it an indication that Jesus came into being and entered life by a miracle, so why wouldn't his departure from it also be via a miracle? When God tells us that Jesus departed life by a miracle, we do not find it surprising. It is not astonishing that something that started miraculously ended miraculously.

Sha'rāwī is spot on that Jesus' life in the Qur'an is permeated by miracles from birth. In fact, his mother conceived him by a miracle. He performed miracles and was the subject of miracles, not least those that protected him. It looks like this high frequency of wonders is what made Ayoub confidently yet unjustifiably declare that, like verse 4.157, all statements concerning Jesus in the Qur'an belong not to history but theology in the broadest sense.[1] It is a fundamental fact in the Qur'an, as it is in the Old and New Testaments and other scriptures, that history is created by the supernatural as well as the natural. In the language, thought, and theology of the Qur'an, the reported miraculous episodes of Jesus' life are accurate biographical history even though history, including Jesus', is mostly written by natural events. I have discussed elsewhere the concept of "miracle" in the Qur'an and the fusion of the natural and supernatural in the lives of some individuals.[2]

To recap, verses 3.54-55 and 5.110 further confirm that 4.157 denies the historicity of the crucifixion. This is the obvious and natural reading of every relevant verse we have studied so far, as is the case with those we are yet to examine. It is not possible to come up with credible interpretations of all these verses that can be aligned with the assumption that Jesus was crucified, let alone get them to confirm that he was!

---

[1] Ayoub, *A Muslim View of Christianity*, 176.
[2] Fatoohi, *Muhammad Al-Muhammad Al-Kasnazan*, 91-130.

22

Crucifying the Wrong Man

The Qur'an's assertion that it was made to appear to the Jews that they crucified and killed Jesus can have one of two meanings. The first is that the plotters experienced some kind of collective illusion, thinking that they got Jesus crucified when in fact no crucifixion ever happened. This purely supernatural interpretation has no supportive evidence and is highly unlikely. A far more likely reading is that the Jews, through the Romans, crucified someone else thinking that he was Jesus.

This natural interpretation of the crucifixion, which is known as the "substitution" theory, has been adopted by most Muslim exegetes. Someone is said to have volunteered or was forced to be crucified instead of Jesus.

Christian sources from as early as the second century also talk about the crucifixion of a substitute. This view, which must go back to the first century, is linked directly or indirectly to the doctrine of docetism, at least in some cases. We touched on this earlier (§16.2). The form of substitution that Muslim exegeses have adopted is not linked to docetism because the Qur'anic Jesus is a human being.

The interpretation of the crucifixion that I advocate is what I call "misidentification". I argue that a man was wrongly identified as Jesus and put on the cross instead of him. In this chapter, I will discuss both forms of substitution first and then the misidentification interpretation.

22.1 Docetic Substitution

The term "docetism" is derived from the Greek "dokeĩn", which means "to seem". It is the doctrine that Jesus only seemed to have a body, which effectively denies his human nature. His crucifixion and suffering can only be an illusion, as both are experiences that only a body can undergo. Docetism is considered heresy even though mainstream Christianity considers Jesus to be both divine and human, which is certainly no less strange and illogical.

Around 110 CE, bishop Ignatius of Antioch, Syria, wrote a letter to the Christians of Smyrna (today's Izmir in Turkey) in which he critically says, "Some unbelievers say that his Passion was merely in semblance".[1] Ignatius talks about docetists who did not accept that Jesus suffered the crucifixion.[2]

The second-century Egyptian Christian gnostic Basilides taught that the Jews crucified a Simon of Cyrene instead of Jesus and that Jesus ascended to God. Writing around 185 CE, Irenaeus, the orthodox bishop of Lyon, has the following to report about Basilides' heretical beliefs about the crucifixion:

> Wherefore he did not himself suffer death, but Simon, a certain man of Cyrene, being compelled, bore the cross in his stead; so that this latter being transfigured by him, that he might be thought to be Jesus, was crucified, through ignorance and error, while Jesus himself received the form of Simon, and, standing by, laughed at them. For since he was an incorporeal power, and the Nous (mind) of the unborn father, he transfigured himself as he pleased, and thus ascended to him who had sent him, deriding them, inasmuch as he could not be laid hold of, and was invisible to all.
>
> Those, then, who know these things have been freed from the principalities who formed the world; so that it is not incumbent on us to confess him who was crucified, but him who came in the form of a man, and was thought to be crucified, and was called Jesus, and was sent by the father, that by this dispensation he might destroy the works of the makers of the world. If any one, therefore, he declares, confesses the crucified, that man is still a slave, and under the power of those who formed our bodies; but he who denies him has been freed from these beings, and is acquainted with the dispensation of the unborn father.[3]

Some have disputed that Basilides held this belief about the crucifixion,[4] but this is a moot point here. What matters is that the belief that someone other than Jesus suffered the crucifixion is likely to have been in circulation very early in the history of Christianity.

Other early sources that advanced a docetic substitute version of events come from a collection of thirteen codices containing fifty-two

---

[1] Ignatius, *Ignatius to the Smyrnaeans*, I, 2.
[2] For other quotes from Igatius, see Goulder, "Ignatius' "Docetists"".
[3] Irenaeus, *Against Heresies*, 1.24.4.
[4] Pearson, "Basilides the Gnostic", 22.

treatises of mostly gnostic nature that were discovered at Nag Hammadi
in Egypt in 1945. The first, *The Second Treatise of the Great Seth*, dated to
the third century, is supposed to be a revelation from Jesus to an audience
of gnostic believers. Like the view that Irenaeus attributes to Basilides,
this text claims that a Simon of Cyrene was crucified instead of a laughing
Jesus:

> And the plan which they devised about me to release their Error and their
> senselessness — I did not succumb to them as they had planned. But I was not
> afflicted at all. Those who were there punished me. And I did not die in
> reality but in appearance, lest I be put to shame by them because these are my
> kinsfolk. I removed the shame from me and I did not become fainthearted in
> the face of what happened to me at their hands. I was about to succumb to
> fear, and I (suffered) according to their sight and thought, in order that they
> may never find any word to speak about them. For my death which they
> think happened, (happened) to them in their error and blindness, since they
> nailed their man unto their death. For their Ennoias (minds) did not see me,
> for they were deaf and blind. But in doing these things, they condemn
> themselves.
>
> Yes, they saw me; they punished me. It was another, their father, who
> drank the gall and the vinegar; it was not I. They struck me with the reed; *it
> was another, Simon, who bore the cross on his shoulder.* I[t] was another upon
> whom they placed the crown of thorns. But I was rejoicing in the height
> over all the wealth of the archons and the offspring of their error, of their
> empty glory. And I was laughing at their ignorance.
>
> And I subjected all their powers. For as I came downward no one saw me.
> For I was altering my shapes, changing from form to form. And therefore,
> when I was at their gates I assumed their likeness. For I passed them by
> quietly, and I was viewing the places, and I was not afraid nor ashamed, for
> I was undefiled. And I was speaking with them, mingling with them through
> those who are mine, and trampling on those who are harsh to them with zeal,
> and quenching the flame. And I was doing all these things because of my
> desire to accomplish what I desired by the will of the Father above.[5]

A second Nag Hammadi book, *The Coptic Apocalypse of Peter*, which
is dated to the second or third century, narrates visions that were seen by
the apostle Peter and interpreted by Jesus. In the second visionary scene,
Jesus explains to Peter that the physical body of the crucified person is

---

[5] Bullard and Gibbons, "The Second Treatise of the Great Seth", 365-366.

distinct from the living Jesus. While someone who looked like Jesus was being crucified, the real Jesus was watching the events in derision from above a tree and was invisible to the ignorant executioners:

> When he had said those things, I saw him seemingly being seized by them. And I said, "What do I see, O Lord, that it is you yourself whom they take, and that you are grasping me? Or who is this one, glad and laughing on the tree? And is it another one whose feet and hands they are striking?"
>
> The Savior said to me, "He whom you saw on the tree, glad and laughing, this is the living Jesus. But this one into whose hands and feet they drive the nails is his fleshly part, which is the *substitute being put to shame, the one who came into being in his likeness*. But look at him and me". But I, when I had looked, said, "Lord, no one is looking at you. Let us flee this place." But he said to me, "I have told you, 'Leave the blind alone!' And you, see how they do not know what they are saying. For the son of their glory instead of my servant they have put to shame".
>
> And I saw someone about to approach us resembling him, even him who was laughing on the tree. And he was (filled) with a Holy Spirit, and he is the Savior. And there was a great, ineffable light around them, and the multitude of ineffable and invisible angels blessing them. And when I looked at him, the one who gives praise was revealed. And he said to me, "Be strong, for you are the one to whom these mysteries have been given, to know them through revelation, that he whom they crucified is the firstborn, and the home of demons, and the stony vessel (?) in which they dwell, of Elohim, of the cross which is under the Law. But he who stands near him is the living Savior, the first in him, whom they seized and released, who stands joyfully looking at those who did him violence, while they are divided among themselves. Therefore he laughs at their lack of perception, knowing that they are born blind. So then the one susceptible to suffering shall come, since the body is the substitute. But what they released was my incorporeal body. But I am the intellectual Spirit filled with radiant light. He whom you saw coming to me is our intellectual Pleroma, which unites the perfect light with my Holy Spirit".[6]

A less direct and detailed reference to a docetic view of the crucifixion is found in a third Nag Hammadi book called *The First Apocalypse of James*. This book is a dialogue between Jesus and his brother James. When James asked about the coming suffering, Jesus replied:

---

[6] Brashler and Bullard, "The Apocalypse of Peter", 377.

And after this I shall appear for a reproof to the archons. And I shall reveal to them that he cannot be seized. If they seize him, then he will overpower each of them.

After the crucifixion, Jesus appeared to a much-distressed James and reassured him:

James, do not be concerned for me or for this people. I am he who was within me. Never have I suffered in any way, nor have I been distressed. And this people has done me no harm.[7]

There are other potential docetic interpretations of the crucifixion in other sources.[8]

It is difficult to tell how widespread this docetic view of the crucifixion was, but it seems that even some New Testament books, including the Gospels, may contain rebuttals of this doctrine.[9]

I would like to propose a new way to understand the development of docetism. This doctrine has always been seen as a theological development and a distortion that *denied the historical* crucifixion of Jesus' body and *introduced the unhistorical* crucifixion of a substitute. Yet this view ignores the fact that the central premise of docetism is the *non-crucifixion*, not the *crucifixion*, of Jesus. The crucifixion of a substitute is used to stress the non-crucifixion of Jesus. It is secondary to the main thesis; it is an interpretational accessory. The standard view of the genesis of docetism needs to be turned on its head. It is not only as legitimate but, in my view, also more convincing to argue that docetism is a theological development and distortion of the *historical belief that Jesus escaped the crucifixion*. The crucifixion of a substitute is used to counter the competing, yet unhistorical, belief that Jesus was crucified.

22.2 Non-Docetic Substitution

Muslim scholars have also claimed that another person was made to look like Jesus and was crucified instead. Ṭabarī (4.157) has preserved several variations of this theory. According to one, when those who came to capture Jesus surrounded him and his disciples, all disciples were transformed into his lookalikes. One of them came out of the house, so

[7] Schoedel, "The First Apocalypse of James", 264-265.
[8] Yamauchi, "Docetic Christology".
[9] Price, *Shrinking Son of Man*, 326-331; Yamauchi, "Docetic Christology", 5-7.

he ended up being killed.

In a similar version that is also attributed to the Successor Wahb Ibn Munabbih, the arresting Jews stormed the house, but God had already made all seventeen disciples look like Jesus. The attackers accused those in the house of practising magic to confuse them and threatened to kill them all unless Jesus stepped forward. Jesus asked a disciple to volunteer in return for a place in paradise. One did and was taken away and crucified.

Ṭabarī attributes to Wahb Ibn Munabbih a different narrative that closely follows the Gospels' story, including Jesus having supper with the disciples and predicting that one of them would betray and surrender him to the Jews. Another person was mistaken for Jesus and was left on the cross for seven days. When Mary and another woman visited the cross and started crying, Jesus appeared to them. He reassured them that God had raised him and he was safe and that the crucified man was someone who was made to look like him to the Jews. The identity of the substitute is not disclosed here.

Ṭabarī ascribes to the Successor Qatāda Ibn Di'āma yet another version of the story. Jesus asked his disciples for a volunteer who would be made to resemble him and be killed instead of him. One duly came forward and was crucified. The Successor Suddī is also said to have claimed that when Jesus and nineteen of his disciples were surrounded, one of them volunteered to take his likeness while Jesus was raised to heaven. The second-century AH historian Ibn Isḥāq is said to have named the disciple who became Jesus' lookalike as Sarjis.

Other versions differ in a few or many details but there is little need to list them here. Ṭabarī prefers one of Ibn Munabbih's two versions in which all of the disciples were made to look like Jesus.

Some of these narratives may be labelled *voluntary substitutionism*, as they involve one of Jesus' disciples, who was made or offered to be made to look like him, volunteering to be crucified instead of him. Ṭabarī mentions a version of *punishment substitutionism* whereby the person who betrayed Jesus is punished by involuntarily being made to look like him and being crucified in his stead. He attributes this claim to "some Christians" and does not link it to any Muslim source. Ayoub notes that over time, a preference for punishment substitutionism developed among

Muslim exegetes.[10]

I should quickly mention another Christian source that also advocates non-docetic substitutionism, the apocryphal *Gospel of Barnabas*. Its version of substitution resembles the one found in Muslim sources. Before Judas Iscariot betrayed Jesus to the authorities, the angels took Jesus to the third heaven. God then made Judas look and speak like Jesus. Not only the soldiers and the disciples but all those who knew Jesus closely, including his mother, mistook Judas for Jesus. The betrayer was then arrested and crucified instead of Jesus.[11]

There are two manuscripts of *The Gospel of Barnabas* from the late sixteenth or early seventeenth century. A book under this name is mentioned in independent sources from the sixth and seventh centuries. Many Muslim scholars accept the claim of the author of this book to have been one of Jesus' disciples,[12] but non-Muslim scholars consider the work to be much later and a forgery.

The supposed Qur'anic basis of the substitute theory, which is found in most exegetical works, is the explanation in 4.157 of what happened:

> They did not kill him, nor did they crucify him, but it was made *to appear so to them.*

The Arabic verb in question is *shubbiha*, which is followed by *lahum* (to them). Unlike my translation, "it was made to appear so to them", some exegetes have understood this verb to mean something like "a likeness was made", i.e. a semblance of Jesus. Those who are more attentive to the language and structure of the verse, such as Zamakhsharī and Fakhr al-Dīn al-Rāzī (606/1209), have rightly pointed out that Jesus could not be the referent of *shubbiha*. Had the verb referred to making a Jesus lookalike, it would have been followed by *lahu* (of him), not *lahum* (to them), in which case the phrase would have meant "a likeness of him was made". Both Zamakhsharī and Rāzī accept that the referent could be the one killed instead of Jesus, which would make him the subject of confusion for the Jews. But they also point out that the victim is not mentioned earlier for the nonspecific reference to be linked to him. The

---

[10] Ayoub, *A Muslim View of Christianity*, 162.
[11] *The Gospel of Barnabas*, 215-217.
[12] Yusseff, *Gospel of Barnabas*.

claim of an indirect and implicit link would require a rather convoluted understanding of the verse.

I find the reading of the verb given in my translation to be far more natural than the alternatives. The phrase does not say anything other than that the Jews misunderstood or got confused about what happened, as no details about what actually happened are given. While the substitute theory is not incompatible with the Qur'an, it is not supported by it either and it cannot be derived from it. One has to twist the phrase *shubbiha lahum* beyond what is linguistically possible to find a substitute in it.

In his commentary on 3.55 and 4.157, the great exegete Rāzī raised a novel objection to the substitute interpretation. He argued that if God makes one person look like another, this would lead to sophistry, undermining trust in social contracts and interactions. This would undermine, among other things, faith in the attributions in the transmission of religious traditions, which is critical for verifying its authenticity.

Incidentally, it has been claimed that Rāzī's criticism of the substitute theory moves him considerably towards affirming the Christian belief that Jesus was crucified.[13] The rush to make such claims about Rāzī, in particular, seems to be an attempt to claim support from this highly regarded exegete. Yet these claims are completely wrong. When discussing a verse in his voluminous exegesis, Rāzī usually mentions all known interpretations and presents arguments for and against them. Some modern scholars seem to misunderstand his presentation of a particular view as an endorsement. This is just one quote, from Rāzī's opening commentary on 4.159, that confirms his understanding that the Qur'an denies Jesus' crucifixion:

> The Almighty mentioned the scandals and bad deeds of the Jews, explained that they intended to kill Jesus peace be upon him, and clarified that *they did not achieve that goal* and that Jesus obtained the highest statuses and finest ranks.

Because the theory of substitution predates the Qur'an by a few centuries and the Qur'an is customarily accused of appropriating Jewish and Christian traditions and sources, it has been claimed that the adoption

---

[13] Lawson, *The Crucifixion and the Qur'an*, 107.

of substitutionism by Muslim scholars is the result of influence by its Christian docetic version.[14] The Qur'an's denial of the crucifixion has itself been said to reflect influence by docetism.[15] It has even been falsely suggested that all Western scholars trace the theory of substitution to docetism.[16] These unsupported claims are based on a misunderstanding of the word *shubbiha*, as explained earlier. Others have rightly pointed out that there is no such evidence,[17] while many accept that the substitution theory in Muslim exegeses cannot be linked to docetism.[18] The Qur'an is unequivocal in its rejection of the divinity of Jesus and its confirmation that he was only a human being, which refutes docetism. Jesus was only human like all other prophets. Considering all relevant Qur'anic texts makes it absurd to trace the substitution theory of Muslim scholars, let alone the broader Qur'an's denial of the crucifixion, to docetism.

22.3 Misidentification

My reading of verse 4.157 shows no reference to any kind of substitution. The verse only stresses that having set out to crucify Jesus, his enemies were somehow confused and thought that they had succeeded. The Qur'an does not say exactly how this confusion came about, hence the appearance of the non-docetic substitution theory as an explanation.

Verse 4.157 does not say whether a miracle was involved in Jesus' avoiding the crucifixion. Verses 4.158 and 3.55 talk about the final and grand miracle of raising him to heaven. Verses 3.45 and 5.110, however, strongly indicate that the crucifixion was foiled by supernatural help, just as other hostilities against Jesus were miraculously circumvented. The indirect reference to this divine intervention in the mention of God's general help to Jesus indicates that it was not of the same scale of the great miracle of raising Jesus to heaven (§21). This, in turn, points to a course of events that was mostly natural but was steered by subtle supernatural input to achieve the goal of saving Jesus. This is the overall picture that I have in mind when proposing the following natural series of events.

---

[14] Yamauchi, "Docetic Christology", 14; Fry, "The Quranic Christ", 219-220; Turek, "Crucifixion of Jesus", 153-156.

[15] Reynolds, "The Muslim Jesus", 238.

[16] Samir, "Theological Christian Influence", 153.

[17] Parrinder, *Jesus in the Qur'an*, 119.

[18] Ayoub, *A Muslim View of Christianity*, 160; Fonner, "Jesus' Death", 444.

The most likely natural explanation is that the authorities arrested and crucified the wrong person. The Qur'an does not say anything about the arrest, so it is possible, though unlikely, that Jesus was arrested but he then somehow escaped and the wrong person was crucified instead. But to avoid unjustified speculation, I will presume that the misidentification happened at the time of the arrest.

Mistaking another man for Jesus was not necessarily because of an amazing resemblance. How could such a misidentification happen, then? Two thousand years ago, a person could be identified only by people who personally knew them, so misidentification was much more likely and frequent than it is today. There are several facts about Jesus that would have facilitated his misidentification. **First**, Jesus was in the public eye for a short period. According to the Synoptists, Jesus' ministry lasted for about one year, and for John, it did not exceed three. I think he was active for a few years, but he was much younger than the Gospels claim (§23.3).

Second, he was a low-profile teacher who had a small following. The Gospels' image of Jesus being followed by thousands is unhistorical. **Third**, according to the Gospels, Jesus' arrest and crucifixion did not happen where he lived most of his life, Galilee. They took place in Jerusalem, which he visited in his ministry once, according to the Synoptists, or four times, according to John. His last visit lasted only five days before he was arrested. His other visits, if there were others, would not have lasted much longer. Given that he did not have many followers even in his hometown, he would have had even fewer in Jerusalem.

Now, if we combine the shortness of Jesus' public activity, his very limited success in attracting followers, and the fact that the arrest and crucifixion happened in Jerusalem, we should conclude that not many people would have been able to identify him. A misidentification would have been further facilitated by two other factors.

Fourth, the Gospels state that the arrest happened during the Passover when numerous Jews came from various places. Looking for one stranger among many others would have made the task of identifying Jesus even more difficult.

Fifth, by that point, God had informed Jesus of the impending danger to his life (§25.4), so he would not have made any public appearances. He must have gone into hiding by the time the search for him was on.

Those who came to arrest Jesus did not know what he looked like. This is what the Gospels suggest was the case, as noted, for example, by Rashīd Riḍā (4.157). According to the Synoptists, Judas Iscariot led the guards to Jesus' place and *identified* him among his disciples by kissing him (Matt. 26:47-50; Luke 22:47-54):

> Immediately, while he was still speaking, Judas, one of the twelve, arrived; and with him there was a crowd with swords and clubs, from the chief priests, the scribes, and the elders. Now the betrayer had given them a sign, saying, "*The one I will kiss is the man*; arrest him and lead him away under guard." So when he came, he went up to him at once and said, "Rabbi!" and kissed him. Then they laid hands on him and arrested him. (Mark 14:43-46)

While John's story differs, it still shows that those who came to arrest Jesus could not identify him. In this version, they had to rely on him to identify himself:

> So Judas brought a detachment of soldiers together with police from the chief priests and the Pharisees, and they came there with lanterns and torches and weapons. Then Jesus, knowing all that was to happen to him, came forward and asked them, *"Whom are you looking for?"* They answered, *"Jesus of Nazareth." Jesus replied, "I am he."* Judas, who betrayed him, was standing with them. When Jesus said to them, "I am he," they stepped back and fell to the ground. Again he asked them, "Whom are you looking for?" And they said, "Jesus of Nazareth." Jesus answered, "I told you that I am he. So if you are looking for me, let these men go." (John 18:3-9)

It looks like the guards were ready to arrest all of the disciples had Jesus not been identified for them. As he was unknown to the guards and authorities, a misidentification could have taken place. That the arrest took place in the darkness of night might have facilitated the mistaken identification.

Furthermore, the Synoptists acknowledge that none of Jesus' followers witnessed his crucifixion. Only John disagrees, but his account of a dying Jesus on the cross being heard by his mother and a disciple is undoubtedly fictional (§1.13).

In addition to substitutionism, which he mentions several versions of, Rāzī states that the other line of interpretation taken by scholars is that the Jews crucified a person other than Jesus and misled people into thinking they killed Jesus. He then goes on to say this deception was possible because Jesus' little interaction with people allowed the crucifiers to pass the victim off as Jesus. This view comes close to the interpretation of misidentification but it advocates deliberate deception instead. Verse 4.157 indicates that the Jewish claimants *genuinely* thought, though they could not be totally certain, that they had killed Jesus, so I find no justification for the assumption that there was deception.

Some contemporary Muslim writers have made the case for misidentification based on the natural resemblance that one of the disciples had with Jesus. In one version of this scenario, a regretful Judas decided not to protest the misidentification when this disciple was arrested instead of Jesus. The fact that those who witnessed the crucifixion had not met Jesus earlier allowed this deception to go unexposed. [19] In another version, a disciple who looked like him volunteered to pretend to be him. The author cites the darkness of the night as a factor that facilitated the misidentification. [20] The theory of misidentification is not new, and these are not its only flavours. Any details about the person who was mistaken for Jesus are pure speculation.

Scholars have also suggested that Jesus was miraculously capable of changing his appearance, which is how he avoided arrest. [21] They note, for example, that some reports of his post-crucifixion appearances indicate that at times his disciples failed to recognise him. Rashīd Riḍā has added that Jesus might have made someone else look like him and had that man arrested and crucified instead of him. [22]

The fact that the crucifixion was hastily carried out, as suggested by the Gospels, would have made it less likely for the authorities to discover that they had the wrong person. The Gospels' claim that the crucifixion took place less than twenty-four hours after the arrest is probably not historical, but there is no reason to doubt the implication that the whole process was wrapped up quickly.

I see misidentification as the most convincing interpretation of 4.157:

And saying, "We have killed the Messiah, Jesus, the son of Mary, the

[19] Ṣidqī, *Naẓariyyatī*, 36–42.
[20] Al-Khaṭīb, *Al-Masīḥ*, 486–488.
[21] Shaʿbān, *Ḥayāt Al-Masīḥ*, 92–94.
[22] Riḍā, *ʿAqīdat Al-Ṣalīb*, 34.

messenger of Allah". They did not kill him, nor did they crucify him, but it was made to appear so to them. Those who differ over it are *in doubt about it.* They have no knowledge of it except the following of *conjecture.* They *did not kill him with certainty.*

Those who conducted the crucifixion had *doubts* that they killed Jesus. They knew that their claim was based on "conjecture" rather than "certainty". I take this to mean that they were not completely certain that it was Jesus that they crucified. Jesus' complete disappearance after the crucifixion did not give them any reason to investigate that uncertainty.

So what role might God's protection of Jesus have played in this scenario to explain Jesus' evasion of arrest in natural terms? One possibility is that God prevented anyone who knew Jesus from accompanying the arresting guards or witnessing his trial or crucifixion. This is one possibility for the apparently natural case of misidentification being subtly facilitated supernaturally.

23

The Dead Jesus

Non-Muslim scholars believe that Jesus died when he was crucified, but they fall into two groups when it comes to what happened to him afterwards. Those of the Christian faith believe that Jesus was raised from death and will return at the end times. Those who do not treat the resurrection narrative in the New Testament as literal history, including confessed Christians, believe that the crucifixion was the end of Jesus' life, as would have naturally happened to any human being.

Most Muslim scholars believe that after rescuing Jesus from the attempt to crucify him, God raised him to somewhere in heaven where he continues to live. He will descend to the earth to play a major role in the eschaton.

The Qur'an partly agrees and partly disagrees with both Non-Muslim and Muslim scholars. It unambiguously denies Jesus' crucifixion, yet it also unequivocally affirms Jesus' mortality and death.

23.1 Jesus' Mortal Nature and Death

There are direct and indirect indications in the Qur'an that Jesus is dead and that he lived a life of normal length.

First, the Qur'an attributes to Jesus mentioning his future death. After becoming pregnant with Jesus, Mary decided to leave her hometown to hide her pregnancy. She would not have convinced people that it was caused by a miracle and did not involve an illicit relationship. After giving birth in an isolated area and witnessing the miraculous nature of her child, she went back with her newborn to her hometown, having been instructed by God through the child not to speak to people and to let him speak instead. When people saw her carrying her newborn, they accused her of fornication, reminding her that she descended from a noble family and that both of her parents were chaste:

> Then she brought him to her people, carrying him. They said, "O Mary, you have committed an abominable thing. (27) O sister of Aaron! Your

father was not a man of evil nor was your mother unchaste". (19.27-28)

Keeping her silence, she signalled to her accusers to talk to the newborn instead. Naturally, they reacted with shock and incredulity to being asked to speak to someone who was still in the cradle. At this point, Jesus started speaking. His miraculous ability to speak in the cradle was itself a defence of his unmarried mother against the accusation of unchastity. It confirmed that he could not have been born of an illegitimate relationship. His descriptions of himself, including as being a servant and prophet of God, particularly stressed that he was human to pre-empt any misconceptions that the impressive miracle could have caused:

> I am the servant of Allah. He has given me the Book and made me a prophet. (30) He has made me blessed wherever I am and has enjoined on me prayer and acts of purification *as long as I remain alive* (31) and to be dutiful to my mother, and He has not made me a wretched tyrant. (32) Peace is on me the day I was born, the day *I will die* (amūtu), and the day I am brought back alive. (19.30-33)

In verse 31, Jesus indirectly stresses that he is mortal and will suffer death like every human being. More significantly, verse 33 mentions only one death and, accordingly, one resurrection, which is the general resurrection on the Day of Judgment when all people are brought back to life. It does not mention an earlier resurrection that is specific to Jesus. This understanding is confirmed by the use of almost identical wording to describe John, whom no one suggests was raised from death as is said to have happened to Jesus after his crucifixion:[1]

> Peace is on him the day he was born, the day he will die, and the day he is brought back alive. (19.15)

Verse 19.33 is, therefore, another confirmation that Jesus was not raised from death.

The mention of *death*, not *murder*, is a further indication that Jesus was not killed. We will analyse this observation in more detail in the next chapter.

Second, in the context of refuting the divinity of Jesus, the Qur'an presents his death as an argument against such a claim. Had he been

---

[1] Robinson, *Jesus*, III, 17.

divine, he would not have died:

> The Messiah, son of Mary, was only a messenger before whom other messengers have *passed on*. His mother was righteous. They both used to eat food. See how We make the signs clear to them, then see how they are deluded. (5.75)

The verb "passed on" (*khalat*) means "died and are no more", as confirmed by its appearances in other verses (e.g. 2.134; 46.17). Jesus' and Mary's need for food to survive is another proof that they were mortal.

The **third** evidence that Jesus died can be read indirectly from a reference to Jesus' age, which appears in two verses. The first of these reports a promise and the second confirms its fulfilment:

> He will speak to people in the cradle and when middle-aged (*kahlan*) and he will be of the righteous. (3.46)
>
> Remember My favour on you and your mother when I supported you with the Spirit of Holiness, making you speak to people in the cradle and when middle-aged (*kahlan*). (5.110)

The word *kahl* does not occur in the Qur'an elsewhere. Lexicographers agree that this word indicates an age of over 30, with some combining with this age the presence of some grey hair. Others consider *kahl* as covering up to the age of 50. The Qur'an has a different word for a very old man, "shaikh" (11.72; 12.78; 28.23), which is why "middle-aged" seems like a reasonable interpretation. It should be noted, though, that "middle age" in modern times covers later years, usually 45–60 years, because of the significantly longer average life expectancy.

Jesus' speaking in the cradle is mentioned because of its miraculous nature, but what is meant by the concomitant reference to his speaking in his middle age when this is normal? God's miraculous gifts to Jesus are the focus of 5.110. If *kahl* refers to an age that is significantly older than Jesus' age at the crucifixion, speaking while *kahl* would serve the purpose of becoming another affirmation that Jesus did not die on the cross and went on to live well past that age. This, in turn, suggests that Jesus was probably much younger at the time of the crucifixion than the traditionally accepted thirty years of age. I discuss this in detail later in this chapter.

Jesus' speaking to people was first mentioned when the angels delivered to Mary the good news about her future miraculous son. She naturally recognised that his speaking in the cradle was a miracle. She had no reason to understand that his speaking as a middle-aged man also referred to a miracle, but she drew reassurance from this promise about her young son's safety as his life was increasingly coming under threat. This news about Jesus' future had a similar function to the promise that God gave to Moses' mother. Having ordered her to put her baby in a chest and cast it in the river, God reassured her that He would return her infant to her and make him grow up to become a messenger:

> We inspired Moses' mother, "Suckle him and when you fear for him, cast him into the river and do not fear or grieve. We will return him to you and We will make him one of the messengers". (28.7)

Also, being an indication that Jesus lived a normal number of years, this reference to him reaching middle age counters the claim that he is still alive. The Christian version of this claim is linked to the belief in his divinity, whereas the Muslim's derives from the belief that he will return for the final eschaton.

Fourth, putting the argument from the term *kahl* aside, while the Qur'an details Jesus' miracles, there is no mention of him living supernaturally longer than usual. This is something that the Qur'an would have mentioned, not only because it mentions other miracles of Jesus but also because it is mentioned in the case of Noah:

> We sent Noah to his people, and he remained among them a thousand years less fifty. The flood seized them while they were wrongdoers. (29.14)

Interestingly, even in the unique case of Noah, Muslim scholars are unanimous that he died at some point.

Fifth, more generally, in the Qur'an, all human beings are mortal. There is no exception even among the prophets:

> We have not granted any man before you [O Muhammad!] immortality. So if you die, would they live forever? (34) Every soul will taste death. We test you with evil and with good as trial; to Us you will be returned. (21.34-35)

This verse is also emphatic that no one before the Prophet Muhammad, which includes Jesus, was immortal. The following verse also talks specifically about God's messengers:

> Muhammad is not but a messenger before whom the messengers have

passed on. So if he dies (*māta*) or be killed, would you turn back on your heels [to unbelief]? (3.144)

The verses that we have reviewed in this section should leave no doubt that Jesus died naturally after living a normal length of time.

23.2 The Unreturning Messiah

The fact that Jesus is dead conflicts with the belief of Christians and Muslims that he will return in the future. The Christian concept of the "returning Messiah" developed for two reasons. First, Jesus' followers accepted his peaceful non-political messiahship and that it was not going to create a seismic change to the world order. Nevertheless, they expected a much bigger impact from their spiritual master than the small one he left on the Jews and Palestine during his life. Second, in addition to knowing that he rose from death after the crucifixion, they took his appearances afterwards to mean that he could and would come back.

Since Muslim scholars accept that Jesus was mortal, it would have been natural to conclude that he died at some point like every other human being. This conclusion should not have been affected by the belief that he was raised to heaven after the crucifixion. Yet the overwhelming majority of Sunni and Shia scholars believe that Jesus' death will take place after he descends at the end times. This means that he is currently some 2,000 years old! As we have already seen, this view is incompatible with the Qur'an, whose language on Jesus is not eschatological.[2]

The belief in Jesus' return is an import from Christian theology, with a corpus of ḥadīths having been developed to support it. Such ḥadīths are found in both Sunni and Shia sources. These narratives talk about Jesus descending to the earth at the end times to put right what had gone wrong, including him killing the antichrist. Only then will Jesus die.

Sunni sources have no less than fifteen different ḥadīths of varying lengths and details about Jesus' second spell on the earth.[3] One states that he will die forty years after killing the antichrist,[4] but another seems to suggest seven years instead.[5] In his commentary on 3.55, Ṭabarī attributes

---

[2] Reynolds, "The Muslim Jesus", 250.

[3] Harās, *Faṣl Al-Maqāl*, 24-46.

[4] Abū Dāwūd, *Sunan*, VI, no. 4324, p. 0378.

[5] Muslim, *Ṣaḥīḥ*, IV, no. 2940, pp. 2258-2259.

to Ka'b al-Aḥbār saying that Jesus would stay for twenty-four years.

Ṭabarī (3.55) also mentions the view that Jesus died for a few hours on the earth, implying that he was then brought back to life, so this was not the natural death that later ended his life. Wahb Ibn Munabbih said that God made Jesus die for three hours and then raised him. Ibn Isḥāq attributes to Christians the view that Jesus died for seven hours and was then brought back to life.

Shia scholars quote Sunni sources and have traditions attributed to their Imams as well.[6] Some Shia traditions link the descent of Jesus to the return of the Mahdī, with the latter leading the prayer and Jesus being among the congregation.[7]

Scholars have also claimed that 43.61 and 4.159 implicitly refer to Jesus' return. Such interpretations are driven by an a priori belief in Jesus' return, rather than representing an accurate reading of the text. I discuss elsewhere in more detail the genesis of the fallacy of Jesus' return in both Christianity and Islam.[8]

23.3 Jesus' Age at the Time of the Crucifixion
I would like now to offer new insight into the age of the historical Jesus at the time of the crucifixion.

I have serious doubts about Luke's claim that Jesus was as old as thirty when he started his public mission. I find it highly unlikely that Jesus started his preaching that late in his life. The Gospels portray Jesus, the Messiah, as an extremely charismatic, highly educated, full-time spiritual teacher. He enthusiastically and relentlessly communicated his reformist teachings and informed interpretations of the Mosaic law to people from all walks of life. He regularly attacked the religious establishment for its distorted teachings and for misguiding people to advance its own interests. How can such a person live like a layperson and have no public activity whatsoever until he is thirty? Certainly, theological arguments could be made as to why his mission had to start suddenly and that late, but it is hard to find any argument outside the realms of theology, and even theology would struggle to offer a convincing answer. There is no

---

[6] Editors, *Mu'jam*, III, 497-501, 511; Majlisī, *Biḥār Al-Anwār*, XIV, 349-350.

[7] Editors, *Mu'jam*, IV, 859; V, 1235.

[8] Fatoohi, *The Messiah in Islam, Christianity, and Judaism.*

suggestion that local circumstances in the first thirty years of Jesus' life would have made his teachings less needed or would have stopped him from sharing them with the largest audience possible, which was the whole point of his mission.

I find support for doubting the image of Jesus suddenly changing from being almost in hiding to a public Messiah in the same Gospel that claims that Jesus started his ministry at thirty. This is what Luke says:

> Now every year his parents went to Jerusalem for the festival of the Passover. And when he was *twelve years old*, they went up as usual for the festival. When the festival was ended and they started to return, the boy Jesus stayed behind in Jerusalem, but his parents did not know it. Assuming that he was in the group of travelers, they went a day's journey. Then they started to look for him among their relatives and friends. When they did not find him, they returned to Jerusalem to search for him. After three days they found him *in the temple, sitting among the teachers, listening to them and asking them questions.* And all who heard him were amazed at his understanding and his answers. When his parents saw him they were astonished; and his mother said to him, "Child, why have you treated us like this? Look, your father and I have been searching for you in great anxiety." He said to them, "Why were you searching for me? Did you not know that I must be in my Father's house?" But they did not understand what he said to them. Then he went down with them and came to Nazareth, and was obedient to them. His mother treasured all these things in her heart. *And Jesus increased in wisdom and in years, and in divine and human favor.* (Luke 2:41-52)

Here we have an extraordinary twelve-year-old with precocious knowledge and enough confidence to daringly engage with religious teachers in an intimidating place in a foreign city with no parental support. Surely, this child would have become even more confident, energetic, enthusiastic, curious, and debate-seeking as he grew older. It is illogical to claim that he went completely silent for eighteen years! Did he not visit the temple in those years? Were there no religious teachers and interested people in his hometown to discuss religious matters with? Could he really have ignored his growing knowledge, energy, and realisation of the need for Judaism to reform for eighteen years? This is unreasonable and unlikely.

Sure enough, the Evangelist contradicts himself when he

acknowledges that as the child grew older, his stature continued to grow not only in God's eyes but also with people. The only way for Jesus' standing with people to have increased would be if he continued to impress them with his knowledge, oratory and debating skills, and charisma. It is only logical to presume that Jesus continued to preach to people, probably with his activity reaching its height towards the end of his teens.

As Jesus was nearing adulthood, he would have become more active and people would have seen him as more credible. The increasing activity and growing credibility of the young teacher became so alarming that the Jewish authorities tried to stop him. Having failed to do that, they decided to eliminate him (§18.7, §5.3).

I find this timeline of Jesus' public life more plausible and realistic than the one in the Gospels. My alternative scenario makes Jesus' life on the earth much shorter and removes the inexplicable large gap in the Gospels' timeline. This proposed timeline is aligned with my view that the misidentification that led to crucifying the wrong person was facilitated by the shortness of Jesus' public activity, during much of which he remained relatively little known (§22.3).

This conclusion can also be linked to my interpretation that the mention of Jesus' middle age in verses 3.46 and 5.110 hints at something miraculous. If Jesus was in his late teens or early adulthood when the crucifixion took place, then the fact that he spoke to people when middle-aged, that is, over a decade or more later, is a reference to his rescue from that plot to kill him. Speaking to "people" also means that he was physically rescued and continued to live normally in a place where he could communicate with others. We will discuss this further later (§25.2). It is difficult to speculate what people these verses talk about as we do not know where he was taken to and its inhabitants.

Jesus' life in his new abode must have been long enough for his deification to have taken hold among some people on the earth. This is evidenced by a dialogue between God and Jesus after He moved him to heaven (§26.2).

We have seen in the first part of the book (§6) that the Gospels offer irreconcilable information about the dates of Jesus' birth and crucifixion. My reasoning that Jesus was in his late teens when the crucifixion took place creates even more tension between the Gospels' statements that relate to the dating of his birth and death.

Mark, the earliest Gospel, and John, the latest, start with Jesus' baptism, so they say nothing about Jesus' birth. Matthew's account of Jesus' birth under Herod the Great is mythical. Luke's claim that Jesus was born during the legateship of Quirinius in Syria, which started in 6 CE, has its own historical problems.[9]

On the other hand, all four Gospels agree that the crucifixion happened during Pilate's prefectship of Judea. Let's see what combining this consensus as a dating reference point with my proposal that Jesus was around eighteen years old at the time of the crucifixion would lead to. One consequence is that Jesus could not have been born during the reign of Herod the Great. The latter died in 4 BCE and Pilate became a prefect in 26 CE. This gap of thirty years is significantly longer than Jesus' eighteen years of age at the time of the crucifixion. Similarly, Jesus could not have been born during the census of Quirinius in 6 CE.

Given that Pilate governed in 26-36 CE, if Jesus was around eighteen years old at the time of the crucifixion, he would have been born in 8-18 CE. Luke also states that the crucifixion was around the sixteenth year of Tiberius, which corresponds to 30 CE. This would date Jesus' birth to 12 CE.

Admittedly, there is quite a bit of speculation here, but the general conclusion that Jesus was a very young man when the Jews tried to crucify him seems to be more plausible than the alternatives.

---

[9] Fatoohi, *The Mystery of the Historical Jesus*, 257-297.

24

God's Taking (*tawaffī*) of Jesus

Except for a small minority of dissenting voices, Muslim scholars deny that Jesus died by crucifixion. An increasing number think that he lived and died on the earth, while the overwhelming majority continue to argue that God took him to live in heaven. At the heart of these differences lie the interpretations of two verbs that describe divine actions concerning Jesus after he avoided the crucifixion:

- *Wfy* (in *tawaffī*): Did God "cause Jesus to die" or "take him"?
- *Rf* (in *rafaʿa*): What does God's "raising" of Jesus mean?

We will examine the former in this chapter and the latter in the next.

The Qur'an uses the verbal root *wfy* to describe God's intervention to protect Jesus from the attempt on his life. Some modern scholars, such as Ibn ʿĀshūr in his commentary on 3.55, have strongly argued that *wfy* can only refer to death. This uncompromising understanding of the verb is a recent phenomenon and is the view of only some. The overwhelming majority still agree that *wfy* does not mean death in the case of Jesus. A very small minority of early scholars, such as the Andalusian jurist Ibn Rushd (520/1126), have differed only in admitting the possibility, not even the plausibility, that it may indicate Jesus' death.[1]

In the story of Jesus, the verb *wfy* appears in two verses from different chapters that report a dialogue between God and Jesus. In the first verse, God is the speaker, whereas in the second, Jesus answers a question from God:

> When Allah said, "O Jesus! I am taking you (*mutawaffīka*), raising you to Me, and cleansing you of those who disbelieve, and setting those who follow you above those who disbelieve until the Day of Resurrection. Then to Me you shall all return, and I shall judge between you concerning what you

---

[1] Ibn Rushd, *Al-Bayān*, XVIII, 448-449. This is the grandfather of the philosopher Averroes.

differed on". (3.55)

I did not say to them other than that which You commanded me, "Worship Allah, my Lord and your Lord". I was a witness over them as long as I was among them; but when You took me (*tawaffaytanī*), You were the observer over them. You are witness over everything. (5.117)

Those who claim that the Qur'an does not deny Jesus' crucifixion and Muslim scholars who, while disagreeing with this view, accept that Jesus is already dead here argue that the verb *wfy* means "cause to die". The others take it to mean something along the lines of "take", as in my translation, which reflects my understanding of this action in these two verses and, more broadly, the context of Jesus' story as a whole.

Some Western scholars have suggested that Muslim scholars are unnecessarily confused by the verb *mutawaffika*, which, according to them, unambiguously means "cause you to die".[2] Most appearances of this term are in connection with death or the separation of the soul from the body, they note, so there is no justification for claiming that the two instances of this verb in Jesus' story do not carry the same meaning.[3] This view ignores the fact that *wfy* has a *broader* meaning in the Qur'an that includes the *specific* meaning of death.[4] This is conceded even by those who argue for Jesus' death on the cross.[5]

Following the hermeneutical principle of "the Qur'an interprets itself", I have summarised in Table 24.1 the eight different forms in which the triliteral verb *wfy* occurs in its sixty-six appearances in the Qur'an.

The verb *wfy* conveys the meaning of "claim in full", "pay in full", and "fulfil". Almost two-thirds of its appearances in the Qur'an are not related to death. The only form that is connected with death is *tawaffā*, which is one of the two instances of *wfy* used with Jesus. The second is *mutawaffī*, which occurs only once in the Qur'an. Leaving the two verses about Jesus aside, there are twenty-three appearances of *tawaffā* in as many verses. We will study these twenty-three occurrences to understand the likely meaning of this verb in the two instances of its use for Jesus.

---

[2] Parrinder, *Jesus in the Qur'an*, 106; Anderson, *The Qur'an in Context*, 247.

[3] Reynolds, "The Muslim Jesus", 239-240. Ironically, this author argues this "is in part due to the prevalent method of studying quranic verses in isolation" (p. 251), yet it is his very view that fails to consider all relevant verses.

[4] McAuliffe, *Qur'anic Christians*, 133.

[5] Ayoub, *A Muslim View of Christianity*, 169; Lawson, *The Crucifixion and the Qur'an*, 30.

Table 24.1: The forms of the verbal root *wfy* in the Qur'an

Arabic	Form	Frequency	Meaning
Tawaffā	Form V verb	24	Take; take the soul; take consciousness
Mutawaffī	Form V active participle	1	Take
Waffā	Form II verb	18	Pay/give in full; fulfil
Awfā	Form IV verb	18	Fulfil; give in full
Yastawfū	Form X verb	1	Take in full
Awfā	Nominal	2	The fullest; more faithful
Muwaffū	Form II active participle	1	Paying in full
Mūfūn	Form IV active participle	1	Fulfilling

Out of these twenty-three verses, twenty use the verb *wfy* to mean *cause to die*. The subject of this transitive verb is God in eight verses (3.193; 7.126; 10.46, 104; 12.101; 13.40; 16.70; 40.77), the angels in seven (4.97; 6.61; 7.37; 8.50; 16.28, 32; 47.27), and the Angel of Death in one (32.11). The angels are agents of God, so He is ultimately the actor. In another four verses (2.234, 240; 22.5; 40.67), the verb occurs in the passive voice, so the subject is implied.

While the verb means "cause to die" in those twenty verses, the other three show that it has a broader meaning of which causing death is a specific case. This is the **first** of the three verses:

> Those of your women who commit an unlawful sexual act, bring against them four witnesses from among you. If they testify, confine them [the guilty women] to houses until death (*mawt*) takes them (*yatawaffāhunna*) or Allah ordains for them another way. (4.15)

As death (*mawt*) is the subject of the verb *wfy* in *yatawaffāhunna*, *wfy* cannot mean "cause to die", otherwise the clause *yatawaffāhunna al-mawtu* would mean "death causes them to die", which makes no sense. The verb *wfy* must be referring to an "action" that, in this context, is caused by death. Accordingly, *yatawaffāhunna* may be translated as "takes them" or "seizes them", which denotes the taking of the soul when death is its context. The target of the verb, therefore, is the "soul", whose separation from the body is death.

This conclusion, which is also drawn by some non-Muslim scholars,[6] is confirmed in the **second** verse that uses the verb in its broad sense. This verse describes what happens to the human being during sleep:

> Allah takes (*yatawaffā*) the souls at the time of their death (*mawt*) and those that do not die during their sleep. Then He keeps those for which He has decreed death and releases the others for a specified term. Indeed, in that are signs for a people who reflect. (39.42)

The verb *wfy* is used in its general meaning of "take" as it defines "death" as the process of *permanently taking the soul* and "sleep" as the *temporary taking of the soul*, despite the two being biologically completely different. The temporary seizing of the soul is associated with the unconsciousness and low sensory and perceptual activity of sleep. As noted by the great exegete Ṭabāṭabāʾī, the Qur'an considers death as the end of the person's life *only in this world*. In this sense, death also is a temporary state of unconsciousness because the person will be brought back to life on the Day of Resurrection.

The Qur'an considers the soul the essence of the person because it is the carrier of their spiritual characteristics; it is the person's spiritual ID. The body is transient, but the soul is immortal. This is why the object of *wfy* can be switched from the "soul" to the "person". Linguistically, *wfy* means "take", but the Qur'an's concept of "soul" being the essence of the person means that it can be replaced with "person" as the object of the verb, as seen in most relevant verses.

Applying *wfy* to a person does not necessarily indicate their death but could denote a death-like state of unconsciousness. This is confirmed again in 6.60, the **third** verse that uses the verb in its general meaning:

> It is He who takes you (*yatawaffākum*) by night and knows what you have committed by day. Then He revives you so that a specified term may be fulfilled. Then to Him will be your return; then He will inform you about what you used to do. (60) He is the subjugator over His servants. He sends over you guardians until when death (*mawt*) comes to one of you, Our messengers take him (*tawaffathu*), and they do not fail [in their duties]. (6.60-61)

---

[6] McAuliffe, *Qur'anic Christians*, 133.

Verse 6.60 uses *wfy* in the sense of the temporary taking of the soul in sleep, whereas 6.61 uses it for the permanent seizing of the soul in death.

Verse 6.61 contains a term that is critical to fully understand *wfy*, which is *mawt*. Forms of this word occur in the Qur'an 165 times—two and a half as many times as the derivatives of *wfy*. *Mawt* refers to death in the strict sense of ceasing to be alive. Its meaning is simple and has no nuances. Verse 6.61 makes a clear distinction between *mawt* as the *state of lifelessness* and *wfy* as the *process of causing death*. One significant difference between the two is that the focus of *mawt* is the *termination of the physical body*, whereas the focal point of *wfy* is the *preservation of the soul*.

This contrast in the sophistication of meaning shows in the use of the two verbs. First, *mawt* is used for all forms of living creatures, i.e. including those that may not have souls, whereas *wfy* is restricted to human beings. Second, *mawt* is used with God as the agent causing the death or, significantly, without an agent. In this case, the person acts as the subject because the focus of the verb is only the change from the state of being alive to the state of being dead. This use shows that the emphasis of the meaning is on the outcome, not the process that leads to it. *Wfy*, on the other hand, is mostly used with a subject as the agent that affects the process of death, i.e. performs the taking of the soul. In the remaining small number of verses in which there is no subject, *wfy* appears in the passive voice, so an agent is implied.

Significantly, Jesus uses *mawt* when referring to his death:

> Peace is on me the day I was born, the day I will die (*amūtu*), and the day I am brought back alive. (19.33)

Yet when God and Jesus refer to the action that ended his contact with his people, they both use *wfy*, whose focus is the taking of the soul:

> When Allah said, "O Jesus! I am taking you (*mutawaffīka*), raising you to Me, and cleansing you of those who disbelieve, and setting those who follow you above those who disbelieve until the Day of Resurrection". (3.55)

> I was a witness over them as long as I was among them; but when You took me (*tawaffaytanī*), You were the observer over them. You are witness over everything. (5.117)

Note that *mawt* can be used with an agent, not only without it, yet both verses use *wfy* instead of *mawt*. This contrast with 19.33, which uses *mawt*, is not meaningless. There are twenty-one verses in which *mawt* appears in verbal form IV. This verb would have been used if Jesus' death was the focus of 3.55 and 5.117. What is being highlighted, rather, is a temporary death-like state. As we shall see in the next chapter, this action is inseparably connected to the action of "raising" Jesus.

There is a verse in which the prophet Abraham describes God as the ultimate cause of whatever happens to him, including death. As expected, and as Jesus does in verse 19.33, he uses *mawt* rather than *wfy*:

> (He) who will cause me to die (*yumītunī*) and then bring me back to life. (26.81)

In his commentary on 3.55, Ṭabāṭabāʾī quotes the following verses:

> Say, "The Angel of Death (*mawt*) who has been entrusted with you takes you (*yatawaffākum*)". (32.11)
> Allah takes (*yatawaffā*) the souls at the time of their death (*mawt*) and those that do not die during their sleep. Then He keeps those for which He has decreed death and releases the others for a specified term. Indeed, in that are signs for a people who reflect. (39.42)

He goes on to note:

> Reflecting on the last two verses shows that *tawaffī* (the infinitive of *wfy*) is not used in the Qur'an to mean *mawt* but to denote the care of taking and preserving. In other words, *tawaffī* is used for the taking involved in death to indicate that the human soul does not cease to exist or perish with death, which an ignorant person would consider to be a state of perishing and end of existence. Rather, Allah Almighty preserves the soul until He resurrects it to return to the person. Accordingly, He (exalted is He) uses the term *mawt* rather than *tawaffī* in places where this care (of taking and preserving) is not the referent.

He then gives four examples of the many such verses, including 19.33 and this verse:

> Muhammad is not but a messenger before whom the messengers have passed on. So if he dies (*māta*) or be killed, would you turn back on your heels [to unbelief]? (3.144)

In summary, it is highly unlikely that *wfy* in verses 3.55 and 5.117 refers to Jesus' death. His death must have happened *after*, not *before*, his raising. His death was not on the earth and it did not happen shortly after the crucifixion.

One of Muḥammad ʿAbduh's prominent students, Maḥmūd Shaltūt, who became the Grand Imam of al-Azhar from 1958 until his death in 1963, argues that the verb *wfy* in the Qurʾan is mainly used for death. When this is not the case, he notes, the verb is associated with something that moves it away from this meaning.[7] Given that this is not the case in the instances in which *wfy* is applied to Jesus, he concludes that the term must refer to death. There are two serious faults with Shaltūt's conclusion. First, it ignores the clear distinction in the Qurʾan between *wfy* and *mawt*.

Second, in a statement such as "it is He who takes you (*yatawaffākum*) by night", for example, the phrase "by night" provides a specific context to clarify the meaning of the verb. Shaltūt's argument, therefore, is that context matters to understanding the verb. But this is exactly one argument made in favour of reading the verb as not meaning death with regards to Jesus! The raising of Jesus by God is a major context for *wfy* in this specific case. "Raising" is a very suggestive term, so it is only wise to resist jumping to the conclusion that Jesus died until the divine action of raising has been interpreted. This is the subject of the next chapter.

Contemporary preacher ʿAdnān Ibrāhīm claims that if Jesus was going to be raised alive to heaven, he would have mentioned this future event in verse 19.33 in which he mentions his death.[8] To show the flaw in this view, we need to study the verse in context. When Mary returned to her people and asked them to speak to her newborn instead of her, they understandably replied with bemusement, "How can we speak to one who is a child in the cradle?" (19.29). At this point, Jesus spoke the following words:

> I am the servant of Allah. He has given me the Book and made me a prophet. (30) He has made me blessed wherever I am and has enjoined on me prayer and acts of purification *as long as I remain alive* (31) and to be dutiful to my mother, and He has not made me a wretched tyrant. (32) Peace is on me the day I was born, the day I will die (*amūtu*), and the day I am brought back alive. (19.30-33)

Jesus' ending statement is intended to stress that he was a human being despite his miraculous birth and wonderful gifts as a small child. This is why he started by stressing his servanthood to God and ended with the

---

[7] Shaltūt, *Al-Fatāwā*, 52.
[8] Ibrāhīm, "ʿAwdat ʿĪsā," 2012.

mention of his resurrection from death, just like every human being.

There was only a subtle hint of future miracles when he said that *he was made blessed wherever he is*. He did not specify any other future miracles because that would have served no purpose. He would not have made a future claim that was not provable then when he was already showing his miraculous ability to speak while still an infant. Furthermore, there is no reason to believe that the newborn knew that one day he would have to be rescued and raised to heaven! Indeed, God's speech to Jesus in 3.55 that he was going to raise him sounds very much like He was informing him of something he did not know. This is why Ibrāhīm's objection is no argument against the physical raising of Jesus.

Muslim scholars, the majority of whom agree that *wfy* does not mean "cause to die" in the case of Jesus, have expressed two views about what exactly the verb *wfy* indicates happened to Jesus. One view is that he was put in a sleep-like state before being raised to heaven. This utilises the Qur'an's use of the verb to describe sleep.

The second view is that he was "seized" (*qubiḍa*) from the earth and raised, with no reference to sleep. This means that he was raised while fully awake. This interpretation derives from the general meaning of *wfy*, which is to pay in full. The object of the verb, i.e. the payment, is usually a debt, reward, retribution, or reckoning. But when Jesus is the object of the verb and God is its subject, the meaning is that God took Jesus in full, as in not lacking wakefulness.

The heterogeneous view that Jesus died for a few hours seems to use *wfy* to mean a temporary death. This use is not found in the Qur'an.

25

The Raising (*raf'*) of Jesus

So far, we have concluded that Jesus escaped the attempt to arrest and crucify him and another man was misidentified and put to death instead. God then *raised Jesus to Himself*, which is the subject of this chapter. We will see that this can only mean that God physically raised Jesus and that this raising was to heaven. This was the final step of the plan to save him from his enemies. Given that Jesus was mortal, like any other human being, and did not come back to the earth, he must have died in heaven.

25.1 A Physical Raising of Jesus

God's raising of Jesus is mentioned in two verses:

> Rather, Allah raised him (*rafa'ahu*) to Himself. Allah is invincible, wise. (4.158)
>
> When Allah said, "O Jesus! I am taking you (*mutawaffika*), raising you (*rāfi'uka*) to Me, and cleansing you of those who disbelieve, and setting those who follow you above those who disbelieve until the Day of Resurrection". (3.55)

Both verses use the same verb to describe the action of "raising" Jesus. The triliteral root *rf'* occurs twenty-nine times in the Qur'an, including twenty-two times in verbal forms. It has two different meanings in the Qur'an:

- The spatial raising of something or someone
- The raising of the standing or status of something or someone

Here is a sample verse of each use:

> In houses that Allah has ordered to be raised (*turfa'a*) and that His name be mentioned therein. (24.36)
>
> We raise (*narfa'u*) in degrees whom We will, and over every person of knowledge is a more knowledgeable one. (12.76)

The first verse talks about building places of worship and the second about the spiritual promotion of individuals.

In the last century or so, some scholars have taken the agnostic position that the text is ambiguous about what exactly happened to Jesus. For instance, in his celebrated book *The Stories of the Prophets*, ʿAbd al-Wahhāb al-Najjār says that God may have caused Jesus to die on the earth, put him to sleep as He did to the sleepers of the cave (18.9-26), or raised him to heaven. He refrains from taking a view because he thinks the Qurʾan is vague on this issue.[1] Another example is the Eygptian Islamic theorist Sayyid Quṭb who, in his commentary on 4.157, states the following:

> The Qurʾan does not give details about this raising. Was it in both the body and the soul while alive? Or was it in the soul only after death? When was this taking/death? Where?

This caution reflects uncertainty not only about the meaning of the divine action of raising Jesus but also about what happened to him after the crucifixion in general.

Muslim and non-Muslim scholars who do not accept that Jesus was physically raised from the earth to heaven argue that his elevation was allegorical. They claim that God raised Jesus in status, not as a person.[2] There are several serious flaws with this view.

First, all seven verses that use *rf* in the sense of raising a person in status, not spatially, include a word that makes this meaning abundantly clear. Six of these verses use the plural word "ranks" (*darajāt*) (also 6.83, 165; 12.76; 43.32; 58.11):

> He has raised (*rafaʿa*) some of them in rank (*darajāt*). (2.253)

The other verse uses "signs" (*ʾāyāt*) as the means by which God would have raised someone in status:

> Recite to them [O Muhammad!] the news of him to whom we gave Our signs (*ʾāyāt*), but he detached himself from them; so, Satan pursued him, and he became one of the tempters. (175) Had We willed, we could have raised him (*rafaʿnāhu*) by them, but he clung [instead] to the earth and followed his own desire. (7.175-176)

Both verses on Jesus' raising do not include such a word. This word

---

[1] Al-Najjār, *Qiṣaṣ Al-Anbiyāʾ*, 512.
[2] Shaltūt, *Al-Fatāwā*, 54-55; Ibrāhīm, "ʿAwdat ʿĪsā".

would have been necessary had the raising been in status, not physical.

Second, given that other prophets had been rescued by God or killed by their enemies, this view does not explain why Jesus is uniquely described as having been raised to God. For instance, the Qur'an explains how God saved Noah, Abraham, Moses, and other prophets from their respective peoples when they tried to kill them. None of these prophets is said to have been "raised".

Others liken Jesus' raising to the case of martyrs who are described as "alive with their Lord" (3.169), i.e. they died on the earth but are spiritually alive in heaven.[3] This semblance is invalid because those scholars still accept that Jesus was not killed to start with. Also, this misguided effort invokes a *general* fact to explain Jesus' *unique* treatment in the Qur'an. Furthermore, no one has even tried to explain what that supposed exaltation of Jesus by God means because there is no mention of it whatsoever in the Qur'an.

Third, raising Jesus is presented in 4.158 as God's reply to the attempt to *crucify and kill* him, not merely *humiliate* him. The Jews would have gone after Jesus again if they knew he had evaded the crucifixion, so the ultimate goal of the rescue operation was to raise him to heaven.

Fourth, in addition to the two verses about Jesus, there is one other instance in which the Qur'an uses the verb *rf'* in the sense of *raising a person to a physical place*. This is what it says about the prophet Idrīs:

> Mention [O Muhammad!] Idrīs in the Book. He was truthful and a prophet. (56) We raised him (*rafa'nāhu*) to a high place (*makānan*). (19.56-57)

Idrīs is identified in Muslim tradition with the Biblical figure of Enoch who was also *taken by God*:[4]

> Enoch walked with God; then he was no more, because God took him. (Gen. 5:24)

The Qur'an does not state or imply that Idrīs died before he was raised by God. As in the case of Jesus, raising a dead body would make little sense for the Qur'an to present as a favour that reflects someone's elevated status with God. Nor is there anything to indicate any dissimilarity between the raising by God of Jesus and Idrīs. Ṭabarī reports that

---

[3] Shalabī, *Al-Masīḥiyya*, 58-59.
[4] Reeves, "Explorations", 44-52; Erder, *Idrīs*, 2, 484.

Mujāhid has said that "Idrīs was raised, so he did not die, as Jesus was raised". Ṭabarī also attributes to others saying that Idrīs was raised to one of the heavens.

The "place" that Idrīs was taken to is described as "high" (*'aliyyan*). Confirmation that the word "place" identifies a physical location comes from the same Qur'anic chapter of the Idrīs verse. It occurs three other times in that chapter and each instance denotes a physical location: the place where Mary lived to dedicate herself to worship God is called "eastern" (19.16), where she went after becoming pregnant is described as "remote" (19.22), and the abode of the disbelievers on the Day of Resurrection is said to be a "worse" place (19.75). The latter instance may be translated as "position" or "state", but that cannot be separated from its reference to hell, which is a physical place. The same word in the Idrīs verse must also denote a physical location.

We have to conclude that the Qur'an is unambiguous that the raising of Jesus was physical.

25.2 A Raising to Heaven

The Qur'an has clear indications that the relocation of Jesus was to somewhere in heaven rather than another place on the earth.

First, the Jesus verses use "raise" rather than "move", "migrate", or any other verb that describes the common practice of moving from one place to another on the earth. The verb *rf* means to "raise" or "lift" to a high place. Unlike other verbs, it emphasises the *upward* nature of the move.

Second, unlike the other actions of relocation mentioned in the Qur'an, Jesus' is attributed to God. I read this to imply that it is an action that could not have been done by Jesus, so God had to do it. This is in line with the view that this is a move from the earth to heaven.

Third, God's description of raising Jesus as being "to Me/Himself" is strong evidence that He elevated him to heaven. Of the twenty-two occurrences of the verbal form of *rf* in the Qur'an, it is followed by the preposition "to" (*ilā*) only in the case of Jesus, and it is used in both Jesus verses! This preposition requires identifying a destination, hence "Me/Himself". The phrase "to Me/Himself" is not used anywhere else with the verb *rf*, yet it is found in both verses about Jesus.

I have not seen any study that rejects Jesus' elevation to heaven make this observation, let alone attempt to explain it. I find this particularly puzzling because Muslim scholars are unanimous that every word and construct in the Qur'an is intended to convey a specific meaning, if not multiple meanings. Exegetes would not claim that this unique use of "to Me/Himself" is a meaningless linguistic quirk! Those who erroneously and confusingly argue that this phrase must not be taken to mean that Jesus was raised to heaven do not tell us why it is there at all!

Fourth, the Qur'an twice describes Jesus as a messenger to the Jews. In one verse, God calls Jesus "a messenger to the Children of Israel" (3.49). In the second, a newborn Jesus tells his people, "O Children of Israel! I am Allah's messenger to you" (61.6). Indeed, Jesus' mission was local to the Jews. Yet when it comes to describing the miracle of him speaking in the cradle and as a middle-aged man, the Qur'an refers to Jesus speaking to "people" rather than "the Children of Israel":

> He will speak to *people* in the cradle and when middle-aged (*kahlan*) and he will be of the righteous. (3.46)
>
> Remember My favour on you and your mother when I supported you with the Spirit of Holiness, making you speak to *people* in the cradle and when middle-aged (*kahlan*). (5.110)

Why is there this pointed distinction between whom Jesus was sent to and whom he spoke to? The obvious general answer is that the two groups are not the same. So, what is the difference? We know that when Jesus spoke in his infancy, that was to his own people, i.e. the Jews. Using the general referent "people" instead of the specific designation "the Children of Israel" must be related to his speaking when a mature adult. We also know that he did not live outside Palestine, so the term "people" could not denote non-Jewish people elsewhere on the earth. It must refer to people he met in heaven who, naturally, could not have been described as "the Children of Israel".

The view that God physically raised Jesus to Himself was ridiculed as implying that God is located there, which contradicts the Qur'an's affirmation that He is not localised.[5] Despite its relative popularity, this is more of a strawman argument. Let me explain.

Adherents of this objection have sought support for their position in the following verse about the prophet Abraham when he decided to emigrate after his people tried to kill him because of his faith (also 29.26):

---

[5] Ibrāhīm, "ʿAwdat ʿĪsā".

He said, "I will *go to my Lord*; He will guide me". (37.99)

They rightly argue that this verse does not mean that God existed only in the place to which Abraham migrated. This euphemism means that he migrated in the cause of Allah to have his full religious freedom. But the same can be said about the raising of Jesus to God! It could not mean that he was raised to where God is. He was raised to where he could be safe from his enemies, which is confirmed by the statement that this would cleanse him of those disbelievers. This interpretation of raising to God is equivalent to one opinion quoted by Rāzī (4.158) as meaning to go or be taken to a place where God is the ruler.

Similarly, the following verse does not mean that God was present only where the Prophet Muḥammad was:

> Whoever leaves his home as an emigrant to Allah and His Messenger and then death overtakes him, his reward has already become incumbent on Allah. (4.100)

God in the Qur'an is beyond time and space, so He is everywhere and with everyone:

> He is with you wherever you are. (57.4)
> To Allah belongs the east and the west. So wherever you turn, there is the face of Allah. Indeed, Allah is encompassing, knowing. (2.115)

Interpreting God's raising of Jesus to Himself to mean taking him to heaven does not imply that God is in heaven any more than verses 29.26, 37.99, and 4.100 do. All these statements are metaphorical.

Furthermore, Abraham's "going" or "migrating" *to his Lord* and the early Muslims "migrating" to Allah and the Prophet in Medina each describes a relocation to another physical place. This can surely only support the interpretation of God's raising of Jesus *to Himself* as physically relocating him.

Rāzī has rightly objected to understanding Jesus' raising to heaven as being equivalent to him being taken to *where God is*. Yet this has been misrepresented as meaning that he favoured the view that Jesus was not raised but died on the earth.[6] Ayoub has claimed that Rāzī's description of the view of a Christian group he calls "Nestorians" implies Rāzī's support for his preference to accommodate the Christian non-historical

---

[6] Shalabī, *Al-Masīḥiyya*, 63-64.

concept of the suffering Messiah over treating the Qur'an's statements as historical.[7] Yet as I have already mentioned (§22.2), Rāzī's exegesis reiterates his belief that the Qur'an denies the crucifixion of Jesus. This is another quote from him, this time about the concept of "taking" and "raising" in his commentary on 3.55:

> His words "I am taking you (*mutawaffika*)" indicate that "taking" (*tawaffi*) took place. This is a type that includes various forms, some of which are caused by death and others by raising to heaven. As He followed those words with "raising you (*rāfi'uka*) to Me", this indicates that this saying identifies the form and is not mere repetition.

Rāzī expressly accepts that *wfy* has a broader meaning than death, that it is used in the sense of "taking" in the case of Jesus, and that Jesus was raised to heaven while alive.

The Qur'an has another potentially relevant story. God sent two messengers and later a third to a certain people. Only one man believed in God's callers and unsuccessfully pleaded with his people to follow suit. The Qur'an then reports how this man was taken to "paradise":

> [The man said to the messengers:], "I have believed in your Lord, so listen to me". (25) It was said, "*Enter Paradise*". He said, "I wish my people could know (26) how my Lord has forgiven me and made me one of the honoured". (27) We did not *send down* on his people after him any soldiers *from heaven*, nor would We have done so. (28) It was only one shout, and immediately they were extinguished. (29) Alas for the servants! There never came a messenger to them but they mocked him. (36.25-30)

Describing the messengers as being from heaven and naming the place to which the man was taken as "paradise" indicate that he was transferred to somewhere in heaven. His speech in paradise, after being spared the punitive fate of his people, implies that he continued to live there. Exegetes often claim that this man was killed by his people, so his speech was after he was taken to where martyrs live (2.154, 3.169). But others, such as Rāzī, have pointed out the possibility that he was taken to heaven alive. Indeed, there is nothing in the verse to suggest he was murdered. If anything, the all-powerful heavenly soldiers who destroyed his people would have protected him before transporting him to heaven.

---

[7] Ayoub, *A Muslim View of Christianity*, 167.

We should finally remember that the Prophet Muhammad is himself reported in the Qur'an to have been taken on a journey to heaven (53.1-18). This ascension followed his night journey from the al-Masjid al-Ḥarām in Mecca to the al-Masjid al-Aqṣā in Palestine (17.1). Unlike Jesus' raising, the Prophet Muhammad's journey was temporary, probably lasting hours, after which he was returned to his house in Mecca.

The Qur'an, therefore, confirms that the earth is not the only place where human beings have lived. Some individuals who were born and lived on this planet were taken, for different reasons, to live elsewhere. Jesus was one of those individuals. His transfer was to save him from a certain danger to his life.

This and the previous section should leave no doubt that God's raising of Jesus was to a physical location in heaven rather than in status. Rashīd Riḍā, 'Adnān Ibrāhīm, and others are wrong in ascribing the interpretation of raising a living Jesus to heaven to Christian influence. This is what the verses, not the Christians, say.

25.3 The Silence on Jesus after the Crucifixion

While the overwhelming majority of Muslim scholars believe that Jesus was raised to heaven, a small but growing minority believe that Jesus died on the earth, so he was not raised to heaven.[8] This view seems to have been first proposed, or at least popularised, by the Egyptian reformist Muhammad 'Abduh in the second half of the nineteenth century. He influenced prominent scholars, such as Muhammad Shaltūt and Muhammad al-Ghazālī, who adopted this interpretation.

The lack of any information on Jesus being active after the crucifixion is natural in the majority view because he was raised from the earth to heaven. The next time people on the earth will hear about him, it is claimed, is when he descends to play out his eschatological role. This complete absence of Jesus after escaping the crucifixion is difficult to explain from the perspective of the small minority view that he died on the earth and did not leave this planet, which is probably why it is rarely raised and discussed. There are two possible explanations for this silence on Jesus after he evaded the crucifixion, but both lack credibility.

First, after avoiding the crucifixion, Jesus kept out of the public eye

---

[8] Shalabī, *Al-Masīḥiyya*, 64-67.

for the rest of his life. This is highly unlikely given what we know about Jesus. He was driven by an unshakable belief in his divine mission, which the Qur'an confirms. This made him preach in public to as many people as he could, speak the truth as he knew it, and not shy away from criticising the Jewish religious authorities. It does not sound credible to suggest that this highly public and determined reformist teacher suddenly and for the rest of his life lived like a nondescript man and concealed his true identity. Furthermore, such a change would mean that the religious authorities prevailed in silencing him, albeit not by death. The Qur'an's repeated confirmation of God's support for Jesus against his enemies does not make such a moral defeat likely.

One contemporary scholar has suggested that Jesus left Palestine to avoid being caught by the authorities.[9] It is reasonable to suggest that Jesus would have escaped from Palestine and settled where he could preach his message without putting himself in harm's way. But why is there no information at all about him after the crucifixion? Even if he was unsuccessful in spreading his message to the non-Jewish population of his new abode, history would have recorded something about him and his activities. He was, after all, not only a charismatic preacher but also a miracle worker. Yet there is virtually zero information about him from any historical or religious source. From the Muslim perspective, the Qur'an also reports nothing about Jesus preaching after the crucifixion. This means that there was no second preaching phase in Jesus' life.

The **second** explanation is that Jesus' natural death happened shortly after the crucifixion. This is equally inconsistent with the letter and spirit of the Qur'anic statement that God intervened to rescue Jesus. It effectively means that God rescued Jesus from his enemies who wanted him dead only to cause him to die! The Jews wanted to humiliate Jesus by the crucifixion, but their ultimate goal was to kill him to put an end to his growing criticism of the religious establishment and his preaching of reformist teachings. By causing Jesus to die, God would have done what the Jews wanted, which was to eliminate Jesus. This would have been a victory for Jesus' enemies and a defeat for him even if his death was not by the most humiliating method of crucifixion. The Qur'an stresses that He did not only prevent the crucifixion of Jesus but also his

---

[9] Ibid., 56.

killing. This means that God protected his life, rather than causing him to die in a different way.

A view that has been adopted by an even smaller group of Muslims states that Jesus was crucified but survived the crucifixion and died naturally later. The first Muslim scholar to advocate this view seems to be Sayyid Ahmad Khan in the nineteenth century. It looks like this view tries to accommodate, albeit unsuccessfully, both the belief in the historicity of the crucifixion of Jesus and the Qur'an's unambiguous statement that the Jews did not kill him. As I have already pointed out (§14.1), non-fatal crucifixion scenarios lack credibility. Also, the Qur'an's denial is of Jesus' crucifixion, not of crucifixion being the cause of his death! Like the suggestion that Jesus died naturally but not by crucifixion, this theory fails to explain the silence of history and the Qur'an on Jesus' life on the earth after escaping the crucifixion.

Mirza Ghulam Ahmad took Sayyid Ahmad Khan's theory further, claiming that, having survived the crucifixion, Jesus travelled as far as the Indian subcontinent and was buried in Kashmir. There is no evidence to substantiate his identification of Jesus' tomb. The failure of this theory to explain the silence of history and the Qur'an on Jesus' life after the crucifixion is further highlighted by its claim that he lived safely away from the Jews in Palestine.

Furthermore, the Qur'an's description of Jesus as a messenger to the Jews is taken by exegetes to mean that his missionary work targeted, by design, only the Jews. I agree that he only preached to Jews, but not because he was not supposed to try to convert Gentiles. It was rather because he lived and conducted his mission among the Jews. Either way, this description dismisses any suggestion that Jesus preached outside Jewish Palestine.

25.4 One Divine Intervention of Taking and Raising

Exegetes have had two views on Jesus' state of consciousness when he was raised: a sleep-like state or wakefulness. The former is derived from the fact that *wfy* is used to describe sleep, while the latter seems to put the emphasis on raising him. It seems reasonable to argue that the mention of *wfy*, as opposed to only the raising, indicates that Jesus must have experienced some alteration to his state of consciousness. These two seemingly different actions are, in fact, inseparably connected.

I would like to highlight something that is, to the best of my knowledge, a hitherto unnoticed observation about the three verses that summarise the end of Jesus' life on the earth, which, for most Muslims, including myself, involved being raised to heaven, not dying. These are the verses listed in their order in the Qur'an:

> When Allah said, "O Jesus! I am taking you (*mutawaffīka*), raising you (*rāfi'uka*) to Me, and cleansing you of those who disbelieve, and setting those who follow you above those who disbelieve until the Day of Resurrection. (3.55)
> Rather, Allah raised him (*rafa'ahu*) to Himself. Allah is invincible, wise. (4.158)
> I did not say to them other than that which You commanded me, "Worship Allah, my Lord and your Lord". I was a witness over them as long as I was among them; but when You took me (*tawaffaytanī*), You were the observer over them. You are witness over everything. (5.117)

In the first verse, after mentioning the plot of Jesus' enemies and His counterplot that foiled it, God goes on to inform Jesus about how He was going to help him: *take* and *raise* him. These are at the heart of understanding what happened to Jesus. *Cleansing* him of the disbelievers is only a consequence of those two actions.

In the second verse, God summarises His intervention as *raising* Jesus. Then in the third and last verse, Jesus summarises God's action as *taking* him.

So, God's intervention is once described as *taking and raising*, a second time as *raising*, and a third as *taking* Jesus. Put differently, the two actions of taking and raising are once summarised as raising, so taking is implied, and another as taking, so raising is implied. Why? What does this surprising reduction tell us?

In my view, this can only mean that these actions are inseparable because they are effectively the integral parts of one divine intervention. When God spoke to Jesus, He told him *in detail* what He was going to do to rescue him. It was necessary to tell him exactly what was going to happen to him to reassure him and, possibly, because Jesus needed to prepare.

When God later referred to His intervention as a counteraction to the plan of the Jewish authorities to crucify Jesus, He only described it as a *raising* of Jesus, having already given the other details. Similarly, Jesus did not need to describe in detail to God what He did to him, so he only referred to the divine rescue as *taking*.

The fact that both actions are treated as one means that it would be incorrect to talk about the action described using *wfy* as separate from that described using *rf*. The *cleansing* of Jesus of the disbelievers was a consequence of the intervention. At some point, Jesus went from being in hiding to living in a different place in heaven, out of the reach of his enemies.

It is fascinating that Jesus' death, resurrection, and ascension to heaven in the Gospels' narrative may be entirely present in the Qur'anic story but in a very different context and order. The Gospels talk about death by crucifixion, followed by resurrection on the earth, and then ascension to heaven. If God's taking of Jesus in the Qur'an meant a loss of consciousness by Jesus that required some kind of awakening, then we have a death-like state, followed by an ascension to heaven, then a resurrection from that state of unconsciousness, and at some future point a natural death. The authors of the New Testament and their sources placed events in the wrong historical context.

This is an instance of what I call "contextual displacement". I have coined this term to denote a special kind of "textual corruption" in Jewish and Christian writings where "a character, event, or statement appears in one context in the Qur'an and in a different context in other sources".[10] Contextual displacements are the result of "the Bible's editors moving characters, events, and statements from their correct, original contexts". This concept is the exact opposite of the popular view among non-Muslim scholars that the Qur'an distorted narratives that it borrowed from Jewish and Christian sources.

It is tempting to equate the New Testament's ascension of Jesus to heaven with the Qur'an's reference to him being raised by God. The divine rescue operation of Jesus became misconstrued and misinterpreted as resurrection from death followed by the ascension of a divine Jesus. This heavenly elevation could have contributed to the edification of Jesus. As we shall see later (§26.2), Jesus was not treated as divine when he was on the earth.

---

[10] Fatoohi, *The Mystery of the Historical Jesus*, 44.

26

After the Crucifixion

In this chapter, we will first discuss Jesus' appearances after the crucifixion that are reported in the New Testament and examine whether they can be related to the Qur'anic version of events. We will then study a dialogue between God and Jesus in the Qur'an that is likely to have happened after Jesus was raised by God.

26.1 Hiding and Appearances

Let's first briefly review something we discussed in detail earlier (§21). At some point, Jesus sensed that the hostility of the Jewish authorities escalated to a dangerous level, so he wanted to make sure that his close followers would not abandon him because of the fear of persecution:

> But when Jesus perceived disbelief from them (the Children of Israel), he said, "Who are my supporters for the cause of Allah?" The companions said, "We are Allah's supporters. We believe in Allah, and you bear witness that we are Muslims. (52) Our Lord! We have believed in that which You have sent down and we have followed the messenger, so write us down among those who bear witness [to the truth]". (3.52-53)

The disciples reassured Jesus that they would support and protect him. God had not informed Jesus yet that He was going to miraculously intervene to help him, although Jesus might have expected this to happen.

The religious authorities decided to eliminate Jesus, but God had already decided to foil their scheme with a plan of His own:

> They (the Children of Israel) planned, and Allah planned; Allah is the best of planners. (3.54)

God then informed Jesus of His rescue plan:

> When Allah said, "O Jesus! I am taking you (*mutawaffika*), raising you to Me, and cleansing you of those who disbelieve, and setting those who follow you above those who disbelieve until the Day of Resurrection. Then to Me you shall all return, and I shall judge between you concerning what you

differed on". (3.55)

The decision to kill Jesus was carried out quickly, being the culmination of a period of growing hostility to him. This hasty implementation of the decision resulted in capturing and crucifying the wrong person.

After being informed by God of the authorities' decision to arrest him, Jesus must have gone into hiding. This continued after the crucifixion as he avoided making any public appearances. He was supposed to be dead and he would not have wanted the authorities to know that they killed someone else. Having not made sufficient effort to ascertain that the crucified man was Jesus, the authorities would have been enraged by the humiliation of their misidentification of Jesus becoming public. They would have ensured that this time they got their man. During his hiding, only a few very close and totally loyal followers would have been able to see Jesus in secret. These were the "supporters" mentioned in 3.52-53.

Let's now turn our attention to the New Testament. Paul's epistles, the Gospels, and Acts report appearances of Jesus after the crucifixion, although they differ about their number, whether they happened in Galilee or Judea, when they happened, and what happened in these appearances (§1.18). Paul's fantastic claim that Jesus appeared to over five hundred people is substantively different from all other accounts and is almost certainly unhistorical. All other accounts are suggestive of a Jesus in hiding, appearing only briefly to a few close followers before disappearing again. Could these appearances be genuine secret meetings with Jesus after the crucifixion, in which case they would be reconcilable with the Qur'an's story? Possibly, if they were not visions.

It is not possible to tell with any confidence how much time passed between the three main events in verses 3.52-55: Jesus' asking for his disciples' support, the crucifixion, and the rescue. We could be talking days, weeks, or even months. His hiding could have lasted any amount of time until God actioned His plan and elevated him from the earth. Jesus' appearances in the New Testament, ignoring Paul's claims, happened at various dates, starting from the dawn of Easter Sunday when Jesus appeared to Mary Magdalene and the other Mary (Matt. 28:9). The last appearance seems to be forty days later (Acts 1:3).

Jesus' appearance to Paul is the only one that is reported by its eyewitness. But this alleged encounter was with a spiritual, not physical, Jesus. Paul did not see Jesus but saw a light and heard a voice that identified itself as Jesus'. Also, this is said to have taken place long after the ascension, possibly a few years later. Whatever this incident was, if it was at all, it does not belong to the same category of the other post-crucifixion appearances.

Linking Jesus' appearances in the New Testament with the Qur'an's narrative may sound more plausible to some than others but, needless to say, it remains speculative.

26.2 Post-Raising Deification
The Qur'an reports the following dialogue between God and Jesus:

> When Allah said, "O Jesus son of Mary! Did you say to people: 'Take me and my mother for two gods besides Allah?'" He said, "Exalted are You! It was not for me to say that which I have no right to say. If I have said it, then You know it. You know what is within myself but I do not know what is within Yours. You know the unseen. (116) I did not say to them other than that which You commanded me, 'Worship Allah, my Lord and your Lord'. I was a witness over them as long as I was among them; but when You took me (*tawaffaytanī*), You were the observer over them. You are witness over everything. (117). If You punish them, then they are Your servants; and if You forgive them, then You are the Invincible, the Wise". (118) Allah said, "This is a Day on which the truthful will benefit from their truthfulness. They shall have gardens beneath which rivers flow in which they will abide forever, Allah being pleased with them and they with Him. This is the great triumph". (5.116-119)

Tabarī favours the opinion of Suddī who thinks that the dialogue in 5.116-5.118 took place after God raised Jesus. But the overwhelming majority of exegetes think that this dialogue will take place on the Day of Judgment. I disagree with this view in favour of the minority view.

Placing this dialogue on the Day of Judgment has led some Muslim scholars to give the verb *wfy* in Jesus' story two different meanings. The overwhelming majority of scholars believe that Jesus was raised to heaven alive or in a sleep-like state, so they interpret *mutawaffīka* in the promise in 3.55 to mean "take" or "put to sleep". The view that the dialogue in 5.117 will happen after the universal resurrection of the dead has led some scholars to understand *tawaffaytanī* in 5.117 to mean "caused me to die".[1] This convenient choice of meaning is unconvincing.

The main argument for considering the above dialogue as a future event on the Day of Resurrection comes from verse 5.119, which unambiguously refers to it. But looking at the surrounding verses supports a different interpretation. Let's briefly review the verses leading to the dialogue in question. Verse 5.110, which we have already studied, is a dialogue after Jesus was raised; 5.111 confirms the belief of Jesus' close followers; and verses 5.112-115 recount the miracle of "the feast", which is probably the historical event that appears as the Last Supper in the four Gospels. Then we have the verses under consideration, 5.116-118. Verses 5.110-118 are all about Jesus. These are then followed by 5.119, which clearly talks about the Day of Resurrection. This is the verse that precedes 5.110-118:

> The Day when Allah will assemble the messengers and say, "What was the response you received?" They will say, "We have no knowledge. It is You who is the knower of the unseen". (5.109)

Like 5.119, 5.109 also talks about the "Day" on which the messengers are asked about how their calls were received. It is perfectly reasonable to read verse 5.119 as following from 5.109, thus considering the Jesus verses, 5.110-118, as *parenthetical*. This style is not uncommon in the Qur'an. In this case, the word "Day" in 5.119 is preceded by the pronoun "this" because it references the same "Day" already mentioned in 5.109.

My observation is also supported by Ṭabarī, who rightly points out that "when" (*ith*), with which 5.116 starts, is used to refer to past events. This is indeed how it is usually used in the Qur'an. It also identifies a change of context. Verses 110, 111, 112-115, and 116-118 all represent past mini-episodes in Jesus' story. Also, moving from one to the other represents a change of context within the story. Indeed, each of these four starts with "when".

Interestingly, God uses "people" instead of "the Children of Israel" in His rhetorical questioning of Jesus when He asks whether he instructed them to worship him and his mother. This has the same significance as the use of the same word in the two verses that talk about Jesus speaking

---

[1] Al-Khālidī, *Al-Qaṣaṣ*, 355-357.

when he is a middle-aged man (§25.2). The belief in the divinity of Jesus spread among pagans, not the Jews, thanks to Paul in particular. Jesus confirmed what God already knew, that he did not do that. Obviously, Jesus lived only among the Jews, so his answer can only refer to them.

We should also recall the man who was transferred to heaven by God's messengers and was reported to have spoken after he was taken up (§25.2). There is an element of similarity between that event and Jesus' speaking after he was raised that is reported in 5.116-118.

Dating this dialogue to after Jesus was raised to heaven means that the distortion of his teachings started in his lifetime, albeit after he had left the earth. Interestingly, the worship of Mary, or Mariolatry, had also already started by then, probably as a result of the edification of her son, Jesus. This change to Jesus' teachings could have started within one or two decades of the crucifixion. This is in line with the generally accepted view that Paul, in particular, played a major role in developing the theology that became dominant in Christianity.

27

Conclusion: A Crucifixion of History by Faith

We will now summarise the findings of this book about the alleged crucifixion of Jesus.

Given the extremely prominent position of Jesus in history in general, not only in Christianity, one would be forgiven for expecting a plethora of early non-Christian resources that mention his crucifixion. Yet in the whole of the first two centuries of the common era, there is only a handful of them, specifically, three! Furthermore, only one of these classical sources, Tacitus, is from the first century following the crucifixion. All three accounts are dependent on Christian sources rather than independent witnesses to the crucifixion or derived from official Roman Imperial records. Josephus' Testimonium is a late Christian forgery that has nothing to do with Josephus. Jesus' small impact during his lifetime is confirmed by the absence of early Jewish sources on the crucifixion.

The popular claim that Jesus' crucifixion is supported by extra-New Testament sources is simply untrue. The mention of the crucifixion in a few external sources that are influenced by Christian tradition does nothing to support the historicity of the crucifixion in the New Testament. This fact often seems inconvenient or hard to acknowledge to those who adamantly argue that the crucifixion of Jesus belongs to history proper.

The Gospels and Paul's letters are the earliest sources of the claim that Jesus was crucified. While Paul's writings are the earliest, they contain very little history, not to mention the fact that their author never met Jesus. Paul claims to have received the teachings he preached from Jesus directly, but he inexplicably fails to give any details about how and when this happened. He recounts only one encounter with Jesus when he was prosecuting Christians, which resulted in his conversion. Even in this lone and momentary incident, he did not see Jesus, as he reported seeing a light that claimed to be Jesus.

This leaves us with the Gospels as the earliest sources on Jesus' life, including his death. We have examined their accounts of the crucifixion, including the events leading up to and following it. We have noted the most serious of the many discrepancies between the four Gospels and the historical fallacies in their narratives of the trial, crucifixion, resurrection, and post-resurrection appearances. The Evangelists' reading of the Old Testament does not fare any better. They inaccurately and even falsely quote several alleged Old Testament prophecies about the suffering of the Messiah. They needed this distorted interpretation and invention of Old Testament passages to support their claim that the now crucified Jesus was the awaited Messiah. The concept of a suffering Messiah never existed in Judaism. It was made up by Christians who anachronistically superimposed it on the Jewish scripture. In summary, individually and collectively, the Gospels are highly unreliable as historical sources.

This being the state of the earliest and main sources on Jesus' life, scholars have devised "authenticity criteria" to help them tell likely historical information from fiction in the Gospels. Yet these criteria have proven to be more successful in enforcing prior biases than in making an objective assessment of the texts and helping scholars converge on some kind of a consensus. The considerable unreliability of the sources has placed unrealistic expectations on such criteria.

The state of the primary sources has even led a small minority of scholars to doubt that Jesus was a historical figure at all! Mythicism, as this view is known, is not taken seriously by scholarship, though. It is an unconvincing attempt to make sense of the poor quality of the early sources on Jesus. It is more reasonable to make sense of these sources by trying to separate the authentic from the unhistorical accounts than it is to declare them all fiction. Mythicism raises more questions than it claims to answer.

With contradictions, inaccuracies, and historical fallacies permeating the Gospels, and with theology, at least partly, driving its authors, developing a *credible* history of Jesus inescapably requires being selective as to what narratives to consider historical and what to dismiss. This is never clearer than it is in the case of the various episodes of the crucifixion narrative, from Jesus' trial to his post-crucifixion appearances. Extracting a consistent account of the crucifixion not only requires high selectivity when it comes to admissible texts but probably also rejecting more material than is accommodated. This is the case, it is important to stress, whether or not one accepts the historicity of the crucifixion. One offshoot of the unreliability of the early sources is that it is not possible to categorically disprove Jesus' crucifixion and it is also impossible to prove it beyond all doubt. The historical Jesus of any scholar, whether they admit it or not, represents *their selective reading* of the Gospels. There are multiple different Jesuses, not only one, in the Gospels, and the same is true in scholarship. Yet while there has been scholarly disagreement on the authenticity and interpretation of almost every detail in the Gospels about Jesus' life, virtually all non-Muslim scholars consider Jesus' death on the cross a historical certainty.

However, the resurrection, which is probably one of the most contentious New Testament claims, has split the unanimity on the historicity of the crucifixion into two camps whose views I will call "natural" and "supernatural". Scholars who accept the Gospels' claims wholesale at face value, thus admitting supernaturality in the world, treat the resurrection as a historical event. Problems in the sources are dismissed or explained away, often unconvincingly, in favour of professing the integrity and authenticity of the text. Those who do not accommodate the supernatural, including some liberal Christians, consider Jesus' death by crucifixion the end of his life; he did not rise. They treat sources critically and are selective in what they accept. Naturally, there are variations of each of the two major approaches that differ in various details.

A tiny minority of scholars has unconvincingly suggested that Jesus survived the crucifixion. This view is not taken seriously by mainstream scholarship, mainly because surviving a crucifixion is highly unlikely, but also because it fails to offer a credible post-crucifixion history.

I have listed these three approaches in Table 27.1. Among the most prominent scholars that represent the "supernatural" and "natural" approaches are N. T. Wright and J. D. Crossan, respectively.[1] For completeness, the table includes the non-fatal crucifixion theory, which is a version of the natural approach. Obviously, the table does not include mythicism and the Muslim view that Jesus was not crucified.

---

[1] Stewart, *The Resurrection of Jesus.*

Table 27.1: The main views that accept the historicity of the crucifixion

Event	Supernatural (N. T. Wright)	Natural (J. D. Crossan)	Non-fatal crucifixion
Crucified?	Yes	Yes	Yes
Died by crucifixion?	Yes	Yes	No
Resurrected and raised to heaven?	Yes	No	N/A
Dead or alive in heaven?	Alive	Dead	Dead
Will descend?	Yes	No	No

I have already pointed out that any credible and consistent narrative of Jesus would have to selectively admit some Gospel material and reject the rest. Similarly, accepting the historicity of the crucifixion means ignoring extra-New Testament Christian sources and traditions, such as those that promote docetism. Another target of this rejection is a source that is particularly of interest to this study, the Qur'an.

The Qur'an's accounts of Old and New Testament figures are typically dismissed by non-Muslim scholars for several reasons. First, the Qur'an is six centuries later than the events it recounts. Second, it is a book of faith rather than history. Third, it is accused of appropriation, often unfaithfully, from written and oral Jewish and Christian sources. Jesus' story is no exception to this sweeping rejection. In fact, the Qur'an's denial that Jesus was killed is probably the main claim in it that unifies the various critics of its historical reliability, all of whom consider the crucifixion a historical certainty. Yet our analysis of Jesus' story in the Qur'an has shown that, unlike the Gospels, it is internally consistent and has every right to be treated as at least on par with the Gospels. Furthermore, we have demonstrated that the Qur'an provides a more credible history of Jesus.

With rare exceptions, Muslim scholars have always understood the Qur'an as denying the crucifixion of Jesus, but they have offered different interpretations of the various verses and, consequently, related episodes of his life. In this book, I have proposed a reconstruction of events that accommodates all relevant verses. Alternative views might appear to convincingly interpret some verses but they fail to account for others. The headline conclusions of my reading of the Qur'an is that Jesus escaped the attempt on his life, somebody else was wrongly crucified in his stead, and Jesus was raised to heaven where he spent the rest of his life until his death. I will now give a more detailed summary of the story of the crucifixion in the Qur'an, integrating details from the Gospels and historical sources that are aligned with the Qur'anic account.

Jesus was a prophet sent by God to the Jewish people. His core teachings were the same as those which Noah, Abraham, Jacob, Moses, and all other messengers of God delivered. One fundamental creed they all thought was that only God is divine. Jesus, like every created being, was a servant of the Divine. He preached a divine book that was revealed to him called the "Injīl". This book complemented, rather than replaced, the Torah. Jesus upheld the Mosaic law but he abolished some prohibitions. He also taught that another prophet called Aḥmad, referring to the Prophet Muhammad, would follow him in the future. He performed impressive miracles, including raising the dead.

Not unlike other prophets, Jesus faced strong resistance to his reformist teachings from both the public and the religious authorities. He was not the popular preacher that the Gospel narratives depict him as. He proclaimed that he was the awaited Messiah, yet his peaceful spiritual teachings disappointed the Jews, who were hoping and waiting for a military Messiah who would restore the glory of the ancient kingdom of Israel. His modern interpretation of the law and being an independent teacher who did not belong to the Pharisees or Sadducees further limited his ability to attract followers. His miracles were dismissed by the majority, who rejected his teachings as a form of magic rather than godly wonders.

The Gospels' claim that Jesus was a nondescript layman who suddenly and inexplicably burst into the public scene in an extraordinary way when he was around thirty is probably fictional. Jesus likely started teaching to the public when he was still a teenager. As he approached adulthood and started to be seen as more credible, his preaching intensified and he engaged and attracted more people.

Yet the Jewish authorities considered Jesus' teachings to be false and dangerous. This view was more driven by concerns for their own standing and privileges in the community than a genuine conviction that

Jesus was a self-appointed teacher who misled people. Jesus exposed the exploitation of Judaism by the religious elite to advance their own interests rather than providing spiritual guidance. He publicly and provocatively proclaimed that the spiritual scene was in dire need of reform and that this was his mission. The Gospels' image of a meek Jesus with the sinners and the poor contrasts sharply with their portrayal of him repeatedly and severely criticising the religious establishment. Jesus' miracles might well have become the target of the envy and ill feeling of rabbis who had nothing wondrous to show to the public as a testimony to their righteousness.

Slowly but steadily acquiring highly committed followers, the young teacher started to alarm the religious authorities. Having failed in their repeated harassment, warnings, and threats to stop him preaching, the Jewish authorities concluded that the only way to end his unwelcome activity and influence was to eliminate him. The Gospels suggest that the hostility of the authorities was accelerated by his move to Jerusalem, the city of the temple and the power base of the priestly authorities.

The Jewish authorities were going to arrest him, conduct a sham trial, and sentence him to death. Sensing the escalating danger to his life, Jesus sought support from his closest followers. God informed him of the plot against him and promised to save him. He stayed out of the public eye as a result, hiding with the help of some of his followers.

One critical claim made by the Gospels is that the soldiers who came to arrest Jesus had to rely on an informant to *identify* him. The arrest is also said to have taken place not in Jesus' hometown but in Jerusalem, where he was even less known, during the extremely busy religious celebration of the Passover. It is not difficult to see how the guards who went to arrest him could have picked up the wrong man.

Equally significant, the Synoptists state that Jesus' followers *did not witness* his crucifixion. None of them was present close to the cross to confirm the identity of the crucified man. In other words, the primary sources on the most famous crucifixion in history imply that the man on the cross was only *presumed* to be Jesus. Remarkably, the Gospels also agree that Jesus' alleged resurrection too had *no eyewitnesses*. It was *concluded* from the empty tomb and Jesus' post-crucifixion appearances. I argue that a critical review of the Gospels demonstrates that the crucifixion of Jesus was a presumption that had certainty conferred on it and was given the status of fact by a faith that made it its central theme; it does not belong to history proper.

The Qur'an alludes to a divine intervention that allowed this misidentification of Jesus to continue, resulting in the wrong man being crucified.

The religious court proceedings against Jesus were designed to deliver a quick guilty verdict, rather than being a proper trial. Having indicted the man they arrested, thinking that he was Jesus, the priestly authorities had to convince the Roman prefect to execute him because the Romans had not delegated the power of capital punishment to the Jews. However, most modern scholars claim that Pontius Pilate decided to crucify Jesus because he conceived him to be a threat to the peace and public order. They greatly minimize or deny the role of the Jews in Jesus' death. This relatively recent trend does not reflect history but it is a remedial reaction to the devastating antisemitism that has been generated by the Jews' responsibility for Jesus' death in the Gospels. Yet the Gospel narratives do not ascribe any political agenda, let alone activity, to Jesus. In fact, the Gospels show him preemptively and expressly rejecting any attempt to attribute to him any political motives. The Romans would have had no interest in a little-known, non-political religious teacher, but the Jewish leaders probably falsely claimed that Jesus was a potentially dangerous instigator of riots. Even if Pilate did not buy the lie, he may have wanted to do a favour to the high priest. Given his brutality, Pilate would have happily sacrificed one innocent life for a political end. It is not unlikely that he also took this opportunity to make an example of Jesus for real would-be troublemakers.

After the crucifixion, Jesus remained in hiding awaiting God's promised intervention to rescue him. The post-crucifixion appearances of Jesus might have been meetings that he had with his close followers while in hiding.

The Qur'an suggests that God put Jesus in a sleep-like state, which was presumably necessary for this miraculous elevation to heaven. Still a young man, he lived there until at least his thirties but probably well beyond that. The idea that Jesus will return to the earth, which most Muslims, like Christians, believe in, is incompatible with the Qur'an's account of Jesus and its general teachings. He never had an eschatological role. His mission was complete; there was nothing left to fulfil.

The Qur'an reports a dialogue between God and Jesus after he was raised to heaven. It informs us that Jesus was still alive when his deification had started to be spread by those who preached in his name, Paul being the most influential among them.

Table 27.2 summarises the main Muslim views. In addition to the majority view, I have identified another three and named their most well-known advocates. The "natural" approach is the same as that which we encountered in Table 27.1. I have also added the scenario I have proposed in this book.

Table 27.2: Muslim views on what happened to Jesus

Event	Majority	Modern (Muḥammad 'Abduh)	Rational (Sayyid Ahmad Khan)	Natural (Mahmoud Ayoub)	This book
Crucified?	No	No	Yes	Yes	No
Died by crucifixion?	N/A	N/A	No	Yes	N/A
Supernatural involvement?	Yes	Yes	No	No	Yes
Resurrected and/or raised?	Raised to heaven alive	No	No	No	Raised to heaven alive
Dead or alive in heaven?	Alive	Dead	Dead	Dead	Dead
Will descend?	Yes	No	No	No	No

My conclusions differ from the majority view of Muslim scholars in that I think Jesus is already dead and there is no eschatological role for him in the future.

I hope that the new Qur'an-based insights offered in this book will help to move the debate of the crucifixion of Jesus beyond its ancient borders. More specifically, this book will have achieved its goals if it assists in liberating the thinking of non-Muslim scholarship from the confines of the New Testament.

References

Abū Dāwūd, Sulaymān b. al-Ash'ath. *Sunan Abī Dāwūd* [Traditions of Abī Dāwūd]. Edited by Shu'ayb al-Arna'ūṭ and Muḥammad Qaraballī. 7 vols. Damascus: Dār al-Risāla al-'Ālamiyya, 2009.

Adler, William, and Paul Tuffin. "Commentary". In *Chronography*, by George Synkellos. Translated by William Adler and Paul Tuffin. Oxford: Oxford University Press, 2002.

Ahmad, Mirza Ghulam. *Jesus in India: Jesus' Deliverance From the Cross & Journey to India.* Surrey: Islam International Publications, 2003.

Al-Khālidī, Ṣalāḥ. *Al-Qaṣaṣ Al-Qur'ānī.* [Qur'anic Stories]. Damascus: Dār al-Qalam, 1998.

Al-Khaṭīb, 'Abd al-Karīm. *Al-Masīḥ fī Al-Qur'an wa Al-Tawrāt wa Al-Injīl.* [The Messiah in the Qur'an, the Old Testament, and the Gospels]. Cairo: Dār al-Kutub al-Ḥadītha, 1965.

Al-Najjār, 'Abd al-Wahhāb. *Qiṣaṣ Al-Anbiyā'.* [The Stories of Prophets]. Cairo: Maṭba't Naṣr, 1936.

Al-Rāzī, Abū Ḥātim. *A'lām Al-Nubuwwa* [Signs of Prophethood]. Edited by Salah Al-Sawy and Gholam-Reza Aavani. Iran: Mu'assat Bazuhshi, 2002.

———. *Kitāb Al-Iṣlāḥ* [The Book of Reform]. Edited by Ḥasan Mīnūchahar and Mahdī Muḥaqqaq. Tehran: Mu'assasat Muṭāla'āt, 2004.

Al-Sijistānī, Abū Ya'qūb. *Kitāb Al-Yanābī'* [The Book of Springs]. Edited by Muṣṭafā Ghālib. Beirut: Al-Maktab al-Tijārī li al-Ṭibā'a wa al-Nashr wa al-Tawzī', 1965.

Al-Wāqidī, Muḥammad b. 'Umar. *Kitāb Al-Maghāzī* [The Book of the Raids]. Edited by Marsden Jones. 3 vols. Cairo: 'Ālam al-Kutub, 1984.

'Alī Ibn Abī Ṭālib. *Nahj Al-Balāgha* [Way of Eloquence]. Edited by 'Abd Allah Al-Ṭabbā' and 'Umar Al-Ṭabbā'. Beirut: Mu'assasat al-Ma'ārif, 1990.

Allen, N. P. L. "Thallus and Phlegon: Solar Eclipse In Jerusalem C. 33 CE?". *Akroterion* 63 (2018): 73-93.

Allison, Dale. "Explaining the Resurrection: Conflicting Convictions". *Journal for the Study of the Historical Jesus* 3, no. 2 (2005): 117.

———. *Jesus of Nazareth: Millenarian Prophet.* Minneapolis: Fortress Press, 1998.

Anderson, Mark Robert. *The Qur'an in Context: A Christian Exploration.* Illinois: InterVarsity Press, 2016.

Avery-Peck, Alan J. "Magic in Rabbinic Judaism". In *The Encyclopaedia of Judaism*, edited by Jacob Neusner, Alan J. Avery-Peck and William Scott Green, 1614-1616. Leiden: Brill, 2005.

Ayoub, Mahmoud. *A Muslim View of Christianity: Essays on Dialogue by*

Mahmoud Ayoub. Edited by Irfan A. Omar. New York: Orbis Books, 2007.

Baljon, J. M. S. *The Reforms and Religious Ideas of Sir Sayyid Ahmad Khan.* Lahore: Orientalia Publishers, 1958.

Bauckham, Richard. "The Eyewitnesses and the Gospel Traditions". *Journal for the Study of the Historical Jesus* 1, no. 1 (2003): 33.

Bermejo-Rubio, Fernando. "Was the Hypothetical Vorlage of the Testimonium Flavianum a "Neutral" Text? Challenging the Common Wisdom on Antiquitates Judaicae 18.63-64". *Journal for the Study of Judaism* 45, no. 3 (2014): 326-365.

Bock, Darrell L. "The Words of Jesus in the Gospels: Live, Jive, or Memorex?". In *Jesus Under Fire*, edited by Michael J. Wilkins and James Porter Moreland, 73-99. Michigan: Zondervan, 1995.

Brashler, James, and Roger A. Bullard. "The Apocalypse of Peter". Translated by James Brashler and Roger A. Bullard. In *The Nag Hammadi Library in English*, edited by James Robinson, 372-378. New York: HarperSanFrancisco, 1990.

Bridger, J. Scott. *Christian Exegesis of the Qur'ān.* Cambridge: James Clarke & Co, 2016.

Bruce, F. F. *The New Testament Documents: Are They Reliable?* Illinois: InterVarsity Press, 1981.

Bullard, Roger A., and Joseph A. Gibbons. "The Second Treatise of the Great Seth". Translated by Roger A. Bullard and Joseph A. Gibbons. In *The Nag Hammadi Library in English*, edited by James Robinson, 362-371. New York: HarperSanFrancisco, 1990.

Bultmann, Rudolf. *Jesus and the Word.* Translated by Louise Pettibone Smith and Erminie Huntress Lantero. New York: Charles Scribner's Sons, 1958.

Carrier, Richard. "Thallus and the Darkness at Christ's Death". *Journal of Greco-Roman Christianity and Judaism* 8 (2011-2012): 185-191.

Case, Shirley Jackson. "The Historicity of Jesus: An Estimate of the Negative Argument". *The American Journal of Theology* 15, no. 1 (1911): 24.

Casey, Maurice. *Jesus of Nazareth: An Independent Historian's Account of His Life and Teaching.* London: T&T Clark International, 2010.

Celsus. *On the True Doctrine: A Discourse Against the Christians.* Translated by R. Joseph Hoffmann. Oxford: Oxford University Press, 1987.

Chapman, David W. *Ancient Jewish and Christian Perceptions of Crucifixion.* Tübingen: Mohr Siebeck, 2008.

Cook, John Granger. *Crucifixion in the Mediterranean World.* Tübingen: Mohr Siebeck, 2019.

Craig, William Lane. *Assessing the New Testament Evidence for the Historicity of the Resurrection of Jesus.* Lewiston: The Edwin Mellen Press, 1989.

———. "Closing Response". In *Jesus' Resurrection: Fact or Figment?*, edited by

Paul Copan and Ronald K. Tacelli, 162-208. Illinois: InterVarsity Press, 2000.

———. "Did Jesus Rise From the Dead?". In *Jesus Under Fire*, edited by Michael J. Wilkins and James Porter Moreland, 141-176. Michigan: Zondervan, 1994.

Crossan, John Dominic. *The Birth of Christianity: Discovering What Happened in the Years Immediately After the Execution of Jesus.* San Francisco: HarperSanFrancisco, 1999.

———. *The Historical Jesus: The Life of a Mediterranean Jewish Peasant.* San Francisco: HarperSanFrancisco, 1991.

Crossley, James "Against the Historical Plausibility of the Empty Tomb Story and the Bodily Resurrection of Jesus: A Response to N.T. Wright". *Journal for the Study of the Historical Jesus* 3, no. 2 (2005): 171-186.

Daftari, Farhad. *Al-Ismā'īliyyūn: Tārīkhuhum wa 'Aqā'iduhum.* [Ismā'īlīs: Their History and Beliefs]. Translated by Sayf al-Dīn Al-Qaṣīr. Beirut: Dār al-Sāqī, 2012.

Dalman, Gustaf. *Jesus Christ in the Talmud, Midrash, Zohar, and the Liturgy of the Synagogue.* Translated by A. W. Streane. London: Deighton, Bell, and Co., 1893.

Danby, Herbert. *The Mishnah.* Oxford: Oxford University Press, 1933.

Dard, A. R. *Life of Ahmad: Founder of the Ahmadiyya Movement.* Surrey: Islam International Publications, 2008.

Doherty, Earl. *Jesus: Neither God Nor Man - The Case for a Mythical Jesus.* Ottawa: Age of Reason Publications, 2009.

Dunn, James D. G. *Jesus Remembered.* Cambridge: Wm. B. Eerdmans Publishing Co., 2003.

Editors. *Mu'jam Aḥādīth Al-Imām Al-Mahdī.* [Compilation of the Traditions of Imām Mahdī]. Qom: Mu'assasat al-Ma'ārif al-Islāmiyya, 2007.

Edwards, William D., Wesley J. Gabel, and Floyd E. Hosmer. "On the Physical Death of Jesus Christ". *The Journal of the American Medical Association* 255, no. 11 (1986): 1455-1463.

Ehrman, Bart D. *Did Jesus Exist? The Historical Argument for Jesus of Nazareth.* New York: HarperOne, 2012.

———. *Jesus, Interrupted: Revealing the Hidden Contradictions in the Bible (and why we don't know about them).* New York: HarperOne, 2009.

———. *Jesus: Apocalyptic Prophet of the New Millennium.* Oxford: Oxford University Press, 1999.

———. *Lost Scriptures: Books That Did Not Make It Into the New Testament.* Oxford: Oxford University Press, 2005.

———. *Misquoting Jesus: The Story Behind Who Changed the Bible and Why.* New York: HarperSanFrancisco, 2005.

———. *The Triumph of Christianity: How a Forbidden Religion Swept the World.* New York: Simon & Schuster, 2018.

Epstein, I. *Hebrew-English Edition of the Babylonian Talmud.* Translated by J. Shachter and H. Freedman. London: The Soncino Press, 1969.

Erder, Yoram. "Idrīs". In *Encyclopaedia of the Qur'an,* edited by Jane Dammen McAuliffe, 484-486. Leiden: Brill, 2002.

Eusebius. *The Proof of the Gospel.* Translations of Christian Literature. London: Society for Promoting Christian Knowledge, 1920.

Evans, Craig. "Hanging and Crucifixion in Second Temple Israel". In *Qumran und die Archäologie: Texte und Kontexte,* edited by Jörg Frey, Carsten Claussen and Nadine Kessler, 481-501. Tübingen: Mohr Siebeck, 2011.

———. "Jewish Burial Traditions and the Resurrection of Jesus". *Journal for the Study of the Historical Jesus* 3, no. 2 (2005): 233.

———. "The Shout of Death". In *Jesus, The Final Days: What Really Happened,* edited by Troy A. Miller, 1-38. Kentucky: Westminster John Knox Press, 2009.

———. "The Silence of Burial". In *Jesus, The Final Days: What Really Happened,* edited by Troy A. Miller, 39-73. Kentucky: Westminster John Knox Press, 2009.

Fatoohi, Louay. *Jesus the Muslim Prophet: History Speaks of a Human Messiah Not a Divine Christ.* Birmingham: Luna Plena Publishing, 2010.

———. *The Messiah in Islam, Christianity, and Judaism: A Theological and Historical Comparison.* Birmingham: Safis Publishing, 2021.

———. *The Mystery of the Historical Jesus: The Messiah in the Qur'an, the Bible, and Historical Sources.* Kuala Lumpur: Islamic Book Trust, 2009.

———. *Shaikh Muhammad Al-Muhammad Al-Kasnazan Al-Husayni: A Life in the Footsteps of the Best of Lives.* Birmingham: Safis Publishing, 2020.

Feldman, Louis. "On the Authenticity of the Testimonium Flavianum Attributed to Josephus". In *New Perspectives on Jewish-Christian Relations: In Honor of David Berger,* edited by Elisheva Carlebach and Jacob J. Schacter, 13-30. Leiden: Brill, 2012.

Fonner, Michael G. "Jesus' Death by Crucifixion in the Qur'an: An Issue for Interpretation and Muslim-Christian Relations". *Journal of Ecumenical Studies* 29, no. 3-4 (1992): 432-450.

Fotheringham, J. K. "The Evidence of Astronomy and Technical Chronology for the Date of the Crucifixion". *Journal of Theological Studies* 35 (1934): 146-162.

France, R. T. *The Evidence for Jesus.* London: Hodder and Stoughton, 1986.

Fredriksen, Paula. *Jesus of Nazareth, King of the Jews: A Jewish Life and the Emergence of Christianity.* New York: Vintage Books, 1999.

Fry, C. George. "The Quranic Christ". *Concordia Theological Quarterly* 43, no. 3 (1979): 207-221.

Furnish, Victor P. *Jesus According to Paul.* Cambridge: Cambridge University Press, 1993.

Goldberg, Gary J. "The Coincidences of the Emmaus Narrative of Luke and the Testimonium of Josephus". *Journal for the Study of the Pseudepigrapha* 7, no. 13 (1995): 59-77.

The Gospel of Barnabas. Translated by Lonsdale and Laura Ragg. Oxford: The Clarendon Press, 1907.

Goulder, Michael. "Ignatius' "Docetists"". *Vigiliae Christianae* 53, no. 1 (1999): 16-30.

———. "Jesus' Resurrection and Christian Origins: A Response to N.T. Wright". *Journal for the Study of the Historical Jesus* 3, no. 2 (2005): 187-195.

Habermas, Gary R. "Resurrection Research from 1975 to the Present: What Are Critical Scholars Saying?". *Journal for the Study of the Historical Jesus* 3, no. 2 (2005): 19.

Harās, Muḥammad. *Faṣl Al-Maqāl fī Nuzūl ʿĪsā wa Qatlihi Al-Dajjāl.* [The Decisive Statement on the Descent of Jesus and His Killing of the Antichrist]. Egypt: N/A, 1969.

Harvey, A. E. *Jesus on Trial: A Study in the Fourth Gospel.* Atlanta: John Knox Press, 1976.

Hengel, Martin. *Crucifixion in the Ancient World and the Folly of the Message of the Cross.* Translated by John Bowden. London: SCM Press, 1977.

Herford, Travers. *Christianity in Talmud and Midras.* New York: Ktav Publishing House, 1975.

Holmén, Tom. "Crucifixion Hermeneutics in Judaism at the Time of Jesus". *Journal for the Study of the Historical Jesus* 14 (2017): 197-222.

———. "Seven Theses on the So-Called Criteria of Authenticity of Historical Jesus Research". *RCatT* XXXIII, no. 2 (2008): 343-376.

Homolka, Walter. *Jewish Jesus Research and its Challenge to Christology Today.* Leiden: Brill, 2017.

Hopkins, Keith. "Christian Number and its Implications". In *Sociological Studies in Roman History*, edited by Christopher Kelly, 432-480. Cambridge: Cambridge University Press, 2018.

Horrell, David. "The Label χριστιανός: 1 Peter 4:16 and the Formation of Christian Identity". *Journal of Biblical Literature* 126, no. 2 (2007): 361–381.

Hussein, Muhammad Kamel. *City of Wrong: A Friday in Jerusalem.* Translated by Kenneth Cragg. London: Oneworld Publications, 1994.

Ibn Ḥazm al-Andalusī , ʿAlī. *Al-Muḥallā bi Al-ʾĀthār* [One Ornamented with Traditions]. Edited by ʿAbd al-Ghaffār al-Bandārī. Beirut: Dār al-Kutub al-

'Ilmiyya, 2003.

Ibn Mansūr al-Yaman, Jaʿfar *Asrār Al-Nuṭaqāʾ* [Secrets of the Speakers]. Edited by Muṣṭāfā Ghālib. Beirut: Dār al-Andalus, 1984.

Ibn Rushd, Abū al-Walīd. *Al-Bayān wa Al-Taḥṣīl* [Clarification and Conclusion]. Edited by Muḥammad Ḥajjī. Beirut: Dār al-Gharb Al-Islāmī, 1988.

Ibn Taymiyya, Taqiyy al-Dīn. *Muqaddima fī Uṣūl Al-Tafsīr* [Introduction to the Sources of Exegesis]. Edited by ʿAdnān Zarzūr. Kuwait: Dār al-Qurʾān al-Karīm, 1972.

Ibrāhīm, ʿAdnān. "ʿAwdat ʿĪsā Bayna Al-ʿIqrār wa Al-Inkār." 2012, accessed 15 September, 2020, https://bit.ly/2FSbfZO.

Ignatius. *Ignatius to the Smyrnaeans*. Translated by Kirsopp Lake. The Apostolic Fathers. New York: William Heinmann, 1919.

Ikhwān al-Ṣafāʾ. *Rasāʾil Ikhwān Al-Ṣafāʾ wa Khillān Al-Wafāʾ* [Letters of the Brethren of Purity and Friends of Loyalty]. Edited by Buṭrus Al-Bustānī. Vol. IV, Qom: Markaz Al-Nashr, 1985.

Instone-Brewer, David. "Jesus of Nazareth's Trial in the Uncensored Talmud". *Tyndale Bulletin* 62, no. 2 (2011): 269-294.

Irenaeus. *Against Heresies* Edited by A. Cleveland Coxe. The Apostolic Fathers with Justin Martyr and Irenaeus. New York: Charles Scribner's Sons, 1885.

James, Montague Rhodes. *The Apocryphal New Testament.* Translated by Montague Rhodes James. Oxford: The Clarendon Press, 1983.

Jerome. *On Illustrious Men.* Translated by Thomas Halton. The Fathers of the Church: A New Translation 100. Washington, D. C.: The Catholic University of America Press, 1999.

John of Damascus. *Fountain of Knowledge.* Translated by Frederic H. Chase. The Fathers of the Church: Saint John of Damascus Writings 37. Washington: The Catholic University of America Press, 1958.

Josephus, Flavius. *Antiquities of the Jews.* Translated by William Whiston. The Complete Works of Flavius Josephus. London: Ward, Lock & CO. Limited, n.d.

———. *Life of Flavius Josephus.* Translated by William Whiston. The Complete Works of Flavius Josephus. London: Ward, Lock & CO. Limited, n.d.

———. *Wars of the Jews.* Translated by William Whiston. The Complete Works of Flavius Josephus. London: Ward, Lock & CO. Limited, n.d.

Kalimi, Isaac. "The Story about the Murder of the Prophet Zechariah in the Gospels and its Relation to Chronicles". *Revue Biblique* 116, no. 2 (2009): 246–261.

Kaltner, John, and Younus Mirza. *The Bible and the Qurʾan: Biblical Figures in the Islamic Tradition.* London: Bloomsbury T&T Clark, 2018.

Kazen, Thomas "The Coming Son of Man Revisited". *Journal for the Study of the Historical Jesus* 5, no. 2 (2007): 155-174.

Kim, Jintae. "The Concept of Atonement in Early Rabbinic Thought and the New Testament Writings". *Journal of Greco-Roman Christianity and Judaism* 2 (2001-2005): 117-145.

Klausner, Joseph. *Jesus of Nazareth: His Life, Times, and Teaching.* Translated by Herbert Danby. New York: The Macmillan Company, 1926.

Lawson, Todd. *The Crucifixion and the Qur'an: A Study in History of Muslim Thought.* Oxford: Oneworld, 2009.

Leirvik, Oddbjørn. *Images of Jesus Christ in Islam.* London: Continuum, 2010.

———. "Jesus in Modern Muslim Thought: From Anti-colonial Polemics to Post-colonial Dialogue?". In *Jesus beyond Nationalism: Constructing the Historical Jesus in a Period of Cultural Complexity*, edited by Halvor Moxnes, Ward Blanton and James G. Crossley, 139-158. New York: Routledge, 2014.

Lucian. *The Passing of Peregrinus.* Translated by A. M. Harmon. The Loeb Classical Library. Cambridge: Harvard University Press, 1962.

Lyons, William John. "A Prophet is Rejected in His Home Town (Mark 6.4 and Parallels): A Study in the Methodological (In)Consistency of the Jesus Seminar". *Journal for the Study of the Historical Jesus* 6, no. 1 (2008): 26.

Macarius, Magnes. *The Apocriticus of Macarius Magnes.* Translated by T. W. Crafer. Translations of Christian Literature Series I: Greek Texts. New York: The Macmillan Company, 1919.

Majlī, Nasīm. *Muhammad Kamel Hussein: Ibn Sīnā Al-Qarn Al-'Ishrīn.* [Muhammad Kamel Hussein: Avicenna of the Twentieth Century]. Cairo: Kutub 'Arabiyya, n.d.

Majlisī, Muḥammad. *Biḥār Al-Anwār.* [Seas of Lights]. Vol. XIV, Beirut Dār Iḥyā' al-Turāth al-'Arabī, 1983.

Mánek, Jindřich. "The Apostle Paul and the Empty Tomb". *Novum Testamentum* 2, no. 3 (1958): 276-280.

McAuliffe, Jane Dammen. *Qur'anic Christians: An Analysis of Classical and Modern Exegesis.* Cambridge: Cambridge University Press, 1991.

Meier, John P. "Jesus in Josephus: A Modest Proposal". *The Catholic Biblical Quarterly* 52, no. 1 (1990): 76-103.

———. *A Marginal Jew: Rethinking the Historical Jesus.* Vol. 1, New York: Doubleday, 1987.

Metzger, Bruce M. *Textual Commentary on the Greek New Testament.* London: United Bible Societies, 1971.

Mevorach, Ian "Qur'an, Crucifixion, and Talmud: A New Reading of Q 4:157-58". *Journal of Religion & Society* 19 (2017): 1-21.

Moss, Candida. *The Myth of Persecution: How Early Christians Invented a Story of*

Martyrdom. New York: HarperOne, 2013.

Mourad, Suleiman A. "The Death of Jesus in Islam: Reality, Assumptions, and Implications". In *Engaging the Passion: Perspectives on the Death of Jesus*, 359-381. Minneapolis: Fortress Press, 2015.

——. "Does the Qur'an Deny or Assert Jesus's Crucifixion and Death?". In *New Perspectives on the Qur'an: The Qur'an in its Historical Context 2*, edited by Gabriel Said Reynolds. Oxon: Routledge, 2011.

Muslim, Abū al-Ḥusain. *Ṣaḥīḥ Muslim* [Authentic Traditions of Muslim]. Edited by Muḥammad 'Abd al-Bāqī. 5 vols. Cairo: Dār al-Ḥadīth, 1991.

Olson, K. A. "Eusebius and the "Testimonium Flavianum"". *The Catholic Biblical Quarterly* 61, no. 2 (1999): 305-322.

Origen. *Against Celsus.* Translated by Frederick Crombie. The Ante-Nicene Fathers IV. New York: Charles Scribner's Sons, 1926.

——. *Commentary on the Gospel of Matthew.* Translated by John Patrick. The Ante-Nicene Fathers IX. New York: Charles Scribner's Sons, 1906.

Parrinder, G. *Jesus in the Qur'an.* Oxford: Oneworld Publications, 1995.

Pearson, Birger A. "Basilides the Gnostic". In *A Companion to Second-Century Christian "Heretics"*, edited by Antti Marjanen and Petri Luomanen, 1-31. Leiden: Brill, 2005.

Peper, Bradley M, and Mark DelCogliano. "The Pliny and Trajan Correspondence". In *The Historical Jesus in Context*, edited by A.J. Levine, Dale C. Allison and John Dominic Crossan, 366-370. New Jersey: Princeton University Press, 2006.

Philo, Julius. *The Embassy to Gaius* Edited by G. P. Goold. Translated by F. H. Colson. The Loeb Classical Library. Cambridge: Harvard University Press, 1991.

Pines, S. *An Arabic Version of the Testimonium Flavianum and its Implications.* Jerusalem: The Israel Academy of Sciences and Humanities, 1971.

Pliny. *The Letters of Pliny the Younger.* Translated by W. Bosanquest. New York: Hinds, Noble & Eldredge, 1931.

Pregill, Michael E. "The Hebrew Bible and the Quran: The Problem of the Jewish 'Influence' on Islam". *Religion Compass* 1, no. 6 (2007): 643–659.

Price, Robert M. *The Incredible Shrinking Son of Man: How Reliable is the Gospel Tradition?* Amherst: Prometheus Books, 2003.

Rahman, Muda Ismail Abd. "The Interpretation of the Birth of Jesus and His Miracles in the Writings of Sir Sayyid Ahmad Khan". *Islam and Christian–Muslim Relations* 14, no. 1 (2003): 23-31.

Reeves, John C. "Some Explorations of the Intertwining of Bible and Qur'an". In *Bible and the Qur'an: Essays in Scriptural Intertextuality*, edited by John C. Reeves, 43-60. Atlanta: Society of Biblical Literature, 2003.

Reynolds, Gabriel Said. "Introduction: The Golden Age of Qur'anic Studies?". In *New Perspectives on the Qur'an: The Qur'an in its Historical Context 2*, edited by Gabriel Said Reynolds, 1-21. Oxon: Routledge, 2011.

———. "The Muslim Jesus: Dead or alive?". *Bulletin of SOAS* 72, no. 2 (2009): 237–258.

———. "On the Qur'ān and the Theme of Jews as 'Killers of the Prophets'". *Al-Bayan* 10, no. 2 (2012): 9-32.

———. *The Qur'ān and the Bible: Text and Commentary*. New Haven: Yale University Press, 2018.

Riḍā, Muḥammad Rashīd. *'Aqīdat Al-Ṣalīb wa Al-Fidā'*. [The Creed of Crucifixion and Redeption]. Cairo: Maṭba'at al-Manār, n.d.

Robinson, Neal. *Christ in Islam and Christianity*. New York: State University of New York Press, 1991.

———. "Jesus". In *Encyclopaedia of the Qurān*, edited by Jane Dammen McAuliffe, 7-21. Leiden: Brill, 2003.

Rodríguez, Rafael. "The Embarrassing Truth About Jesus: The Criterion of Embarrassment and the Failure of Historical Authenticity". In *Jesus, Criteria, and the Demise of Authenticity*, edited by Chris Keith and Anthony Le Donne, 132-151. London: T&T Clark, 2012.

Rosenblatt, Samuel. "The Crucifixion of Jesus from the Standpoint of Pharisaic Law". *Journal of Biblical Literature* 75, no. 4 (1956): 315-321.

Samir, Samir Khalil. "The Theological Christian Influence on the Qur'an: A Reflection". In *The Qur'an In Its Historical Context*, edited by Gabriel Said Reynolds, 141-162. Oxon: Routledge, 2008.

Samuelsson, Gunnar. *Crucifixion in Antiquity: An Inquiry into the Background and Significance of the New Testament Terminology of Crucifixion*. Tübingen: Mohr Siebeck, 2011.

Sanders, E. P. *The Historical Figure of Jesus*. New York: Penguin Books, 1996.

———. *Jesus and Judaism*. Philadelphia: Fortress Press, 1985.

———. "Jesus and the First Table of the Jewish Law". In *The Historical Jesus in Recent Research*, edited by James D. G. Dunn and Scot McKnight, 225-237. London: Eisenbrauns, 2005.

———. *Jewish Law from Jesus to the Mishnah: Five Studies*. London: S CM Press, 1990.

Sanders, E. P., and Margaret Davies. *Studying the Synoptic Gospels*. London: SCM Press, 1985.

Schäfer, Peter. *Jesus in the Talmud*. Princeton: Princeton University Press, 2007.

Schoedel, William R. "The First Apocalypse of James". Translated by William R. Schoedel. In *The Nag Hammadi Library in English*, edited by James Robinson, 260-268. New York: HarperSanFrancisco, 1990.

Schürer, Emil. *The History of the Jewish People in the Age of Jesus Christ (175 B.C-A.D. 135).* Edited by Géza Vermes, Fergus Millar and Matthew Black. Vol. I, London: Bloomsbury T&T Clark, 2014.

———. *The History of the Jewish People in the Age of Jesus Christ (175 B.C.-A.D. 135).* Edited by Géza Vermes, Fergus Millar and Matthew Black. Vol. II, London: Bloomsbury T&T Clark, 2014.

Schweitzer, Albert. *The Quest of the Historical Jesus: A Critical Study of its Progress from Reimarus to Wrede.* Translated by W. Montgomery. London: Adam and Charles Black, 1911.

Shaʿbān, Ḥ. *Ḥayāt Al-Masīḥ ʿĪsā Ibn Maryam Min Manẓūr Islāmī.* [The Life of the Messiah, Jesus Son of Mary, from an Islamic Perspective]. Beirut: Dār al-Kutub al-ʿIlmiyya, 2004.

Shalabī, Aḥmad. *Al-Masīḥiyya.* [Christianity]. Cairo: Maktabat al-Nahḍa al-Miṣriyya, 1988.

Shaltūt, Maḥmūd. *Al-Fatāwā: Dirāsa li Mushkilāt Al-Muslim Al-Muʿāṣir fī Ḥayātihi Al-Yawmiyya Al-ʿĀmma.* [The Rulings]. Cairo: Dār al-Shurūq, 2004.

Ṣidqī, Muḥammad Tawfīq. *Naẓariyyatī fī Qiṣṣat Ṣalb Al-Masīḥ wa Qiyāmatihi min Al-Amwāt.* [My Theory about the Story of the Crucifixion of the Messiah and His Rising from Death]. Edited by Khālid Muḥammad ʿAbdu. Al-Jīza: Matkabat al-Nāfitha, 2006.

Smallwood, E. Mary. "Introduction". In *The Jewish Wars*, by Flavius Josephus. Translated by Williamson, G. A. London: Penguin Classics, 1981.

Spong, John Shelby. *Resurrection: Myth or Reality?: A Bishop's Search for the Origins of Christianity.* San Francisco: HarperSanFrancisco, 1994.

———. *Why Christianity Must Change or Die: A Bishop Speaks to Believers in Exile.* New York: HarperSanFrancisco, 1998.

Stark, Rodney. *The Rise of Christianity: How the Obscure, Marginal Jesus Movement Became the Dominant Religious Force in the Western World in a Few Centuries.* New York: HarperSanFrancisco, 1997.

Stein, Robert H. "The Ending of Mark". *Bulletin for Biblical Research* 18, no. 1 (2008): 79–98.

———. "Jesus, the Destruction of Jerusalem, and the Coming of the Son of Man in Luke 21:5-38". *The Southern Baptist Journal of Theology* 16, no. 3 (2012): 18-27.

Stewart, Robert B., ed. *The Resurrection of Jesus: John Dominic Crossan and N. T. Wright in Dialogue.* Minneapolis: Fortress Press, 2006.

Strauss, David Friedrich. *The Life of Jesus.* Translated by George Eliot. London: Swan Sonnenschein & Co. Lim., 1902.

Strauss, Mark L. *Four Portraits, One Jesus: A Survey of Jesus and the Gospels.*

Michigan: Zondervan, 2009.

Suetonius. *The Lives of the Caesars*. Translated by J. C. Rolfe. The Loeb Classical Library. Cambridge: Harvard University Press, 1959.

Synkellos, George. *Chronography: A Byzantine Chronicle of Universal History from the Creation*. Translated by William Adler and Paul Tuffin. Oxford: Oxford University Press, 2002.

Ṭabāṭabāʾī, Muḥammad. *Al-Mīzān fī Tafsīr Al-Qurʾan*. [The Balance in Interpreting the Qurʾan]. Vol. I, Qom: Jamaʿat al-Mudarrisīn fī al-Ḥawza al-ʿIlmiyya, n.d.

Tacitus, Cornelius. *The Annals*. Translated by John Jackson. Cambridge: Harvard University Press, 1962.

Theissen, Gerd, and Annette Merz. *The Historical Jesus: A Comprehensive Guide*. London: SCM, 1998.

Turek, Przemysław. "Crucifixion of Jesus – Historical Fact, Christian Faith and Islamic Denial". *Orientalia Christiana Cracoviensia* 3 (2011): 131-156.

Van den Broek, Roelof. *Pseudo-Cyril of Jerusalem on the life and the Passion of Christ: A Coptic Apocryphon*. Leiden: Brill, 2012.

Van Voorst, Robert E. *Jesus Outside the New Testament: An Introduction to the Ancient Evidence*. Grand Rapids: W.B. Eerdmans, 2000.

Vermes, Géza. *The Changing Faces of Jesus*. New York: Viking Compass, 2001.

———. *Jesus in His Jewish Context*. Minneapolis: Fortress Press, 2003.

———. *Jesus the Jew: A Historian's Reading of the Gospels*. Philadelphia: Fortress Press, 1981.

———. *Jesus: Nativity, Passion, Resurrection*. 2010.

———. *The Passion*. New York: Penguin, 2005.

———. *Searching for the Real Jesus: Jesus, the Dead Sea Scrolls and Other Religious Themes*. London: SCM Press, 2009.

Wassen, Cecilia. "The Jewishness of Jesus and Ritual Purity". *Scripta Instituti Donneriani Aboensis* 27 (2016): 11–36.

Wells, George Albert. *The Historical Evidence for Jesus*. New York: Prometheus Books, 1988.

Whiston, William. "Commentary". In *Life of Flavius Josephus*, by Flavius Josephus. Translated by Whiston, William. London: Ward, Lock & CO. Limited, n.d.

Winter, Paul. *On the Trial of Jesus*. Berlin: Walter De Gruyter, 1961.

Wright, N. T. *The Resurrection of the Son of God*. London: SPCK, 2003.

Wróbel, Mirosław. "The Rabbinic Anti-Gospel in the Context of the Polemic between the Synagogue and the Church". *The Person and the Challenges* 4, no. 2 (2014): 45–59.

Yamauchi, E. M. "The Crucifixion and Docetic Christology". *Concordia*

Theological Quarterly 46, no. 1 (1982): 20.

Yusseff, M. A. *The Dead Sea Scrolls, The Gospel of Barnabas, and the New Testament.* Indiana: American Trust Publications, 1993.

Zeitlin, Solomon. "The Duration of Jesus' Ministry". *The Jewish Quarterly Review* 55, no. 3 (1965): 181–200.

———. *Who Crucified Jesus?* New York: Bloch Publishing Company, 1964.

Index of Qur'anic Verses

Index of Old Testament Verses

Index of New Testament Verses

Matthew

1:1-16, 65
1:18-25, 65
1:23, 37
2:6, 37
2:15, 37
2:18, 37
2:23, 37
3:3, 37
3:7-10, 74
4:15-16, 37
5.17-19, 72
8:17, 37
10:5-6, 130
10:41, 192
11:10, 37
12:1-8, 72
12:12-17, 71
12:18-21, 37
12:22-28, 72
12:38-40, 26
13:14-15, 37
13:34-35, 37
15:1-20, 71
15:8-9, 37
15:13-14, 73
15:24, 192
16:1-4, 28, 74
16:5-6, 74
16:28, 69
18:3, 77
19:28, 106
20:28, 50
21:4-5, 37
21:8-11, 76
22:21, 76
23:2-7, 74
23:29-37, 204
23:37-39, 144
24:1-2, 15, 70
26:5, 63, 67

26:14, 106
26:15, 19
26:19-50, 11
26:31, 37
26:31-57, 12, 42
26:47-50, 19, 245
26:57-59, 13
26:58, 23
26:59-61, 43
26:60, 14
26:61, 14, 70
26:63-64, 14
26:63-65, 46
26:64-65, 14
26:65-66, 17
26:69-74, 23
27:1, 12
27:3-10, 20
27:9, 56
27:9-10, 37-38
27:11, 77
27:11-14, 18
27:15, 47
27:17-26, 56
27:18, 75, 198
27:26, 166
27:32, 21
27:37, 19
27:44, 22
27:45, 92, 146
27:45-50, 21
27:51-53, 92
27:55, 22-23
27:56, 24, 30
27:57-60, 25
28:1, 26
28:1-8, 30
28:2, 164
28:6-17, 31
28:9, 33, 280
28:11-15, 164

Index of Rabbinic Passages

General Index

316

Ignatius, bishop of Antioch, 139, 236
Ikhwān al-Ṣafā', 213
Infancy Gospel of Thomas,
  apocrypha, 197
Injīl, Jesus' Book, 193-195, 197-198,
  231, 289
Irenaeus, bishop of Lyon, 90-91,
  181, 236-237
Ismāʿīlism, 211-214
Israel, 20, 28, 38, 40, 46, 51, 69, 83,
  106, 113, 130, 152, 192, 195, 197,
  199, 203, 229-231, 233, 271, 279,
  282, 289

Jacob, prophet, 65, 192, 289
Jaʿfar al-Ṣādiq, Imam, 211
Jaʿfar Ibn Mansūr al-Yaman, 213
Jerome, priest and historian, 132,
  134
John of Damascus, monk, 181
John the Baptist, 13, 44, 89, 93, 102,
  108, 122, 124, 174, 196
Joseph of Arimathea, 25, 35, 162,
  165
Joseph, prophet, 218
Josephus, Flavius, v, 4, 44-45, 48, 68,
  81-83, 86, 117, 119-135, 137, 148,
  155, 162, 177, 285
Judas Iscariot, 9, 19-20, 32, 35, 38,
  56, 106, 241, 245-246
Julius Africanus, chronographer,
  146-149

Lucian, writer, 119, 140-142, 155

Mahdī, 212, 215, 254
Mara Bar Serapion, 119, 143-145
Mary Magdalene, 24, 29-33, 35-36,
  280
Mary, mother of Jesus, 24, 28-29,
  35, 65, 78, 142, 152, 192-193, 195,
  197, 202, 206, 208, 223, 229, 231-
  233, 240, 246, 249, 251, 265, 270,
  281, 283
Māwardī, ʿAlī, 210

Mirza Ghulam Ahmad, 215, 276
Mishnah, 41-43, 67, 82, 151
Moses, prophet, 14, 27-29, 46, 66,
  72, 74, 192-194, 201-203, 209,
  218, 252, 269, 289
Muhammad, prophet, 181, 187-188,
  196, 202, 204-205, 224, 230, 252,
  274, 289
Mujāhid Ibn Jabr, 210, 270

Najm al-Dīn Kubrā, 210
Nazareth, 15, 19, 63, 78, 153, 175,
  245, 255
Nero, emperor, 80, 81, 137-139
Noah, prophet, 65, 192, 252, 269,
  289

Origen of Alexandria, theologian,
  131, 134, 142, 153

Palestine, 65, 68, 87, 106, 123-124,
  140, 151, 155, 253, 271, 274-276
Peregrinus Proteus, philosopher,
  140-141
Pharisees, 16, 26-28, 68-69, 71, 73-
  74, 83, 154, 204, 245, 289
Philo of Alexandria, 42, 45, 83, 85,
  154
Pliny the Younger, governor, 80-81,
  149-150, 157
Pontius Pilate, prefect, 9, 11-12, 16-
  19, 21, 30, 39, 42, 47-48, 55-61,
  75-85, 87, 89-90, 92-93, 122, 124,
  126, 132, 135, 138, 145, 154, 157,
  162, 167, 175, 178, 198, 226, 257,
  291

Qāʾim, 212-214
Qatāda Ibn Diʿāma, 210, 240
Quirinius, governor, 44, 90, 93, 257
Qurṭubī, Muḥammad, 210
Qushayrī, ʿAbd al-Karīm, 210

Rashīd Riḍā, Muḥammad, 245-246,
  274

www.ingramcontent.com/pod-product-compliance
Lightning Source LLC
Chambersburg PA
CBHW021216090426

42740CB00006B/252